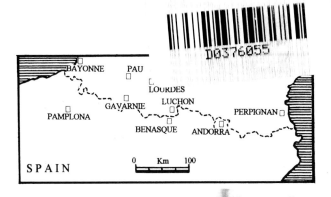

BAYONNE · PAU · LOURDES · GAVARNIE · LUCHON · PERPIGNAN · PAMPLONA · BENASQUE · ANDORRA

0 · Km · 100

S P A I N

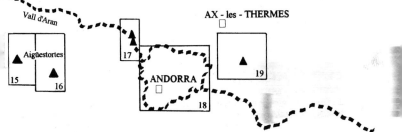

Vall d'Aran

AX - les - THERMES

Aiguestortes

15 · 16

17

ANDORRA

18

19

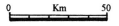

0 · Km · 50

Walks and Climbs in
THE PYRENEES

Walks and Climbs in
THE PYRENEES

by
Kev Reynolds

2 POLICE SQUARE, MILNTHORPE, CUMBRIA LA7 7PY
www.cicerone.co.uk

ABOUT THE AUTHOR

Kev Reynolds, author of this guide, is a freelance writer, photojournalist and lecturer who lives in the Kent coutryside when not trekking or climbing in distant mountain regions. A prolific compiler of guidebooks, *Walks and Climbs in the Pyrenees* was his first title for Cicerone Press, and his enthusuasm for these mountains now spans more than 30 years and dozens of visits. A member of the Alpine Club, Austrian Alpine Club and Outdoor Writers Guild, he is also first Honorary Member of the British Association of European Mountain Leaders. Most winters find Kev travelling around Britain sharing his love of wild places through his lectures.

Cicerone Press guidebooks by the same author:
Walking in the Alps
100 Hut Walks in the Alps
Walks in the Engadine – Switzerland
The Valais – Switzerland
The Jura (with R.Brian Evans)
The Bernese Alps
Ticino – Switzerland
Central Switzerland
Alpine Pass Route
Chamonix to Zermatt – the Walker's Haute Route
Écrins National Park
Tour of the Vanoise
The Wealdway & The Vanguard Way
The South Downs Way & The Downs Link
The Cotswold Way
Walking in Kent Vols I & II
Walking in Sussex
Annapurna – a Trekker's Guide
Everest – a Trekker's Guide
Langtang, Helambu & Gosainkund – a Trekker's Guide
Kangchenjunga – a Trekker's Guide
Manaslu – a Trekker's Guide

MOUNTAIN SAFETY

Every mountain walk has its dangers, and those described in this guide-book are no exception. All who walk or climb in the Pyrenees should recognise this and take responsibility for themselves and their companions along the way. The author and publisher have made every effort to ensure that the information contained herein was correct when the guide went to press, but they cannot accept responsibility for any loss, injury or inconvenience sustained by any person using this book.

International Distress Signal
(To be used in emergency only)
Six blasts on a whistle (and flashes with a torch after dark) spaced evenly for one minute, followed by a minute's pause. Repeat until an answer is received. The response is three signals per minute followed by a minute's pause.

The following signals are used to communicate with a helicopter:

Help needed:
raise both arms above head to form a 'V'

Help not required:
raise one arm above head, extend other arm downward

Note: *mountain rescue can be very expensive – be adequately insured*

© Kev Reynolds 2002
ISBN 1 85284 328 4

First published 1978
Second edition 1983
Reprinted 1986
Reprinted (Revised) 1988
Third edition 1993
Reprinted (Revised) 1997
Fourth edition 2001
Reprinted (Revised) 2002, 2005

A catalogue record for this book is available from the British Library.

DEDICATION

This book is for Alan Payne who has shared
some of the best walks and climbs.

Advice to Readers

Readers are advised that while every effort is taken by the author to ensure the accuracy of this guidebook, changes can occur which may affect the contents. It is advisable to check locally on transport, accommodation, shops, etc, but even rights of way can be altered.

The publisher would welcome notes of any such changes.

Front Cover: Lac d'Estaing (Routes 45, 46, 47, 48)

CONTENTS

PREFACE TO THE FOURTH EDITION

The growth of activity within the Pyrenees during the past decade has been astonishing, and commercial interests on both sides of the international border have mushroomed in order to service that activity. Where in the past information was hard to come by, numerous publications in a choice of languages, and maps of varying degrees of accuracy are now readily available. The range of accommodation has expanded and improved, and scores of roadheads have been equipped with information boards detailing trail options. There are now hundreds of clear trails by which to explore valley systems that were formerly unmarked, with waymarks and signposts of a standard equal to many regions of the Alps. As a consequence the Pyrenees has lost much of its wilderness quality, but happily none of its grandeur.

In the 3rd edition of this guide I rejoiced in the knowledge that more enthusiasts were able to experience some of the previously hidden corners of these mountains, but voiced a fear that this increased popularity might result in a negative effect on the Pyrenean environment. Whilst it is impossible to ignore the plethora of well-marked paths and tracks that score through the honeypot areas, it is encouraging to find that in many instances there appears to have been very little in the way of negative environmental impact. Long may this be so.

However, the Pyrenean environment remains a very fragile one, and it behoves all of us who go there to walk or climb to do so with a heightened awareness of our responsibilities. Our aim should be to leave no sign of our passage, and to ensure that future generations enjoy the same unspoilt glories of these mountains that we experience today.

This latest volume contains a number of changes, additions and revisions to previous editions in order to keep up to date, and with each new visit I discover new routes to include. The boundaries to some chapters included in earlier editions have been expanded here, and in certain cases now absorb neighbouring areas which formerly had chapters of their own. A few routes have been deleted.

As ever I am indebted to many fellow Pyrenean enthusiasts for keeping me up-to-date with changes that occur, or for suggesting new areas for inclusion. The lively correspondence of more than three decades of *Pyrénéisme* provides a constant source of pleasure.

My thanks then to the following people who have added much to my days among the mountains, either by their company, by supplying me with useful information, or by simply sharing their experiences through the media of letters: Michael Adams, Henri Baudrimont, David Brown, Sam Collett, Robin Culverhouse, Brian Davis, Peter Derbyshire and Jude Lock (at Borderline Holidays in Barèges), Gustav Dobrzynski who drew the original maps, Rosemary Durose for countless translations, Nigel Fry, Mike Hobby, Philip Humble, Paul Lucia, Colin Mortlock, Robert Ollivier, the staff at Rando Éditions (formerly Randonnées Pyrénéennes) in Tarbes, Alan Payne, Anne Shipley, Pete Smith, Keith Sweeting, Les Telford, Chris Townsend, Hugh Walton, John Willis and, of course, my wife and daughters. I am deeply grateful to them all – but I owe a particular debt of gratitude to Jean and Pierre Ravier, the ultimate *Pyrénéistes*, whose flow of information, advice and encouragement has been a regular and much-valued source of pleasure since the early 'seventies. Their devotion to all things Pyrenean is a true inspiration.

Kev Reynolds

Pic du Midi d'Ossau – view from below Refuge d'Ayous
(Routes 18, 24, 26 and High Route 4)

INTRODUCTION

For centuries the Pyrenees basked in the mystery of the unknown. Unaccountably dismissed as holding little of importance to the climber, mountain walkers ignored them almost completely. But all that has changed and the Pyrenees have now become the focus of attention for mountain activists of all degrees of commitment. Not just walkers and climbers, but *parapente* enthusiasts, mountain bikers, white-water kayak buffs, bird-watchers, butterfly and flower lovers, cavers and those who gain a thrill from descending horrific waterfalls and seemingly inaccessible canyons – the sport known as *canyoning*. As an arena for outdoor adventure the Pyrenees fulfills so many dreams.

The Alps they are not, and it would be a mistake to attempt comparisons. These are mountains of another order, with something to offer every climber and walker. There are peaks in excess of 3000 metres that are within reach of most hill-walkers weaned on the heights of Snowdonia or the Lakeland fells, but also vertical faces of awesome stature to test the stamina and expertise of the ardent rock specialist. There are valleys lost in the transient mists where weeks of high summer pass with barely a visitor – though these admittedly are growing fewer with the passage of time. There are tracts of unspoiled upland to answer the dreams of the devoted backpacker, and acres of alpine flowers of such rich variety that the botanist could happily spend months of worthwhile exploration there.

This guide is an introduction to one of Europe's finest mountain ranges. It offers suggestions for walks, multi-day tours and moderate ascents of some of the principal summits in the section known as the Central, or High Pyrenees. Those whose ambitions lie in scaling the more extreme faces are directed to *Rock Climbs in the Pyrenees* by Derek L.Walker (Cicerone Press), and to various publications in French and Spanish on sale in Pyrenean resorts that list possibilities of routes outside the scope of this present volume.

'Europe ends at the Pyrenees' is a well-established cliché born of a geographical half-truth. For the mountain barrier stretching for some 400 kilometres between the Atlantic and the Mediterranean acts as a natural frontier dividing Western Europe from the Iberian peninsular, separating a mosaic of northern cultures from those of Spain, whose expanse is dusted with the hot dry breath of Africa.

The generally accepted picture of the range is one of a solitary chain of mountains spreading in a line aiming roughly eastwards from the Atlantic. In fact the axis consists of two lines of virtually equal length; one running a little south of east from the sharp corner of the Bay of Biscay to end in the peaks of Saboredo; the other overlapping by about 12 kilometres and stretching to the Mediterranean at Cape Cerbere. Where the two lines overlap runs the Vall d'Aran, and the gap is bridged by the Port de la Bonaigua (2070m). With a few notable exceptions the frontier traces the watershed and, generally speaking, the major peaks are positioned along it. There are, however, important massifs – and these include the very highest – that are separated to the south of the international boundary by parallel valleys.

The range is one of startling contrasts. On the northern slopes mountains fall steeply to the plains, while the Spanish side is confused by a series of successive ridges – or sierras – which run in a maze away from the main crest to subside in the badlands of the Ebro basin. In the west the Basque country receives heavy, moisture-laden winds from the Atlantic, but the eastern sector has a truly Mediterranean climate with low rainfall confined to the winter months, and summers that are very hot.

Scenically the landscape is full of diversity, offering a rich variety of features guaranteed to excite and entice the first-time visitor. Forests of oak, pine and beech in the west are far removed from vineyards and orchards that dress the sun-baked plateaux of Catalonia. But between these two extremes the High Pyrenees – the area covered by this guide – contain all the attractions of alpine scenery; sharp, irregular peaks splashed with snow, shallow glaciers, deep, trench-like canyons, great amphitheatres (cirques), and many hundreds of glistening mountain tarns.

The High Pyrenees is that portion of the chain bordered by Pic d'Anie (2504m) in the west, and the Carlit (or Carlitte) massif to the north-east of Andorra. It contains three National Parks and all the 3000 metre summits – recently listed as 129 principal peaks and 67 secondary summits, with 82 ridge projections; a total of 278.

NATIONAL PARKS

In 1967 the French authorities designated an irregularly shaped area as National Park. The *Parc National des Pyrénées* (PNP) stretches mostly as a thin ribbon from the mountains south of Lescun eastwards as far as the Néouvielle massif; a distance of around 100 kilometres with an area of 45,700 hectares. Within its boundaries rise perhaps the finest individual peaks north of the watershed; Pic du Midi d'Ossau, Balaitous, Vignemale, Marboré and the complete Cirque de Gavarnie as well as the neighbouring cirques of Estaubé, Troumouse and Barroude. There are more than 100 mountain tarns. On its eastern edge lies the Néouvielle Nature Reserve with its own wild appeal, which has been preserved since 1935.

Whilst centres of tourism, particularly the establishment of winter sports facilities, are encouraged up to the Park's limits, the PNP itself remains a sanctuary where the natural beauty of the mountains receives official protection, albeit against increasing pressure from outside interests.

South of Gavarnie lies the *Parque Nacional de Ordesa y Monte Perdido*. Although the smallest of the three Pyrenean parks, it is the most visually stunning from the sheer grandeur of its vibrantly coloured walls and the drama of the three canyons, Ordesa, Anisclo and Escuain, contained within it. Ordesa was granted National Park status as long ago as 1918, before any major development could detract from the upper reaches of the Arazas river. Today the only concessions to tourism are the Visitor Centre, restaurant and car park at the end of a four-kilometre stretch of road. Paths are plentiful, but the magnificent forests of beech, silver fir and pine are quite unspoiled, and the open meadows at the head of the valley display a host of alpine plants. Anisclo is a more recent addition (1982), and was included within the park's boundaries in time to save this glorious deep trench from being flooded for hydro-electric purposes. Less well-known is the remote slice of the Escuain gorge, accessed by a narrow 15 kilometre road that ends at the all-but deserted hamlet of Escuain whose population is numbered in single figures. North of this the upper reaches of the Valle de Pineta above Bielsa are also contained within the park's boundaries.

Of the mountains which loom over the park, mention should be made of the cliffs of Mondarruego (2848m) that form a spur separating the canyon of Bujaruelo (Ara) from that of Ordesa, the stark wall of Tozal del Mallo with its 400 metres of dramatically exposed South Face, the Fraucata Face of Arruebo (2751m) and, overlooking Ordesa, Anisclo and the Valle de Pineta, Monte Perdido (Mont Perdu; 3355m) third highest mountain in the Pyrenees.

The third National Park is also found on the Spanish slopes. The *Parc Nacional d'Aigües Tortes i Estany de Sant Maurici* lies farther to the east in Catalonia and is a wild, tangled country wedged between the valleys of the Noguera Ribagorzana and the Noguera Pallaresa, with the Vall d'Aran to the north. This National Park was established in 1955, but was extended in 1986 and again ten years later; a region of numerous lakes – many of which have been dammed – sudden jagged peaks and idyllic intimate cirques. In the Encantados will be found climbs of quality, yet the whole region abounds with opportunities for scrambles at varying degrees of difficulty, while walkers have a veritable wonderland to explore for days on end.

Though not strictly a National Park, the establishment of the *Parque Natural Posets-Maladeta* in the 1990s put a girdle of protection around the two highest massifs. The boundaries of this extend from the Valle de Gistau on the west to the Noguera Ribagorzana, with just one road intruding along the Valle del Esera north of Benasque. West of the Esera the Posets massif rewards walkers, climbers and trekkers with some wonderful wild country, while to the east the Maladeta attracts on account of its bulk and superior height. Both cradle numerous tarns in their remote hidden corries, and display a remarkable alpine flora.

MOUNTAINS, FLOWERS AND ANIMALS

The range is of similar vintage to the Alps, being formed during the Tertiary upheavals of 50–100 million years ago. Broadly speaking it has a distinct central core of crystalline rocks against which were thrust sedimentary blocks brought to the surface during processes of folding. (See, for example, the aggravated strata of the Cirque de Gavarnie.) These folds were intensified by restrictions imposed from the north by the Central Plateau, and from the south by the Spanish Meseta. There is, however, a complex distribution of rock types throughout the range. While limestones dominate at the western end, granite of varying qualities is generally found in the heart of the chain; but anomolies exist in a number of massifs.

Glaciers sculpted the valleys and were responsible for eroding sharp alpine summits. As with the Alps, the Pyrenees were most affected by glaciation during the Quaternary Ice Age, when a front of almost 300 kilometres was spread with ice. Evidence is everywhere to be seen. U-shaped valleys, hanging valleys and abundant cirques tell just part of the story, and there are well over a thousand glacial lakes left behind by the last Ice Age to add a prominent and picturesque feature.

With somewhere in the region of 180 plant species endemic to the Pyrenees there is much of interest for botanists. Not only are there plants normally associated with lowland areas of Western Europe, but also species representative of other alpine regions, as well as plants usually found farther south in the Iberian Peninsular, together with those of a more specific Mediterranean identity. Each has made its way into the mountains to join those Pyrenean endemics lodged there since successive Ice Ages isolated the range from its neighbouring land mass.

Among the southern foothills lavender, rosemary and other aromatic plants prosper alongside stunted conifers and coarse grass, but the vegetation of the montane belt is quite different. Meadows here correspond to the 'alps' of Switzerland with a luxurious growth of shrubs and smaller individual plants. Among wild fruits that add a tasty bonus to the walker's day are strawberries, raspberries, bilberries and red currants. But it is the true alpine flower varieties that are of major interest to the botanist.

In springtime masses of narcissi flood hillsides with their drifts of bloom – especially in the Vall d'Aran. Gentians, crocus, orchids and anemones are found in several extravagant forms. In limestone crevices the beautiful *Ramonda myconi* survives to add a splash of violet-blue, and on limestone too may be seen the white pyramid spray of the Pyrenean saxifrage, or perhaps delicate bells of campanula. In summertime high meadows are coloured by the bright blue mountain iris, *Iris xiphioides,* and the tall, feathery plumes of the Pyrenean asphodel. Low-growing clumps of *Daphne mezereon* spread their sweet scent about them and *Arenaria tetraquetra* form hard white cushions on exposed rocks. Juniper and alpenroses confuse with calf-high cover on steep slopes; amongst the screes pink clusters of the Moss campion, *Silene acaulis,* break the monotony of naked rock. Every level has its own dimension of colour and fragrance.

For more in-depth information on the flora of the Pyrenees, the *Bulletins* of the Alpine Garden Society, the field guide *Flowers of South-West Europe* by Oleg Polunin and B.E.Smythies, *The Alpine Flowers of Britain and Europe* by Christopher Grey-Wilson and Marjorie Blamey, and A.W.Taylor's *Wild Flowers of the Pyrenees* are all worth consulting, as is *Mountain Flower Holidays in Europe* by Lionel Bacon.

Native fauna is best represented by the izard, the chamois of the Pyrenees. Herds are to be found in many areas of the higher valleys or roaming the edge of the permanent snowline. No less shy than their cousins of the central European mountain ranges, in the less-frequented corners of the High Pyrenees it is sometimes possible to observe individual animals closely from the shelter of boulders.

There are still a few brown bears *(Ursos arctos)* left, but their numbers have diminished to an intolerably low level and it is questionable whether any more will breed here in the wild. On the other hand, marmots are on the increase and mouflon have recently been reintroduced. Wild boar, pine marten and wild cats are said still to exist in remote regions. Both red and roe deer inhabit the heart of the range.

Smaller creatures include the brightly coloured fire salamander, with its yellow and black patches, various lizards, and the very rare desman. This last-named is unknown elsewhere in Europe outside the Caucasus and is about as large as a rat, but with mole-like features having a long snout and webbed feet. It is an aquatic creature that requires clean, untainted streams in which to live.

Ornithologists are attracted to several Pyrenean sites during the spring and autumn migrations when huge flights of birds funnel through selected passes. Eagles are represented by the golden, booted and Bonelli's, while of the vulture family the Pyrenees boast the Egyptian, griffon and bearded (Lammergeier). Linnets, goldfinches, ptarmigan, capercaillie, black redstarts, nightingales and hoopoes are also seen or heard in various locations. In Ordesa 171 bird species have been recorded.

PIONEERS

A little over two hundred years ago the maze of valleys of the Central Pyrenees were unknown to all but a few izard hunters, shepherds and smugglers. One or two notable passes were used regularly by itinerant merchants, but the mountains themselves held little of interest and were considered to be hostile barriers to trade and communications. But in the summer of 1787 – a year after Paccard and Balmat's historic first ascent of Mont Blanc – Louis-Francois Ramond de Carbonnières (1755–1827) arrived to dispel some of their mystery.

Ramond was the first of the true mountain poets. A politician, aspiring geologist and botanist, he had an enthusiasm for wild country which had developed during an early visit to Switzerland. In five weeks of Pyrenean exploration he made an ascent of Pic du Midi de Bigorre, one of the earliest sightings of Monte Perdido and the first recorded attempt on the Maladeta. Though his achievements were modest when compared with those of some later pioneers, Ramond's name will forever be associated with the exploration of large tracts of hitherto unknown territory. Later he returned to the Pyrenees for a much longer stay, in temporary exile from the bloodbath of the Revolution. During this period he was the inspiration behind the first ascent of Monte Perdido in 1802, repeating the ascent himself a few days later.

Coinciding with Ramond's first visit were the geographers, Reboul and Vidal, from the Academy of Toulouse. It was they who climbed the first 3000 metre peak here, Touron de Néouvielle in 1787, and also encouraged an unknown shepherd from the Aspe Valley to make the ascent of Pic du Midi d'Ossau. Ramond met them on the summit of Pic du Midi de Bigorre.

Prior to the explorations of Ramond, Reboul and Vidal, a few isolated ascents had been achieved, but it was not until the early decades of the nineteenth century that survey officers and 'men of science' initiated a campaign that saw the easiest mountains won. Local hunters were employed as guides by a few tourists prepared to foresake the charms of the valleys, yet with few exceptions professional guiding rarely matched standards attained in the Alps. Guides reached the summit of the Vignemale in 1837 and the following year led an English spinster, Miss Anne Lister, on the first tourist ascent.

In 1842 the highest summit of the range, Pico de Aneto (3404m), was climbed by a Russian, Platon de Tchihatcheff, together with Albert de Francqueville and the guides Argarot, Redonnet and Ursule.

By 1858 all the highest summits had been climbed, yet in many ways the 'Golden Age' of exploration was yet to begin. This, when it came, was largely shouldered by two men; Charles Packe and Count Henry Russell. Packe was a serious, scientific man, "a mountaineer in the best and noblest sense of the word; he was the Tyndall of the Pyrenees." The wealthy squire of Stretton Hall in Leicestershire, Packe was a barrister and an author before he came to the Pyrenees, but once seen, he was prepared to devote his considerable energies to unravelling their mysteries. His great contribution to general knowledge of the range was the publication in 1862 of his *Guide to the Pyrenees,* a work of depth and later enlarged. Before long no-one knew the mountains better than he. His journeys were countless, the Spanish heights in particular coming under scrutiny, and his map of the Maladeta massif which he produced in 1866 was far more accurate than many of its successors, covering an area of "no less than 1000 square kilometres, where none but chamois hunters had gone before him."

Early in his career Packe met Russell by Lac Bleu near Barèges and a friendship was cemented by a common bond of the mountains, but friends though they became, they were of widely differing temperaments.

Count Henry Patrick Marie Russell-Killough (1834–1909) was the most enthusiastic of all the early pioneers. Born at Toulouse of a French mother and Irish father, he became a relentless advocate of the range from 1861 on, and in the broad history of mountaineering must surely contend for the title of the sport's greatest eccentric. His new ascents were numerous, his love of solitude legendary. But the passion which he held for the Vignemale above all others is unparalleled. It was a passion which inspired many madcap escapades including being half-buried alive on the summit, and the excavation of a number of grottoes in which he lived for long periods during the summer, holding dinner parties there on the edge of a glacier and also celebrating Mass with a congregation of friends kneeling on the ice outside his cave. In 1889 Russell leased the mountain from the *syndicat* of the Valley of Barèges, "without right to forbid trespass" for a total of 99 years at the sum of one franc per year. In obvious delight he wrote, "It is certainly the highest estate in Europe and, despite its sterility, I would not exchange it for the finest in France."

A statue of Russell stands just above the road at the entrance to Gavarnie, gazing with longing towards the Vignemale, while several of his grottoes remain to this day in the walls of his mountain.

Mention should also be made of Henri Brulle (1854–1936) who was responsible, along with his guide Célestin Passet, for raising the standard of climbs in the Pyrenees over a very long period. Brulle and Passet spearheaded the 'Heroic Age' with a number of daring routes, many of which were well ahead of their time. Among these was the classic Couloir de Gaube on the North Face of the Vignemale. This route, climbed in August 1889, was not repeated in its entirety until 1933. Brulle made hard first ascents in the Posets, Maladeta and Encantados regions. On Pic du Midi d'Ossau he and Rene d'Astorg forced a North Face route via La Fourche, and on the North Face of Monte Perdido another hard ascent by way of the dangerous icefall – now much diminished. Brulle travelled far and climbed in many other ranges, particularly in the Alps where he died after encountering foul weather conditions during an attempt on Mont Blanc. He was 82.

Célestin Passet (1845–1917) came from Gavarnie. Always popular, he accompanied both Brulle and Russell on many of the most difficult climbs of the period, and his expertise was constantly in demand. With his cousin, Henri (Packe's favourite), the standard of Pyrenean guiding rose. Célestin and Henri both climbed in the Alps and were invited by Whymper to join him on his trip to the Andes. Neither wished to be away from the Pyrenees for long and declined the offer.

After the turn of the century the five brothers Cadier emerged from the tranquillity of the Aspe Valley with enterprising new climbs. Sharing fresh levels of determination they created notable routes on the Maladeta and Balaitous, among others, and recorded their exploits in the classic, *Au Pays des Isards*.

In the twenties and thirties one name stands out above all others. Dr Jean Arlaud (1896–1938) achieved an outstanding number of new climbs at a consistently high standard. In the heart of the range his exploits – and those of the *Groupe des Jeunes* which he headed – were of an almost frantic nature, but his activities were brought to a premature end by a fall from a ridge in the Gourgs Blancs two years after he'd taken part in the first French Himalayan expedition to Hidden Peak.

In 1933 the *Groupe Pyrénéiste de Haute Montagne* (GPHM) was formed, the nucleus being that elite band of climbers who had repeated Brulle's Couloir de Gaube route. Robert Ollivier, Roger Mailly, Henri Barrio and their compatriots led the next stage of

Pyrénéisme, searching for aiguilles and blank faces on which to pursue their sport. The Ravier twins, Jean and Pierre, from Bordeaux carried the momentum through the second half of the twentieth century with the 'Age of Extreme Climbing'.

Today climbers from France and Spain, from Britain and elsewhere, are attracted more and more by the promise of sun-baked sandstone, andesite, limestone or granite, by vast canyon walls or curious thumb-like projections, as much as the classic north faces that soar in uncompromising sweeps of perfection from green tranquil valleys. And although all the summits have been climbed and no-one is ever likely to gain a reputation from their exploits on these mountains, there remains a wealth of still-to-be-explored rock on which to expend one's energies, while the range itself continues to exude that air of benevolent mystery that won the hearts of men like Ramond and Russell, Packe and Brulle and all other pioneers, known and unknown, through two centuries and more of activity.

NOTES FOR WALKERS AND CLIMBERS

The weather here is rather more predictable than that of the Alps, the summer season more settled. However, every mountain area has its own climatic peculiarities, and in this respect the Pyrenees is no exception. Since the range has a southerly latitude summer days tend to be hot, particularly in the Spanish valleys. Mediterranean brilliance lights the skies and southerly breezes drift with a *mañana* indolence. Yet the northern slopes are washed with a rather different influence – illustrated so clearly by contrasts of vegetation – as moist air gusts from the west, bringing with it rainclouds that may persist throughout the afternoon. Many are the times that I have basked in the sun's warmth on a Spanish summit and gazed over cloud-seas that swamped French valleys.

But there is a danger in generalisation, and a danger too in adopting a misguided complacency over a day that begins warm and cloudless. Thunderstorms form rapidly south of the watershed when the hot, dry air of the Ebro rises in the upper valleys to mix with vagrant cooler airstreams washing from the north. These thunderstorms come with little advance warning and may be quite violent. As they form, summits and exposed ridges should be vacated quickly. It is best, therefore, to plan the day's activity with the possibility of storms in mind. Few of the routes described in this guide require a full day's commitment. With minimal snow and ice cover pre-dawn starts are rarely required, and it should normally be possible to have the main difficulties of a climb over by midday. The lower slopes and valleys have sufficient of interest in them to extend one's enjoyment far beyond that of the ascent itself.

In the higher mountains the climbing season does not begin until about mid-June. Snow conditions should by then be generally good and the weather settling into a pattern of predictability. July and August will be hot with a minimum of snow on the peaks and a maximum of flies in the valleys. September sees the first real night frosts and the occasional day of snow. When the weather is good in September it has a golden brilliance and the air vibrant with a mixture of sun and the hint of frost. October marks the lead-in to winter with days of low cloud and rain, unless autumn has managed to extend an Indian summer to the valleys, in which case the mountains will be superb.

Winter stretches through to March or early April when selected areas are given over to skiing. But snow conditions are notoriously unpredictable here and as one year may be almost too-heavily endowed with snow, and the next have practically nothing, there is a question mark hanging over the future of commercial ski resorts. Spring bursts with a vengeance in late March–early April. Then is the time for the botanist who will find the next three months – depending on the altitude of interest – an ever-evolving pattern of colour and fragrance.

Choice of equipment to take depends, of course, on the activity planned. On most of the ascents described one will need no more than is normally used on fell-walks at home. Where additional items of equipment are recommended, for example ice axe or crampons, a note will be found at the head of the relevant route description. A rope is not always necessary, although one ought to be packed as insurance against an unexpected difficulty or in the event of need for psychological aid. Safety helmets are advised on certain routes where loose stones are to be found. The ordinary route on Pic du Midi d'Ossau is a classic case in point, for there are one or two gullies to be climbed that hold no particular difficulty or danger in themselves, but because of the popularity of the mountain and the loose rock in the gullies, a very real danger exists of receiving a stone on the head dislodged by parties above.

Rock climbers will know what is required by way of hardware – again depending on the scale of their commitment. Bivouac gear will only be needed on the most severe of climbs.

To summarise, for summer ascents of the higher peaks, activists will probably be comfortable wearing light clothing, but they should carry warm, windproof and waterproof gear too, as the weather can change rapidly. Take plenty of high factor suncream, sunglasses and lip salve, plus hat to shield the sun. Emergency food, torch and spare batteries should be carried in the rucksack as well as compass, map of the area and whistle. A first aid kit should always be carried.

Since the Pyrenees offer one of the finest wilderness camping areas in Europe, a lightweight tent will be of great value. Sleeping bags adequate for the vagaries of a British summer in the mountains should be sufficient when camping here. Should the plan be to spend your entire holiday in the mountains, as opposed to travelling from region to region by car, you are strongly advised to carry sufficient fuel for all your cooking. Otherwise it may well be necessary to travel great distances in order to restock diminished supplies. Do not cook on open fires, avoid fouling water supplies, and leave no trace of your having spent a night in any wild campspot.

LONG ROUTES FOR WALKERS

Three long-distance traverses of the Pyrenees are worth the consideration of backpackers. The first of these is the *Haute Randonnée Pyrénéenne* (HRP), a classic 45-day trek leading from the Atlantic coast to the Mediterranean. This is the trekker's route *par excellence*. It requires well-practised navigation skills, demands stamina and the ability to carry camping equipment and several days' supplies at a time, and as it follows the frontier crest wherever possible, a knowledge and understanding of mountainous terrain is imperative. But what a route to tackle! The full traverse is treated to a route guide by Georges Véron (consult the Bibliography), but within the pages of the present guidebook will be found descriptions of the High Route as it passes through the very best of the Pyrenees – from Lescun to Andorra.

GR10 *(Grande Randonnée 10)* also travels from Atlantic to Mediterranean but at lower altitudes than the HRP. It covers around 860 kilometres from start to finish, and has the luxury of roofed accommodation at the end of most day stages – usually *gîtes d'étape*.

The GR10 is waymarked throughout and is treated to an English-language guidebook, *The Pyrenean Trail GR10* by Alan Castle (Cicerone Press).

Gran Recorrido 11 is Spain's answer to the GR10; a tremendous backpacker's route through some of the finest and wildest scenery south of the watershed. See *Through the Spanish Pyrenees – GR11* by Paul Lucia (Cicerone Press).

There are also three long routes that cross the Pyrenees from north to south. The *Chemin de Saint Jacques de Compostelle* (GR65) wanders over the Basque mountains south of St Jean-Pied-de-Port by way of the Roncesvalles pass. A guidebook to this route, in French, has been produced by Rando Éditions. (See also: *The Way of St James: Le Puy to Santiago* by Alison Raju, published by Cicerone Press.) GR7 makes a north–south traverse via Andorra and heads as far south as Barcelona, while GR36 makes a traverse of the Eastern Pyrenees from Albi to Montserrat.

MOUNTAIN HUTS AND GÎTES D'ÉTAPE

Facilities on offer at mountain huts vary greatly. Some are quite luxurious with guardians in summer residence offering a complete meals service, while others may be little more than four walls and a roof. A few of the older CAF buildings manage still to convey some of the atmosphere of the pioneers who first used them a century or so ago (Refuge Bayssellance near the Vignemale is a good example), and yet one or two of the more recent huts erected by the PNP authorities – and also by some of the Spanish climbing clubs – offer a greater degree of comfort.

Information regarding individual refuges in the areas covered by this guide will be found under specific regional details. For a list of all mountain huts, the specialist publisher Rando Éditions, whose headquarters is in Tarbes, publishes a very useful book: *Gîtes d'étape Refuges – France et Frontières*.

In the lower mountain areas north of the frontier a whole chain of *gîtes d'étape* have been established for the outdoor fraternity. Not to be confused with Gîtes de France (holiday homes) *gîtes d'étape* are rather like private youth hostels and are often found on farms or in quiet villages. Every *gîte* should have facilities for self-catering, but in addition many offer a meals service too. Dormitory accommodation is the norm, but some also have private bedrooms. Showers are provided. Large-scale IGN maps indicate the position of *gîtes d'étape* on them.

Where possible it is advisable to arrive at your chosen refuge during the afternoon – especially at the height of the season (mid-July to end of August) when the more popular huts will be extremely busy. Bed space is allocated on a first-come, first-served basis. Leave your boots in the porch rack provided, changing into either trainers or the communal hut shoes usually issued for that purpose. Then seek out the guardian to order bed space for the night, and also indicate what meals, if any, are required. These may be surprisingly good, or dismal efforts, depending upon the abilities and/or interest of the guardian, or how recently supplies were brought from the valley. Most will be high in calorific value. Not all huts have self-catering facilities, so if it is your intention to cook your own food, you must be prepared to be self-sufficient with regard to equipment and utensils as well as food.

Access to dormitories is often restricted until early evening, and rucksacks are not allowed in them. Standard sleeping accommodation is a long communal bunk with mattresses laid side by side upon it. Blankets will be provided. A sleeping bag liner will be found very useful, as in most cases a 'camping' quality sleeping bag will be too warm for summer use. Dormitories are not normally segregated for men and women.

Payment is usually settled with the guardian on the morning you leave, but if you plan to make an early start, arrange to pay your bill the evening before. It can be frustrating to wait an hour or more after you want to leave because the guardian is still sound asleep in his room! Members of mountain clubs that enjoy reciprocal rights will receive discounts on overnights, but not on meals provided. Members of the British Mountaineering Council (BMC) can buy a special reciprocal rights card which is valid in CAF and most Spanish club huts.

Most huts that have a guardian in summer residence will usually be partially closed out of season, although a basic winter room or rooms with bunks and a fireplace or stove will normally be available for use.

Most manned huts (if not all) are now equipped with telephones, and guardians expect walkers and climbers to reserve accommodation in advance – especially in the high season. Usually the guardian will phone ahead for you to the next hut on your itinerary. You are advised to take advantage of this facility.

EMERGENCY SERVICES

In certain respects the Pyrenees offer climbers a greater degree of commitment than will be experienced in many other European ranges, and the question of rescue in the event of accident can be of particular importance. In some areas the possibility of rescue depends solely on the proximity of other climbers capable of rendering assistance. In the PNP it is often a fairly speedy process to call up trained rescue services, for most (if not all) the popular huts are in radio contact with the gendarmerie and a highly efficient, helicopter-aided service can be set in action within minutes of the alarm being raised. On the other hand, some areas are so isolated that even the mildest of accidents can have serious results if the party involved is incapable of providing adequate self-help. Off-season ascents in even the summer-popular Maladeta region, to name but one, should be undertaken with an awareness of the serious nature of the expedition and of the consequences arising from an accident. In valleys where there are no huts and few visitors outside aid may be impossible. The moral is clear: know the capabilities of your party and climb within them.

The rescue service, where it exists, can be extremely expensive to call out, and should only be requested where absolutely necessary. Rescue insurance is advisable.

In the event of an accident and a manned hut is not near to hand, make for the nearest inhabited valley and, when a telephone is at last located – it may be a very long way from the scene of the accident – call the gendarmerie (when in France), explain that an accident has happened, give the name of the place from where you are phoning, then wait for their arrival. By means of an accurately-marked map show where the accident has occurred and give what details you can. In Spain contact the nearest Gardia Civil station. Telephone numbers are as below:

France

Western Pyrénées:	05 59 39 86 22
Hautes-Pyrénées:	05 62 92 41 41
Haute Garonne:	(PGHM Luchon) 05 61 79 28 36
	(CRS Luchon) 05 61 79 83 79
Eastern Pyrenees:	(CRS Perpignan) 04 68 61 79 20

Spain

Navarre:	112
Aragon:	062
Jaca:	974 31 13 50
Catalonia:	085

The international distress signal is six blasts on a whistle, or six torch flashes after dark, per minute, followed by a minute's pause, then repeat until a reply is received. The reply is three blasts or flashes followed by a minute's silence. Helicopters may be visually summoned with the use of arm signals. If assistance is needed raise both arms in the air; but one arm raised, the other lowered, means assistance is not required (see box on Mountain Safety at the front of the book).

GETTING THERE

By air, the Pyrenees are most easily accessible via Tarbes–Lourdes and Toulouse. There are good railway connections from both towns.

Road routes through France to all sections of the Pyrenees are straightforward. Most autoroutes are toll roads, but the cost of using them may well be deemed worthwhile for the time saved. Off autoroutes beware of exceeding the speed limit as radar traps operate everywhere and infringements usually bring about an instant fine.

Note that roads are excessively busy on weekends between mid-July and mid-August.

Travel by car brings numerous advantages to those planning to base themselves in one or more areas, but is not such a good idea if you want to make a long cross-country journey such as tackling part of the HRP. Access by bus or rail comes into its own then.

Eurolines express coaches operate summer services from London Victoria to Lourdes, Toulouse and Andorra. These journeys take around 20 hours and offer the cheapest scheduled fares for public transport (Eurolines, 52 Grosvenor Gardens, Victoria, London SW1W 0AU Tel: 020 7730 8235 – Website: www.eurolines.co.uk). Tickets are bookable through National Express agents.

From London to the Pyrenean rail-head takes less than twenty-four hours, whereas the same distance by car will normally take almost twice as long. French trains are fast and clean, and the SNCF has a range of discount fares which are worth enquiring about (French

State Railways, 179 Piccadilly, London W1V 0BA Tel: 0891 515 477). If planning a journey by rail, consider travelling by Eurostar from London (Waterloo) to Paris.

Rail links from Paris (Gare d'Austerlitz) to areas described in the following pages are given below. Note that the super-fast TGV also has a service (TGV Atlantique) which could be useful. This runs five times a day at up to 300km per hour from Paris (Montparnasse) to Lourdes via Pau. There are TGV services also to Hendaye, Toulouse and Perpignan.

Aspe Valley & Cirque de Lescun
By main line to Pau and change for Oloron-Ste-Marie. SNCF bus from Oloron to Bedous or Etsaut in the Aspe Valley.

Pic du Midi
Main line to Pau, and branch line to Oloron-Ste-Marie. Then by bus to Laruns.

Balaitous
As for Pic du Midi for western approaches.

Marcadau–Vignemale–Lutour
Direct to Lourdes by train, thence by SNCF bus to Cauterets.

Gavarnie–Ordesa–Monte Perdido
By rail to Lourdes, thence by SNCF bus to Gavarnie.

Estaubé, Troumouse and Barroude
By rail to Lourdes, then take the Gavarnie (SNCF) bus as far as Gèdre for a western approach.

Néouvielle
By rail to Lourdes, then by SNCF bus to Barèges for a northern approach. For the eastern side of the area go to Lannemezan on the Tarbes–Toulouse railway line, bus to Arreau, and again bus to St Lary or Fabian.

Posets–Maladeta
Rail to Luchon via Toulouse.

Andorra
By rail to L'Hospitalet and connecting bus to Andorra.

Carlit
By rail to Ax-les-Thermes, L'Hospitalet, Porté Puymorens or Porta. Or

by the 'little yellow train' *(petit train jaune)* to Mont Louis from either Latour de Carol or from Perpignan via Villefranche-les-Conflent.

USING THE GUIDE

The aim of this guide is to introduce the walker and climber to one of Europe's finest mountain ranges. By its very nature it has to be selective, for to cover all the possibilities the Pyrenees have to offer would require a volume far too bulky to be of practical use. Areas chosen for inclusion have been selected to provide as wide a choice of country as possible, with the principal peaks highlighted with descriptive routes. That is not to suggest there are no other regions worthy of inclusion, but it is hoped that those who are drawn again to these mountains will be eager to seek out other peaks and valleys for which there are no route guides available. Then an even greater sense of personal involvement may be experienced.

Ascents described are mostly of limited difficulty, but a moderately difficult outing is not necessarily an uninteresting one, and if approached with an open mind the unique character of the Pyrenees will reveal itself.

Regions included are described geographically in massifs travelling from west to east, irrespective of their position with regard to the watershed. In describing ascent routes the international (French) adjectival system has been adopted for grading overall expeditions. Individual rock pitches, where their inclusion dictates a specific standard, are bracketed as Roman numerals. These symbols are shown below against the corresponding U.K. grading system.

International

F:	facile (Easy)
PD:	peu difficile (Moderately difficult)
AD:	assez difficile (Fairly difficult)
D:	difficile (Difficult)
TD:	très difficile (Very difficult)
ED:	extrément difficile (Extremely difficult)

Rock climbing grades

I	Easy and Moderate
II	Moderately difficult and Difficult
III	Very difficult

Estany Tort de Rius (Route 138 and High Route 18)

IV	Hard very difficult to Medium severe
V	Hard severe to Mild very severe
VI	Very severe to Hard very severe

Where times are shown for approach marches to huts, a generous allowance has been made on the assumption that one is heavily laden. On ascents it is assumed that the climber is fit and good conditions prevail. No allowance has been made for rests, and of course all times depend on circumstances relevant to each individual.

Likewise, times given for walks make no allowances for rest stops or photographic halts.

Distances throughout are quoted in kilometres and heights in metres, and are based on the recommended map for the area where possible. Certain errors are judged to have crept in on some maps, particularly those for the Spanish mountains, and in such instances heights have been obtained from other sources deemed reliable at the time. Maps for each area are shown at the head of individual sections. Map suppliers are listed in Appendix A.

In route descriptions, directions given for 'left' and 'right' apply to the direction of travel in ascent, descent or traverse. However, when used with reference to the banks of glaciers or streams 'left' and 'right' indicate the direction of flow; ie: looking downwards. Where doubts may occur a compass direction is also given.

Finally, the word 'stream' is used throughout, irrespective of the size or volume of flowing water. In some cases this indicates little more than an indolent brook, while at other times it refers to a raging torrent. Conditions vary greatly, and what is a silver trickle one year may well be a flooding river the next.

Abbreviations appearing in the following pages are listed below:

CAF	Club Alpin Francais
CEC	Centre Excursionista de Catalunya
EA	Editorial Alpina
EDF	Electricité de France
FAM	Fédéracion Aragonesa de Montanismo
FEM	Fédéracion Espanola de Montanismo
FFM	Fédération Française de la Montagne
GR10	Grande Randonnée 10
HRP	Haute Randonnée Pyrénéenne
ICONA	Instituto de Conservacion de la Natura
IGN	Institut Géographique National
PNP	Parc National des Pyrénées
RE	Rando Éditions
TCF	Touring Club de France
kms	kilometres
m	metres

ASPE VALLEY AND CIRQUE DE LESCUN

Position:	In France, north and north-west of the Col du Somport
Access:	N134 south from Oloron-Ste-Marie. For Lescun take minor road heading west, 6kms upstream of Bedous. By train from Pau to Oloron-Ste-Marie, and bus from Oloron to Lescun-Cette-Eygun. No public transport to Lescun itself.
Maps:	IGN Carte de Randonnées No 3 'Béarn' 1:50,000 IGN TOP 25 Series no: 1547OT 'Ossau, Vallée d'Aspe' 1:25,000
Bases:	Etsaut (597m), Borce (650m), Lescun (900m)

The Vallée d'Aspe is the most westerly of the High Pyrenees, a green, fertile region of deciduous forest and pasture where some of the last remaining European brown bears are said still to roam. The head of the valley is topped by a lovely wall of peaks that slope down to the easy saddle of the Col du Somport, but the finest mountains of all are those that form the so-called Cirque de Lescun, unseen from the valley itself but discovered on rising up the western hillside on the way to the village from which the cirque takes its name.

Lescun commands an enchanting panorama, and one which makes the best possible introduction to the range. Set upon a sloping shelf of hillside it focuses the eye away across meadows to the dark green of woodlands and up to a fairy-tale backcloth of sudden grey mountains crowding the horizon. These peaks are not high; they reach above 2000 metres, but only Pic d'Anie to the west of the village attains the significance of 2500 metres. Their undeniable attraction lies rather in their moulding, and in the contrast which they

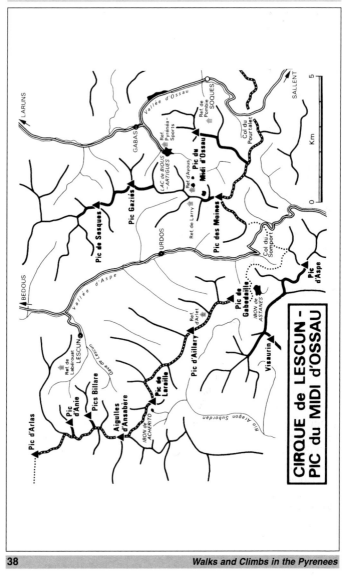

CIRQUE de LESCUN –
PIC du MIDI d'OSSAU

present between lush pastures and apparently barren rock and screes. Their walls are steep – seductively so to the rock-climbing specialist – but many of their summits may be gained by the modest scrambler too. As for the walker, the valleys that nestle and wind among their bases, and the green ridges that link one neighbouring peak with another, offer pleasures of a very special kind.

Among the most prominent mountains in the neighbourhood of Lescun and the Aspe Valley are, from west to east: Pic d'Anie (2504m), reached by a long walk from the village; the Pics Billare which rise immediately above Lescun with a lovely form and appearance; the superb Aiguilles d'Ansabère shyly hiding above their own personal little cirque to the south-west; several neat mountains that linked together form the Franco/Spanish border; Pic d'Aillary and Pic d'Arlet, both over 2200 metres rising above the Refuge d'Arlet; and the delightful Cirque d'Aspe, west of the Somport. South of Pic d'Aillary, and separated from it by the valley of the Rio Aragón Subordán in Spain, is the Visaurin (2668m), the highest of the Aspe group which is reached by way of a path from Sansanet on the northern side of the Somport.

Valley Bases:

ETSAUT (597m) nestles in the bed of the Aspe Valley, about 3.5 kilometres south of Cette-Eygun. It has a small foodstore, the 2-star Hotel des Pyrénées (Tel: 05 59 34 88 62) which houses the only restaurant, and two *gîtes d'étape*, both of which are open all year: the 68 bed Maison des Jeunes et de la Culture/Auberge de Jeunesse (Tel: 05 59 34 88 98) and the smaller 20-bed Maison de l'Ours (Tel: 05 59 34 86 38). The disused railway station contains a Maison du Parc National whose exhibits feature the European brown bear.

BORCE (650m) occupies a terrace on the western hillside overlooking Etsaut. It's an attractive medieval village of thick stone-walled houses visited by walkers tackling the GR10. There are two *gîtes d'étape:* Gîte Communal (18 places; Tel: 05 59 34 86 40) and Gîte de groupe de l'Hôpital de St-Jacques (Tel: 05 59 34 88 99). Just above the village there's a campsite usually open July to mid-September (Camping de Borce, Tel: 05 59 34 87 29).

LESCUN (900m) has a small grocery store and a post office, the 2-star Hotel du Pic d'Anie (Tel: 05 59 34 71 54) with dormitory accommodation in Refuge du Pic d'Anie opposite; dormitories also in the Maison de la Montagne (Tel: 05 59 34 79 14) and the Gîte du Lauzart which is annexed to the excellent campsite a little south-west of the village (Tel: 05 59 34 51 77). The Maison de la Montagne also acts as the local *Bureau des Guides*. A walk of about 1½hrs upvalley leads to the *Refuge de Labérouat* – see below. Lescun has limited parking space by the post office, and the classic view of the village with the Cirque de Lescun beyond is to be found by following a narrow road behind the church. This curves to the right to a few houses, then a footpath continues, from which the panoramic view is enjoyed.

Other Accommodation:

There are several other *gîtes d'étape* in and around the Vallée d'Aspe; notable among these are at **BEDOUS**, **ACCOUS** (the valley 'capital'), **URDOS**, and just below the **COL du SOMPORT**.

Mountain Huts:

REFUGE DE LABÉROUAT (1442m) is situated on the GR10 about 1½ hours' walk above Lescun. Open between January and mid-October with a guardian, it can accommodate 30 and is often busy with children's holiday groups. Meals may be provided (Tel/Fax: 05 59 34 50 43).

REFUGE D'ARLET (2000m) occupies a grassy site above the Arlet tarn almost on the frontier ridge on the route of the HRP. Built by the National Park authorities to accommodate 43 it is open from mid-June to mid-September when a guardian is in residence. Meals may be provided. Out of season the winter quarters can sleep 10 (Tel: 05 59 36 00 99).

REFUGE DE LARRY (1724m) is a small, simple, unguarded hut with few facilities but is capable of sleeping 10. Owned by the PNP it is situated on the right flank of the valley, reached in about 3½ hours from Peyrenère on the Somport road.

Route 1: Lescun (900m) – Refuge de Labérouat (1442m)

Distance:	**4 kilometres**
Height gain:	**542 metres**
Time:	**1¼–1½ hours**

This walk follows the route of GR10 all the way from Lescun and is waymarked with red–white paint flashes. It begins in the heart of the village near the Maison de la Montagne and climbs above it on a stony path between fields heading roughly north-west, and soon comes onto the narrow road which services the refuge. (There's ample parking space just before reaching the refuge, should you prefer to drive.) Follow the road to the right, but when it forks take the left branch. Soon after it bends note a waymark sending you into the right-hand meadow. The way progresses through a tree-lined gully, then up to a farm track from which you gain fine views of the Cirque de Lescun, the Pics Billare and Pic d'Anie.

The track brings you above a farm where you cut off to the right on a narrow path slanting uphill and onto a second track above another farm. Come onto the road once more at a hairpin bend. About 30 metres up the road break left on the continuing waymarked path which soon takes you across an open boggy patch, through a belt of woodland, then emerges to a broad grass path slanting uphill to the right. After passing through another belt of woodland come to a view of Pic Oueillarisse directly ahead. The path eventually makes a couple of zig-zags before spilling onto the road for the last time. Turn left. The refuge is reached in another 200 metres or so (*refreshments usually available*). An orientation table names the high points in an extensive view.

PIC D'ANIE (2504m)

Significant as first of the High Pyrenees, Pic d'Anie requires little more than a long walk to reach its summit by the standard route. With a dusting of winter snow upon it the mountain looks grand from Lescun; in fact it appears much more majestic from afar than it does on close inspection where it is revealed as a chaos of scree and limestone pits. From the summit views look over the Basque country which rolls off to the west. Below, to the north-west, is the entrance to the Gouffre de la Pierre St-Martin, one of the world's most extensive underground caverns.

Route 2: Lescun (900m) – Pic d'Anie (2504m)

Grade:	**F**
Distance:	**10 kilometres**
Height gain:	**1604 metres**
Time:	**5 hours**

From Lescun follow Route 1 as far as Refuge de Labérouat, and then beyond it to pass through woodland beneath the strange organ-pipe rocks of the Orgues de Camplong. About 1hour 15mins beyond Labérouat along the GR10 come to a simple hut, Cabane d'Ardinet (1570m), with spaces for about five people and a water supply. The path climbs on and reaches a second hut, Cabane du Cap de la Baitch (1680m), where there's room for about eight.

The GR10 here strikes north towards Pas de l'Osque and Arette la Pierre St-Martin, but the path to Pic d'Anie swings south-west and rises between Pic du Soum Couy and Pic de Countende towards Col des Anies (2030m) on the route of the HRP (an impressive karst landscape). Pic d'Anie stands to the south of the col and is reached in about 2 hours from it; the route traverses the scree-ridden north face, curves round its west face and makes the final climb from the southwest. (Allow about 3 hours for the descent.)

Route 3: Lescun (Parking Nabia; 1040m) – Lac de Lhurs (1691m)

Distance:	**5 kilometres**
Height gain:	**651 metres**
Time:	**3 hours**

Lac de Lhurs is hidden below the Table des Trois Rois in a small cirque shown on the map as Montagne de Lhurs south-west of Lescun. This walk to it is quite strenuous, but it makes for an entertaining day out. To get to the start follow signs from Lescun marked 'Lhurs (Lac)'. These take you onto one of several minor lanes cutting through the pastures. Out of Lescun there are no more road signs, but you simply remain on the initial lane ignoring alternatives. Soon after crossing a sub-valley you come to a sign pointing to the right along a track marked 'Parking Nabia 100m'. (The continuing lane goes to Pont de Masousa and Ansabère.)

Just beyond the parking space bear left where the track forks. As it makes a long loop you can make a short-cut by taking a narrow, somewhat vague path left up through a meadow to regain the track a little higher. Remain on the track now as it makes a scenic contour of hillside overlooking the great pastureland bowl of the Cirque de Lescun. When it begins a short downward slope, note a small parking space with a minor track/footpath cutting right and waymarked with yellow stripes.

Turn right here and walk uphill, soon alongside a minor stream which you cross on stepping stones and continue on its left-hand side, now in woodland. Before long the path hugs the woodland edge and joins a crossing track where you turn left. This contours for a while, then forks. Take the right branch – this too contours within the woods. After the track divides, with one stem cutting hard back to the left, the way slants uphill and maintains a steady gradient through the Bois de Larrangus. There are several alternative paths and tracks breaking away, but the main path is obvious at all junctions – keep alert for waymarks.

About 1hour 20mins from the start you come to the woodland edge near an abrupt rock wall. Here the path zigzags up to the head of a track (1455m) where you turn left. A stony path now contours immediately below an upper section of rock wall, and at the far end it curves right and resumes uphill. After passing through scrub cross an open avalanche runnel, on the far side of which you gaze into a ravine which supports the unseen Lac de Lhurs.

The path dips into the ravine entrance and crosses to its left-hand side, rising again (a very flowery stretch) in zigzags to gain a high grassy shoulder. Looking back you can see the unmistakable Pic du Midi d'Ossau to the south-east. From the shoulder the path (now broken into several braidings) cuts along the steep left-hand wall of the ravine, crosses sections of limestone pavement and brings you to the lake's outflow stream. Cross on partly-submerged rocks and follow the stream to the Lac de Lhurs. The lake is surrounded by pastures topped by screes and mountain peaks. A small unmanned cabane is seen at the far end. Most notable of the walling peaks is the tilted, semi-pointed summit of the Table des Trois Rois on which it is said the kings of Navarre, Aragón and Béarn met to agree the frontiers of their respective territories. (Allow 2 hours to descend by the same route.)

Route 4: Lescun (900m) – Cabanes d'Ansabère (1560m)

Distance:	**9 kilometres**
Height gain:	**660 metres**
Time:	**3 hours**

This walk takes you to the base of the Aiguilles d'Ansabère, those dramatic limestone pinnacles to the south-west of Lescun that appear to have been transported from the Dolomites. It's an easy walk along a country lane, through woodland and into a pastureland bowl before making a final climb to the shepherds' cabanes.

Leave Lescun by the road which branches off south-westward just below the village and goes to the campsite on the south side of the Gave de Lescun. Continue along the surfaced lane following signs to 'Masousa-Ansabère'. This leads to an official (but unpaved) parking area by the Pont de Masousa. Immediately before the parking area break away left on a forest track rising through woodland – this is not recommended for low-slung vehicles. Remaining well above the true right bank of the Gave d'Ansabère follow this track all the way to Pont Lamary where there are a few parking spaces (about 1½ hours from Lescun).

Cross the bridge and follow a clear path in and out of the woods as it gains height with the Ansabère needles now luring you on. At the top of a rise a large pastureland clearing is reached; a lovely mountain bowl with streams meandering through, dark woods on the far side and the Aiguilles d'Ansabère rising dramatically above.

Descend to the stream, cross it and climb steeply through the woods beyond. Continue climbing on the left bank of the stream until the Cabanes d'Ansabère are located below the screes fanning from the base of the needles.

PIC D'ANSABÈRE (2377m)

Routes on the Ansabère pinnacles are too extreme to fall within the scope of this guide, but their near neighbour, Pic d'Ansabère, offers an interesting, albeit easy ascent for the ordinary scrambler via Col de Pétragème, with some dramatic views to heighten the day.

Route 5: Cabanes d'Ansabère (1560m) – Pic d'Ansabère (2377m)

Grade:	F
Distance:	2.5 kilometres
Height gain:	817 metres
Time:	2½ hours

The cleft of Col de Pétragème is clearly seen from the cabanes; lying below and to the left of the Petite Aiguille soaring a short distance above to the west. The path to it winds away from the shepherds' huts bearing right, and leads among boulders and scree to reach the col after a sudden, steep pull passing directly underneath the teetering pinnacle that rears in an unbelievable gesture of defiance over the walker's shoulder.

Col de Pétragème (2082m) provides an appalling visual contrast, with a scene of decaying mountains wallowing in the sun to the south, in place of the splendour witnessed only moments before. Pass through the col which forms the frontier, and soon bear right to climb bleached limestone terraces that lead without incident to the bald summit block.

From the summit a grandstand view is gained of the Grande Aiguille directly in front. Beyond are the pastures and woodlands that roll off to the northern foothills, while out to the east Pic du Midi d'Ossau offers its unmistakable signature.

Routes on the Ansabère Aiguilles:

Experienced climbers intent on tackling some of the advanced routes here should consult the French-language guide, *Passages Pyrénéens* by Rainier Munsch, Christian Ravier and Rémi Thivel (Éditions du Pin à Crochets, 1999) which describes a number of the hardest climbs. There are several extreme routes; the original (1923) West Face on the northern aiguille is graded VI- and there are numerous others of varying degrees of length and difficulty that would reward the attention of climbers with the necessary expertise. *Les Pyrenees – les 100 plus belles courses* by Patrice de Bellefon gives two routes on the Grande and one on the Petite Aiguille to illustrate the quality of climbing to be found here. The only hard route details seen in English appeared in the ACG publication *Alpine Climbing* in 1971. A copy of this is retained in the Alpine Club Library in London.

Route 6: Lescun (Pont Lamary; 1170m) – Lac d'Ansabère (1859m) – Ibon de Acherito (1875m)

Distance:	**5 kilometres**
Height gain:	**862 metres**
Height loss:	**157 metres**
Time:	**3–3½ hours**

Two delightful mountain tarns, separated by an unnamed col on the frontier ridge, provide highlights of this walk. But there are other highlights too; views of the Aiguilles d'Ansabère and the charm of a Spanish valley stretching one's gaze to far blue sierras. It will be a good day out, for you'll need about two hours for the return to Pont Lamary, plus time spent enjoying the views. If you walk all the way from Lescun, as opposed to driving to Pont Lamary, add another 2½–3 hours for the round-trip (about 8 hours in all).

To reach Pont Lamary, see Route 4 above (but note the comment in regard to low-slung vehicles on the track between Pont de Masousa and Pont Lamary). Follow that route's continuing directions to the Cabanes d'Ansabère, then take the path which goes between the cabanes heading south to cross pastureland, rising steadily and growing clearer until the little tarn of Lac d'Ansabère is reached, about 30mins from the cabanes. (Fine view across the head of the Cirque d'Ansabère to the aiguilles.)

Leaving the tarn behind continue to climb steeply up the hillside towards the frontier ridge, and emerge on it at a point near spot height 2032m. Views south are much more pleasant than those from Col de Pétragème, as experienced on Route 5. Go left along the narrow ridge a short distance, then make a descending traverse southwards over steep grass slopes, taking great care especially should the grass be wet. Aim towards a jutting spur beyond which lies the lake of Ibon de Acherito. To reach the lake a steep descent is guided by red–white paint flashes down to its outflow at the southern end. The tarn is set in a superb amphitheatre of cliffs, while views along the valley of the Rio Aragón Subordán below extend an atmosphere of calm.

Alternative Return to Pont Lamary:

Instead of retracing the outward route, an alternative return could be made by heading round the western side of the tarn and climbing north-east to the ridge at Brèche de Hanas (2054m). Unmarked on

Aiguilles d'Ansabère

the map, this is found below, and to the north-west of, Pic de Laraille. The descent from here leads north-eastward down a steep slope with few waymarks, over scree to cross a spur projecting from Pic de Laraille, then by way of the Vallon de Lazerque whose stream joins that of the Gave d'Ansabère near Pont Lamary. (A challenging route, only for experienced mountain walkers; about 2–2½ hours from Ibon de Acherito.)

Route 7: Cabanes d'Ansabère (1560m) – Col de Burcq (2063m) – Refuge d'Arlet (2000m)

Distance:	**14 kilometres**
Height gain:	**915 metres**
Height loss:	**475 metres**
Time:	**7½ hours**

The High Route across the Pyrenees (HRP), described in detail from Lescun to Andorra elsewhere in this book, incorporates this particular walk. It's a very fine stage, but it makes for a hard day; a day of extensive views over much remote, uninhabited country. It is not a walk to consider lightly, nor one to tackle in inclement weather. Good visibility is required. Carry food and plenty of liquids, and do not leave the Acherito tarn without refilling your water bottle.

Follow Route 6 as far as Ibon de Acherito (1875m; 1 hour 45 mins). Cross the stream flowing from the southern end of the tarn and wander along the path heading south-eastwards, soon losing height but still a considerable way above the valley. At a point about 1620m (30–45 mins from the lake) a well-vegetated area with clumps of box is reached. Do not lose any more height, but instead take the narrow path which heads vaguely north-east and begins to climb through a combe, or shallow 'valley'. Above this hillsides are broad, open pastures with the frontier ridge enlivened by rocky crests. The path disappears, but crossing these pastures heading east you will see Pic de Burcq (2105m) with a col on either side of it. To the left is Col de Pau (1942m) with its frontier stone; to the right is Col de Burcq (2063m).

Through Col de Burcq (4–4½ hours) join a clear path on the French side and follow it to the right (fine views to Pic du Midi d'Ossau). The way leads round the head of the Labadie Valley first among rocks, then grass, on the ridge itself. At Col de la Cuarde (1970m) cut across to Col de Saoubathou (1949m) seen off to the east. Once through this col (6 hours 15 mins) the path rises and falls in varying degrees on a south-easterly course, until at last a sharp series of twists brings you onto a grassy plateau with Refuge d'Arlet set above its lake on the right.

The hut is owned by the PNP and has dormitory space for 43 in summer. A guardian is in occupation from mid-June until mid-September when meals may be provided (Tel: 05 59 36 00 99).

Note: For an interesting view south into Spain, wander above the hut heading west to reach Col d'Arlet (2095m) on the frontier ridge in about 15 minutes.

Route 8: Lhers (950m) – Col de Saoubathou (1949m) – Refuge d'Arlet (2000m)

Distance:	**10 kilometres**
Height gain:	**1050 metres**
Time:	**4½ hours**

An alternative approach to the Arlet refuge, this walk could be shortened by more than an hour by driving from Lhers along the Labadie Valley and parking near the National Park boundary. Lhers itself is reached by a narrow twisting road that branches south from the Lescun road about 800 metres after turning out of the Aspe Valley. It is a scattered hamlet of farms which the GR10 crosses on the way from Lescun to Borce and Etsaut. Just south of the hamlet there's a *gîte d'étape*, the Gîte de Lhers, with 18 places (Tel: 05 59 34 77 27) and facilities for camping.

Walk through Lhers heading south, passing the 18th-century village chapel on your left. The road continues beyond the last houses and about an hour or so later enters the National Park. Remain on the track, drawing ever deeper into the valley, and about 45 minutes from the PNP boundary you will reach Cabane de Caillau (1450m). Col de Saoubathou lies near the junction of ridges above to the south-east and is reached by a steeply climbing shepherds' path about 1½ hours from the cabane. Cross the col and follow the PNP path described above in Route 7 for a further hour or so to reach Refuge d'Arlet.

Other Routes to Refuge d'Arlet:

One route marked on the map leads from **LESCUN**, at first following the GR10 towards Lhers, but then breaks away from it heading south on a narrow road which leads to a parking area at 1112m about 4 kilometres from Lescun. A path continues, and enters the National Park at Pont d'Itchaxe. From here to **COL de PAU** takes about 1½ hours, and from the col the way to the refuge bears left and soon joins Route 7 at Col de Burcq (4½ hours to the hut from the end of the road).

Another approach may be made via the **VALLÉE DU BARALET**, a glen reached by minor road snaking off the Somport road at Pont d'Urdos (699m). It's possible to drive as far as Lamourane (1150m) where there is room to park a few cars. An obvious trail heads through the valley on the west bank of the stream until crossing near the head of the valley and climbing into the cirque of Montagne de Banasse. The trail joins a major route near Cabane des Caillaous where you bear right and soon after come to the Lac and Refuge d'Arlet (3 hours from the roadhead at Lamourane).

Finally, by reversing Route 10 below, it would be possible to reach Arlet in about 5½–6 hours from **SANSANET** (1320m) on the old Somport road

Route 9: Refuge d'Arlet (2000m) – Forges d'Abel (1068m)

Distance:	**9 kilometres**
Height loss:	**932 metres**
Time:	**3½ hours**

Les Forges d'Abel stand at the northern entrance to the new road-tunnel beneath the Somport, a short distance from the original valley road. This walk to it is the shortest route into the Aspe Valley from Refuge d'Arlet.

Leaving the hut go down to the tarn and walk along its left-hand shore. The continuing path heads round the Cirque de Banasse, passes several rough cabanes, then rises slightly to cross Col de Lapachouaou. The way now bears south-east on a traverse of mountainside towards an obvious spur which has to be crossed. On the south side descend into a minor glen, cross a stream below Cabane Grosse, climb over Col Plâtrière and then walk down into the shade of the Espélunguère forest (2½ hours from Arlet). The forest path brings you to a road at Pla d'Espélunguère. Bear left and follow this as it winds all the way down to Les Forges d'Abel.

Route 10: Refuge d'Arlet (2000m) – Sansanet (Aspe Valley;1320m)

Distance:	**10 kilometres**
Height loss:	**680 metres**
Time:	**4½ hours**

An easy but scenically interesting descent to the Aspe Valley below the Somport, used by the HRP. It follows the path of Route 9 for the first 2½ hours before taking a different course.

Follow the path described from Arlet to Pla d'Espélunguère (Route 9). Cross the stream which flows from the frontier peaks (there is a footbridge), and keep on the continuing trail for about 400 metres until a signpost directs you left towards Sansanet. The way climbs to a grassy saddle bordered by trees, then in a south-easterly direction comes to a forest clearing. Follow a forest track until a waymarked path leads from it to a rough pasturage in which you'll find Cabane d'Escouret (1413m; 3 hours 45 mins).

A short way beyond the cabane a signpost directs the route down to Sansanet. It is a straightforward path, mostly among trees, and it brings you to a bridge over the Aspe and the parking/picnic area of Sansanet.

Note: There is a *gîte d'étape* about 3.5 kilometres upvalley near Col du Somport. (Gîte du Somport, 12 places, open all year; Tel: 05 59 36 00 21)

Route 11: Lescun (900m) – Lhers (997m) – Etsaut (597m)

Distance:	**14 kilometres**
Height gain:	**701 metres**
Height loss:	**1004 metres**
Time:	**6 hours**

This walk follows the route of the GR10 as far as the lovely medieval village of Borce, then finishes with a short stretch of road down into the Aspe Valley. There is a climb to be made to cross the wooded Col de Barrancq (1601m), midway between Lhers and Borce, and this will be quite strenuous. The rest of the day makes use of a combination of minor roads, tracks and footpaths winding among pasture and forest.

Descend south-westward out of Lescun on a narrow road (waymarked red–white) to Pont Moulin and down to a crossroads. Go straight ahead but break away left soon after, still with waymarks, to Ferme Lestremeau. From here you wander through woodland to round a spur of hillside, and come to the southern end of the hamlet of Lhers. The climb to Col de Barrancq begins, but it is worth pausing now and then to enjoy views back to Lescun seen on its slope of hillside. The col is reached in a little under two hours from Lhers. Unfortunately there are no views to be had from it, but if you head to the right for about 200 metres you'll emerge from the woods for a fine panorama. Pic du Midi d'Ossau is seen off to the east.

Descend easily to Borce in about 1½–2 hours. The village is worth exploring for a few minutes. *(Refreshments available.)* It is a sturdy-walled place of 15th- and 16th-century houses; it has a shop, restaurant, *gîte d'étape* and a campsite. To reach Etsaut in the valley below walk down the road which heads off to the left. Once down in the valley bear right into the village.

Route 12: Etsaut (597m) – Hourquette de Larry (2055m) – Refuge de Larry (1724m)

Distance:	**13 kilometres**
Height gain:	**1458 metres**
Height loss:	**331 metres**
Time:	**6½ hours**

Part of a longer circuit (the *Tour de la Haute Vallée d'Aspe* – see Route 13), this particular stage is worth tackling on its own account, but note that it will be necessary to carry sleeping bag, food and cooking equipment for an overnight in the simple Larry refuge.

Walk upvalley along the Somport road for almost two kilometres to Pont de Cebers (637m). The former main road crosses the river here, but an old road keeps to the east bank and is waymarked as for the GR10. Follow this for about 800 metres, then join a path that rises through pastures and curves eastward round a rocky spur. Ahead the path has been carved along a steep cliff face (the Chemin de la Mâture), a remarkable section dating from the 18th century. It could cause problems for those who suffer vertigo, but the path is mostly broad enough to ignore the steep drop on the right.

Above the Chemin de la Mâture the path climbs on, and in about 50 mins reaches the converted refuge of Borde de Passette with places for 28 (Tel: 05 59 39 32 49). The valley curves and the path continues to work a way into it before coming to the PNP boundary at the Cabane de la Baigt de Saint-Cours (1560m; 4 hours from Etsaut). Above the cabane the valley begins to narrow while the trail heads south through it, first on the right, then the left bank of the stream.

So reach Hourquette de Larry (2055m; 5 hours 45 mins) where

the path divides. Bear right (west) and continue for about 40 minutes to gain Refuge de Larry.

Note: There are two ways to descend from here to the Aspe Valley. The first takes a path which cuts north-westward behind the hut and reaches the valley at Urdos; the second follows a clear trail (HRP) west round Col de Gouetsoule, then south via Cabane d'Arnousse to reach the valley at Peyrenère below Col du Somport. The first is much shorter than the second.

Multi-Day Tours in the Aspe Valley:

The Aspe Valley and Cirque de Lescun regions lend themselves to a number of fine multi-day tours. By combining well-marked trails used by the GR10 and Pyrenean High Route, with less-travelled paths, the keen trekker could create several journeys of delight, either making the most of mountain huts and *gîtes* for accommodation, or by carrying a tent and pitching it (with discretion) in assorted wild corners. Campers should be aware, however, that in the PNP wild camping is officially forbidden, although it is deemed acceptable more than an hour's walk from the nearest road.

Etsaut in the Vallée d'Aspe (Routes 12, 13, 15)

Route 13: Tour de la Haute Vallée d'Aspe

Start/Finish:	**Etsaut**
Time:	**4 days**
Accommodation:	**Mountain huts and *gîtes d'étape***

On this tour food and cooking equipment will need to be carried for use on the first night. It's a delightful circuit and one that will reveal a number of superb views as well as unfolding the varied nature of this corner of the Pyrenees.

Day One: This has already been outlined as Route 12 above. It leads from Etsaut by way of the Chemin de la Mâture through the valley of the Sescoue stream, crosses Hourquette de Larry (2055m) and descends to Refuge de Larry, an unguarded hut with space for about 10 (6½ hours). A good water supply is found immediately outside the hut.

Day Two: Much of this stage is downhill heading south with the Cirque d'Aspe growing in stature ahead. The path is clear and uncomplicated; some height gain, but mostly downhill or level. It comes onto the Somport road at Peyrenère (1430), but for overnight accommodation it will be necessary to walk uphill towards the Col du Somport for a *gîte d'étape*, Gîte du Somport, 12 places open all year (Tel: 06 08 22 23 31) (4½–5 hours).

Day Three: From the Somport *gîte* descend back to the parking/picnic area at Sansanet (1320m). Cross the bridge over the stream and bear right to follow the path described in reverse for Route 10; this leads by way of the Cabane d'Escouret, Pla d'Espélunguère and Col de Lapachouaou to reach Refuge d'Arlet (2000m). The hut has a guardian from mid-June until mid-September when meals may be provided (Tel: 05 59 36 00 99) (6½ hours).

Day Four: This stage leads first to Col de Saoubathou below the frontier ridge north-west of Arlet. Now walk north along the ridge dividing the valleys of Labadie and Belonce (fine views to Pic du Midi d'Ossau and the Aspe Valley) as far as Col de Barrancq. Bear right and descend to Borce and Etsaut (7–7½ hours).

Route 14: Cirque de Lescun and the Frontier Ridge

Start/Finish:	**Lescun**
Time:	**4 days**
Accommodation:	**Camping, mountain hut and** *gîte*

This circuit explores some of the finest pastoral landscapes of the western Pyrenees, as well as an interesting section of the frontier ridge. The first half follows the High Route as far as Refuge d'Arlet, then drops into a glacier-carved valley that is one of the tributaries of the Aspe, before returning to Lescun.

Follow Routes 4, 6 and 7 (Lescun–Cabanes d'Ansabère–Refuge d'Arlet), spending the first night either bivouacking or camping near the Cabanes d'Ansabère, and the second at Refuge d'Arlet. On the third day retrace your steps towards Col de Saoubathou, but soon break away from this path to follow an alternative PNP trail cutting away in a northerly direction to lead down into the valley of the Gave de Belonce, a pleasant green valley. Towards its northern end come onto a narrow road and follow it down to Borce; an easy, but pleasant day's walking. The final stage follows the course of the GR10 westward, up and over Col de Barrancq, down to Lhers, then on to Lescun.

Routes Across the Frontier Ridge:

From **LES FORGES D'ABEL** and the parking/picnic area of **SANSANET**, footpaths lead south into Spain. **LAC D'ESTAENS** (1754m) makes an obvious goal for a short day's walk. By following a path from Sansanet to a junction of trails just short of Cabane d'Escouret, then heading west to a grassy saddle (1785m), the tarn may be reached in about 1½–2 hours. In order to make a 4 hour circuit continue round the eastern side of the tarn and cross back into France by way of a metal ladder at the Pas de l'Echelle (1775m), descend towards Pla d'Espélunguère, then traverse round the hillside through forest heading east to Sansanet again.

Another route from **SANSANET** heads up to the col above Lac d'Estaens, goes down into the Valle de los Sarrios on a line of cairns, then west below the ridge of Sierra de Berner before climbing steadily to reach the summit of the **VISAURIN** (2668m); about 5–5½ hours from Sansanet.

An ascent of **PIC D'GABEDAILLE** (2258m) is possible from Pla d'Espélunguère above **LES FORGES D'ABEL**. Take the Arlet path

Cirque d'Aspe at the head of the Aspe Valley
(Routes 12, 15, 16 and High Route 4)

heading north-east to Col Plâtrière and Cabane Grosse, then north-west, climbing to reach the frontier ridge at Col de la Contende (2019m). Pic d'Gabedaille rises to the south and is gained in about 40 minutes from the col (2½ hours from Espélunguère). Superb views from the summit. Descend southward with care to the Puerte de Escale (1670m) where you bear left and drop down to Pla d'Espélunguère. (Allow 4½ hours for the full route.)

Trekkers' Routes East to the Pic du Midi Region:

Three recommended routes described below offer interesting ways for the trekker to cross the eastern wall of the Aspe Valley in order to reach the justifiably popular neighbouring region dominated by Pic du Midi d'Ossau. None will take more than a day to achieve, and as there are guarded huts to use around Pic du Midi it should be possible to travel lightly laden during the summer period. (For full hut details see Pic du Midi section below.)

Route 15: Etsaut (597m) – Col d'Ayous (2185m) – Refuge d'Ayous (1982m)

Distance:	**13 kilometres**
Height gain:	**1588 metres**
Height loss:	**203 metres**
Time:	**6–6½ hours**

This crossing follows the waymarked route of the GR10. From Etsaut to Hourquette de Larry (2055m) follow directions given for Route 12. At the pass bear left, climb a little further on a continuing path to gain Col d'Ayous (2185m), from which point you have the first magnificent view of Pic du Midi standing proud to the east. A clear, well-trodden trail descends directly to Refuge d'Ayous, a PNP hut overlooking Lac Gentau, one of the Lacs d'Ayous.

Route 16: Aspe Valley (Sansanet; 1320m) – Col d'Ayous (2185m) – Refuge d'Ayous (1982m)

Distance:	**15 kilometres**
Height gain:	**865 metres**
Height loss:	**203 metres**
Time:	**5½ hours**

Used by the HRP this route provides a very fine day's walking. Leave the parking/picnic area of Sansanet below the Col du Somport and walk uphill along the road as far as the next major hairpin bend. Just beyond Centre Rene Soubre where there is a lay-by car park and a PNP notice board, a path goes off to the left (north) signposted to Refuge de Larry, which you follow. In 1½ hours come to Col de Lazaque; descend into forest, cross the Arnousse stream and veer north again.

The path continues without diversion, crosses Col de Gouetsoule (1845m) and reaches Refuge de Larry (1724m) in 3½ hours. Now heading roughly eastward rise easily at first, then with zig-zags, to gain Col de Larry. Continue round to the right and gain more height to reach Col d'Ayous about 15 minutes later. Descend the obvious trail to Refuge d'Ayous.

Route 17: Col du Somport (1632m) –
Col des Moines (2168m) – Refuge d'Ayous (1982m)

Distance:	7 kilometres
Height gain:	536 metres
Height loss:	186 metres
Time:	3½–4 hours

The shortest crossing offered here, this route is also tackled by one of the HRP *variantes* and is useful for trekkers who may have spent the preceding night in the Somport *gîte*.

Cross into Spain and bear left to walk along the road heading north-east into the Valle del Astun, whose southern slopes are cluttered with mechanical lifts serving an ugly ski development. A waymarked path leaves the road after about two kilometres to rise northward, following the course of a stream (but some distance from it) which drains the lake of Ibon del Escalar. Skirt the lake shore and climb to the obvious saddle of Col des Moines, reached about 20 minutes above the lake (2 hours 15 mins from the Somport road). Pic du Midi is seen to the north-east.

Descend on the French side of the col towards a small tarn, pass to the left of Pic Paradis (2056m) and climb to a col below and to the west of Pic Casteret. The path to the col is clear and well-used, and continues alongside Lac Bersau before dropping to Refuge d'Ayous.

PIC DU MIDI D'OSSAU

Position:	**Entirely in France, east of the Aspe Valley and north of the Col du Pourtalet**
Access:	**By train from Pau to Oloron-Ste-Marie and bus from there to Laruns. By road south from Pau to Laruns and Gabas in the Vallée d'Ossau where the valley forks. South-west to Bious-Artigues, south-east to Col du Pourtalet. Both lead to paths of access. Seasonal bus service from Laruns to Bious-Artigues and Col du Pourtalet.**
Maps:	**IGN Carte de Randonnées No 3 'Béarn' 1:50,000**
	IGN TOP 25 series no: 1547OT 'Ossau, Vallée d'Aspe' 1:25,000
Valley Bases:	**Laruns (530m), Gabas (1027m)**

Despite its lack of glacier or any permanent snowfield, Pic du Midi d'Ossau (see map p38) has all the ingredients of a classical mountain. It stands alone, isolated from its nearest neighbours; a magnificent peak defended by great rock walls that rise abruptly from flower-strewn pastures and jewel-like tarns. Even for the Pyrenees its altitude is modest, but its highly individual outline and the impressive way it dominates the landscape invest it with a stature far greater than that of many higher mountains.

Jean-Pierre, as it is affectionately known by enthusiasts, is among the most satisfying of all Pyrenean mountains. In its *voie normale* will be found an interesting, yet easy scramble. The surrounding valleys provide numerous walks of great variety and beauty, while for those with more energetic and acrobatic ambitions, the various buttresses, gullies and faces hold climbs of practically every degree of difficulty. Pic du Midi, in fact, boasts more rock climbs than any other mountain in the range.

Seen in profile it appears as a great rust-coloured peak with two main summits, the Grand Pic (2885m) and the Petit Pic (2812m), separated by the deep cleft of La Fourche (2705m). Two further summits (Pointe d'Aragon and Pointe Jean Santé) overlook the bowl of the South Cirque, but these are not evident except from limited viewpoints. The southern shoulder is crossed by the stony Col de Peyreget (2300m), the eastern by the grassy saddle of the Col de Suzon (from where the *voie normale* begins), while the northern slopes descend to forests that throw shade into the lower valleys.

As the rock climber's peak *par excellence,* it is understandable that Pic du Midi should attract so much attention today. What is more surprising, however, is that it should have received its first attempt as long ago as the 16th century. In the spring of 1552 François de Foix (the Count de Candale and Bishop of Aire), organised an expedition to determine its height. Equipped with ladders, grapnels, 'climbing irons and certain hooked sticks' the Count and his entourage climbed high enough to see clouds beneath them, but the "cold and rarefied air...caused them sensations of giddiness which made them fall down in their weakness". The attempt failed.

Nevertheless, in about 1787 the geographers Reboul and Vidal from the Academy of Toulouse encouraged an unnamed shepherd from the Aspe Valley to climb the mountain and erect a triangulation cairn on the summit. Ten years later Guillaume Delfau and another shepherd named Mathieu made the second ascent; a climb unusual for the time in that it was made for purely sporting reasons and without any scientific pretension.

But whether your ambitions lie in climbing, wandering the glorious valleys or simply dreaming beside one of the gleaming tarns, Pic du Midi d'Ossau has a way of demanding a return – again and again.

Valley Bases:

LARUNS (530m) lies about 15 kilometres north of the mountain at the foot of the Col d'Aubisque. A lively and attractive village when the sun shines, it has a few hotels and a *gîte d'étape* (l'Embarradère, Tel: 05 59 05 41 88), several campsites, tourist information, post office, shops, cafes and its own *Bureau des Guides* (Place de la Mairie, 64440 Laruns. Tel: 05 59 05 33 04). However, it's really too far from Pic du Midi to serve as a useful base unless you have your own transport.

GABAS (1027m) is a small farming community about 12 kilometres upvalley from Laruns, close to the junction of the route to Bious-Artigues and that of the main Pourtalet road. Because of its proximity to Pic du Midi, and its siting on the GR10, accommodation is always in great demand in summer. There are two small hotels, and the Chalet-Refuge de Gabas, a 50-place refuge owned by the CAF, open all year (Tel: 05 59 05 33 14). Apart from the two hotels there is an independent restaurant, a Maison du Parc National with plenty of information for walkers, and an interesting local natural history exhibition housed in the Centre d'Ecologie Montagnarde. A campsite with a food store is located south-west of Gabas below the dammed Lac de Bious-Artigues: Camping de Bious Oumettes (Tel: 05 59 05 38 76).

Mountain Huts:

REFUGE de BIOUS-ARTIGUES (1430m), as its name implies, is situated at the roadhead near the dammed lake north-west of Pic du Midi. Owned by the Club Pyrénéa Sport of Pau, it's extremely popular on account of its ease of access. Open with a guardian from mid-June until the end of September, it can sleep 45 in two dormitories. Meals may be provided (Tel: 05 59 05 32 12).

REFUGE d'AYOUS (1982m) is owned by the PNP, has a guardian between 15th June and 15th September when meals may be provided, and can accommodate 30 in its dormitories. Best suited to the walker, rather than the climber, it stands to the west of Pic du Midi above Lac Gentau, one of the Lacs d'Ayous, on the route of both the GR10 and HRP (Tel: 05 59 05 37 00).

REFUGE de POMBIE (2032m) is the climbers' hut. Looking onto the great South Face from its perch above the Pombie tarn, it is owned by the CAF, has a guardian from June to the end of September (full meals service) and can sleep 55 in its dormitories and tent 'annexe' (Tel: 05 59 05 31 78). Outside the main season the winter quarters can accommodate 20. **Note**: Wild camping is restricted to a period of 48 hours within the vicinity of this hut.

Route 18: Lac de Bious-Artigues (1415m) – Refuge d'Ayous (1982m)

Distance:	**5 kilometres**
Height gain:	**567 metres**
Time:	**2 hours**

A very fine approach, this walk is worth tackling even if you have no intention of spending a night at the refuge.

From the roadhead at Lac de Bious-Artigues (4kms from Gabas) walk ahead along the broad path leading south-west with Pic du Midi soaring above you to the left. The way rises into woodland shade and emerges soon after on the edge of the lovely Bious pastures. When the path forks near a footbridge over the stream, bear right to climb among trees. Coming out of the forest you gain magnificent views to Pic du Midi again. About 1½ hours from the road you should reach the first of the Lacs d'Ayous, Lac Roumassot (1845m). A ribbon of stream can be seen pouring from the second (unseen) tarn, and the continuing path climbs beside it. This second tarn (Lac du Miey) is the smallest of the three. The path does not stray to it but continues heading a little north of west, soon to reach Lac Gentau and the Refuge d'Ayous with its classic view of Pic du Midi mirrored in the water.

Route 19: Lac de Bious-Artigues (1415m) – Col de Suzon (2127m) – Refuge de Pombie (2032m)

Distance:	**6 kilometres**
Height gain:	**712 metres**
Height loss:	**95 metres**
Time:	**3 hours**

A clear path (signposted) at the northern corner of the lakeside car park heads up into forest. After climbing for a short distance it comes out of the open levels of Col Long de Magnabaigt (1650m), and bears south into the pleasant Magnabaigt glen. Wandering through this valley Pic du Midi comes into view, but appears so different from its generally accepted outline.

At the upper level of the valley the path climbs to Col de Suzon.

The hut is seen from the pass standing below to the south. The way to it traverses below the massive East Face of the mountain, twists among the chaotic boulders of the Grande Raillère, and arrives beside the Pombie refuge.

Route 20: Lac de Bious-Artigues (1415m) – Col de Peyreget (2300m) – Refuge de Pombie (2032m)

Distance:	7.5 kilometres
Height gain:	885 metres
Height loss:	268 metres
Time:	3½ hours

This is a particularly fine walk which serves as part of the Tour of Pic du Midi. Scenically there are numerous contrasts, and underfoot too there is a diversity of terrain; one moment you're bouncing over soft turf, the next you're boulder-hopping or scuffing your boots on scree. There are leafy paths and meandering streams, small tarns and long views, the secret inner recesses of the mountain to peer into and far views of hinted valleys and peaks rinsed blue with distance.

From the end of the road at Bious-Artigues walk upvalley with the lake to your right. The broad path takes you through woodlands and emerges at the northern end of the Bious pastures, close-cropped and level as a Surrey lawn. Cross the footbridge (Pont de Bious) about 40 minutes from the roadhead, and wander across these pastures, veering left at the far end to climb steeply among trees, then with views down to the shepherds' hut of Cabane de Peyreget off to the right. Another path joins ours from the direction of the cabane.

A little over two hours from the roadhead come to the tarn of Lac de Peyreget. Leave the path and go north-eastwards, led by cairns to cross an area of huge blocks that have long been deposited here by Pic du Midi. Cairns lead the way up to Col de Peyreget, an obvious saddle in the south-dipping ridge of the mountain.

Descend to the east by a clear path that takes you past a couple of tarns, and brings you in half an hour to Lac de Pombie and the hut standing just above it.

Route 21: Ossau Valley (Caillou de Soques; 1400m) – Refuge de Pombie (2032m)

Distance:	**2.5 kilometres**
Height gain:	**632 metres**
Time:	**2 hours**

Caillou de Soques is a simple cafe (infrequent opening) situated beside the Pourtalet road opposite some large boulders about 9 kilometres south of Gabas. Cars may be left here, pulled off the road beside the boulders.

Go down to the stream flowing through the valley, cross it by a footbridge and follow the path up into woods above the left bank. The path veers away to the right and then enters the Pombie glen, gaining height steadily. It crosses and recrosses the stream and climbs through the glen with Pic du Midi gradually rising in stature ahead. Without difficulty reach Refuge de Pombie about two hours from the road.

Route 22: Col du Pourtalet (Anéou Pastures; 1750m) – Refuge de Pombie (2032m)

Distance:	**3 kilometres**
Height gain:	**380 metres**
Height loss:	**98 metres**
Time:	**1½ hours**

Cars may be left at a small parking area in the Anéou pastureland, about 1.5 kilometres north of Col du Pourtalet. Turn off the main Pourtalet road at a point marked 'Cabane de l'Araille' on the map. There is a small hut on the east of the road with a short track leading down to the stream opposite. (PNP notice board.)

A well-trodden path leaves the parking area by way of a bridge across the stream and rises gradually over broad rolling pastures towards a grassy ridge to the north. The path is obvious and cannot be missed, and once you top the ridge just west of Soum de Pombie the full impact of Pic du Midi confronts you. The hut is seen below.

Lescun enjoys a view of limestone peaks across the pastures, Routes 1–4

Pic d'Anie (2504m), first of the High Pyrenees, Route 2

Pic du Midi at dawn, Routes 18, 24, 26 and High Route 4

The south-east side of Balaitous, seen from Pic de Cambales, Route 55

PIC DU MIDI D'OSSAU (2885m)

Whilst there are numerous routes on Pic du Midi, only one is given here, the *voie normale*. All others require a certain degree of expertise on rock. Climbs range from the classic North Face pioneered in 1896 by Henri Brulle and graded AD, to a fierce line on the West-North-West Face (ED) achieved in July 1960 by Patrice de Bellefon and Sylvain Sarthou. There are reasonably short, agile lines, and long, demanding routes on the big faces. The Petit Pic has its own special-ities, especially on the North Buttress, developed in the 1960s. Many of the major routes have now been climbed solo, and the mountain attracts plenty of attention in winter too. Derek L. Walker's *Rock Climbs in the Pyrenees* (Cicerone Press, 1990) describes nearly 30 routes on the mountain and is recommended to all English-speaking climbers drawn to the area.

Route 23: Refuge de Pombie (2032m) – Pic du Midi d'Ossau (2885m)

Grade:	**F sup. (Grand Pic, *voie normale*.** **Includes 2 short pitches of grade III)**
Distance:	**3 kilometres**
Height gain:	**853 metres**
Time:	**3–3½ hours**
Equipment:	**Safety helmets advised**

Although this is the easiest route to the summit of the mountain, it is not without interest; a varied ascent that involves moderate scram-bling. Helmets are recommended on account of the very loose rock encountered and the fact that the way leads through gullies where stones could be dislodged by parties above.

Head north from the Pombie hut through the boulder barricade of the Grande Raillère and walk up to the grassy spine which links Pic du Midi with Pic Saoubiste. At Col de Suzon turn left and follow the ridge to the foot of the mountain proper. Climb a short steep gully, then a slab to the left in which there are a number of drilled holes with several moveable pegs which may be utilised to ease the ascent. *(Take care on the descent as these can lead to problems if not placed correctly.)* A clear path then leads round to the right, gaining height to the foot of an open chimney with a broken slab to its right. Climb the slab, which may be easier than the chimney, and continue up a line of cairns.

Having almost reached the North Face a cairn indicates the start of a long sloping groove to the left of a broken gully. *(Beware stonefall.)* Climb the groove without difficulty (one or two pegs will be found, but will probably not be required) and emerge at the top of the gully where a large metal post advertises the correct route of descent.

The ascent now continues via a path winding half-left from the top of the gully, and leads up the dome of the mountain across a region of rough boulders and screes until the very edge of the South Cirque is reached. Follow this ridge round to the saddle between the two summits of the mountain. The highest point, Pointe d'Espagne, is gained by way of a short ridge broken by two steep gullies.

The summit is flat and characterless; a surprise after the many superb aspects of the mountain when seen from below. But the views, especially to the east where the Balaitous dominates a sea of peaks, are splendid. Westward you gaze over the Lacs d'Ayous and far-off to the Aiguilles d'Ansabère.

Care should be exercised on the descent, and only climbers with a clear knowledge of the mountain and considerable experience of ropework, should contemplate any way down other than by the route of ascent. When descending the gullies take every precaution against dislodging stones onto those below.

Route 24: Ayous Lakes Circuit

Start/Finish:	**Lac de Bious-Artigues**
Distance:	**12 kilometres**
Height gain/loss:	**680 metres**
Time:	**4½–5 hours**

West of Pic du Midi the high country beneath Pic d'Ayous, Pic Hourquette and Pic des Moines contains several idyllic tarns; the three Lacs d'Ayous, Lac Bersau and the smaller Lac Casterau. There are others, but they lie beyond this particular circuit. It's a tour that has plenty to commend it. For a start, it's not as strenuous as the full Tour of Pic du Midi (Route 25), but it offers plenty of variety and some of the finest mountain views in all the Pyrenees. The time quoted for the walk is, of course, exclusive of halts, but as there will be numerous places where you'll want to relax simply to absorb the views, a full day must be set aside for it.

Leave Lac de Bious-Artigues heading south-west and follow directions already given (Route 18) as far as Refuge d'Ayous. This will take about two hours. From the hut take the path leading south-west up rock-strewn slopes, passing a number of pools and come to Lac Bersau trapped in a wild corner of the mountains. The path continues along the east shore and rises to a minor, unnamed col behind Pic Casterau. Descend the long loops of path to a rough pastureland and Lac Casterau.

The trail now bears north-west for a surprise view of Pic du Midi, and descends steeply in zig-zags. The Cabanes de la Hosse are seen off to the right, and soon after you come to the Bious stream (3½ hours). A path bears left to follow the stream down into the flat Bious pastures, and across these you rejoin the woodland path that takes you back to Lac de Bious-Artigues.

Route 25: Tour of Pic du Midi d'Ossau

Start/Finish:	**Lac de Bious-Artigues**
Distance:	**13 kilometres**
Height gain/loss:	**885 metres**
Time:	**5½ hours**

The Tour of Pic du Midi is one of *the* classic walks of the Pyrenees, either in its shortened version, as here, or in its full extended length as given below in Route 26. The unique character of the mountain is revealed on the walk with the various faces and ridges being seen from a choice of angles. In addition some fine valleys are explored and three widely differing cols crossed. In previous editions of the guide this particular walk was described in a clockwise direction beginning at Refuge de Pombie. Having since walked it several more times in both directions, I'd now recommend an anti-clockwise circuit, if beginning at Bious-Artigues, or clockwise as before if starting from Pombie. Paths are mostly clear and well-used, so there should be no difficulty with route-finding should you decide to tackle it in the reverse direction to that given here.

Pic du Midi seen from the west

The walk begins at the roadhead at Bious-Artigues, heads south-west beyond the end of the lake and arrives at the Bious pastures. From the roadhead to Refuge de Pombie, follow directions given above for Route 20. This route takes you across the pastures, up to Lac de Peyreget and then steeply to Col de Peyreget from where you can see into the great rocky South Cirque of the mountain. The descent to Refuge de Pombie allows you to gaze east across the depths of the Ossau Valley to the Balaitous.

From Refuge de Pombie (3½ hours) head north across the boulder tip of the Grande Raillère and continue on the path to Col de Suzon. Once over this the way leads down into the green Magnabaigt glen. Towards its northern end the path veers left, crosses Col Long de Magnabaigt, and descends through forest to the car park at Lac de Bious-Artigues.

Route 26: Extended Tour of Pic du Midi

Start/Finish:	**Lac de Bious-Artigues**
Distance:	**20 kilometres**
Height gain/loss:	**1416 metres**
Time:	**8–8½ hours (2 days recommended)**

It would be possible for fit walkers to complete this route in a single day, but it would be a pity to do so. It's far too good to rush; there are magnificent views to enjoy, tarns to relax by, cols to gaze from, alternative corners to explore. Better take two days and enjoy it at a leisurely pace. My recommendation would be to set out for an afternoon stroll from Bious-Artigues to Refuge d'Ayous (2 hours) and spend a night there (book a place in advance by phone). Rise early to capture the magic of sunrise on Pic du Midi's shoulder, seen clearly from the hut itself, and spend the rest of Day Two wandering the remainder of the circuit.

The walk from Bious-Artigues to Refuge d'Ayous has already been described above (Route 18); an easy two hour approach with plenty of fine views to photograph.

Leaving the hut take the path which rises south-westward and brings you to Lac Bersau (2078m). Continue on the path skirting the eastern shore and cross a minor col below Pic Casterau. The path descends easily to Lac Casterau, then more steeply to the Bious stream which flows from a small valley on your right. Cross the stream, below which an indented 'valley' cuts back to the south near the Cabane de Cap de Pount (1½ hours from Refuge d'Ayous). Climb the grassy gully which rises above the cabane. Where it begins to level out bear south-east to gain another pastureland overseen by Cabane de Peyreget. Lovely views of Pic du Midi from here.

Heading east on a mostly level stretch, join a major path and bear right along it. This rises to Lac de Peyreget. Now head north-east following a line of cairns across an area of huge rocks and climb to Col de Peyreget. Descend on the eastern side without difficulty, and reach Refuge de Pombie. For the final stage of the walk over Col de Suzon and through the Magnabaigt glen, follow directions given in Route 25.

Alternatives:

One recommended variation leaves the main route at Lac de Peyreget and heads off to the right to skirt round Pic Peyreget, crossing **COL de l'IOU** (2194m) and the grassy saddle west of Soum de Pombie, to rejoin the described route at Refuge de Pombie.

From Col de Peyreget, head to the right and make an uncomplicated 25-minute ascent of **PIC PEYREGET** (2487m) for a magnificent view of Pic du Midi's four peaks.

BALAITOUS

Position:	East of the Ossau Valley and south of Gourette and the Eaux-Bonnes massif. Astride the frontier.
Access:	All approaches are of necessity by foot. From the west leading out of the Ossau Valley north of the Col du Pourtalet. From the north via Arrens-Marsous and the Vallée d'Arrens (Val d'Azun), and from the east by way of the Marcadau Valley and Col de Cambales. The approach from Spain is by way of Sallent de Gallego and the valley of the Aguas Limpias.
Maps:	IGN Carte de Randonnées No 3 'Béarn' 1:50,000 IGN TOP 25 series no: 1647OT 'Vignemale, Ossau, Arrens, Cauterets' 1:25,000 Editorial Alpina 'Panticos Formigal' 1:25,000
Valley Bases:	None

In the heart of one of the wildest and most inaccessible regions of the whole chain, the Balaitous – 'this threatening and proud peak' – is a big mountain protected by extensive granite ridges and crowding lesser peaks which serve only to complicate all routes of approach. As an example of the difficulties of access, Charles Packe (who made the second ascent) spent so many days searching for a way to penetrate the barricade of ridges in 1862, that he finally withdrew without even discovering the right mountain, and two years later when at last he managed to force an ascent, it was only after wandering for seven days 'on and almost round the mountain before setting his feet on its real summit'.

The first ascent was achieved in 1825 by the military surveyors, Peytier and Hossard, but their actual route remained largely unknown for many years, and even Packe – that most enquiring of Pyrenean historians – was unaware that the Balaitous had previously been climbed until he arrived on the summit to find a cairn already there.

The attractions of the mountain lie in its height (it's the most westerly of the 3000 metre peaks), and in the very savagery of its surroundings. The normal route by way of the West Ridge involves a complicated approach through grand yet austere scenery, followed by an interesting scramble up broken gullies to the bald summit, whose views are vast indeed. From the north a short but very steep glacier leads to great slabs that rise to the lofty summit ridge, while the long, gendarme-crusted ridges themselves are among the mountain's most notable features.

Mountain Huts:

REFUGE D'ARRÉMOULIT (2305m) occupies boulder country on the north shore of Lac d'Arrémoulit below the West Face of Pic Palas, about 3½ hours from the Ossau Valley. Built by the CAF a guardian is in occupation from mid-June to mid-September (Tel: 05 59 05 31 79). Meals may then be provided. The hut can accommodate 45 in its dormitories.

REFUGE DE LARRIBET (2070m) belongs to the Lourdes section of the CAF. A popular hut enlarged in the early 1990s to take 62. There is a guardian on duty at weekends in April and October, and throughout the summer period from May until end-September, with meals provision (Tel: 05 62 97 25 39). It occupies a small grassy basin, the Pla de Larribet, on the north side of the mountain, used as the site of Peytier and Hossard's base camp while they worked on the Balaïtous survey.

REFUGE LEDORMEUR (1970m), also known as Refuge Balaïtous, is the smallest hut in the region, a simple unguarded shelter to the northeast of the mountain. It can accommodate 12. All equipment and food must be carried in.

REFUGE MIGOUÉLOU (2290m) is too far north of the Balaitous to be of use to climbers planning routes on the mountain, but it lies in good walking country on the north-east shore of Lac de Migouélou. Owned by the PNP with a guardian from mid-June to mid-September offering full meals service. The hut can sleep 40. Out of season there's room for 10 (Tel: 05 62 97 44 92).

REFUGIO RESPOMUSO (2200m) is a well-appointed Spanish hut

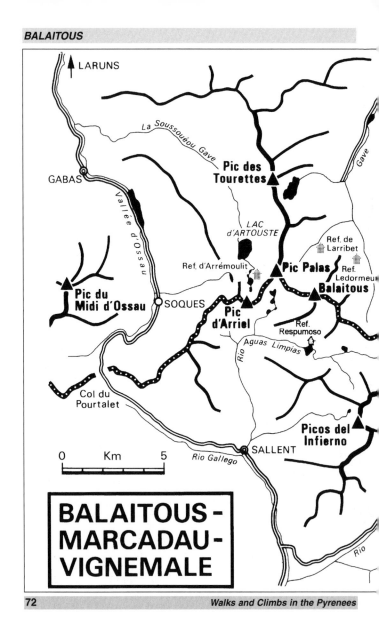

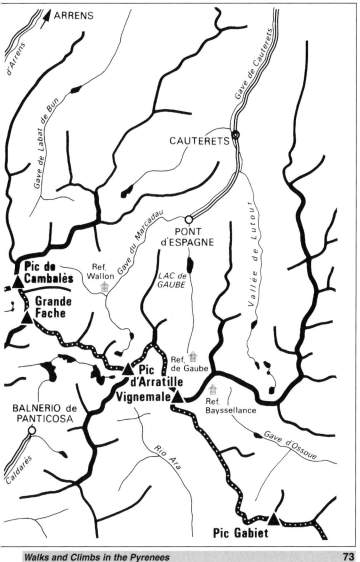

situated above the north shore of the Respomuso reservoir south of Balaitous. Built in 1994 by the Federación Aragonesa de Montañismo (FAM) this large and comfortable refuge is permanently open and wardened. Meals provided, places for 120 (Tel: 974 49 02 03). It serves the GR11 and is on a *variante* route of the HRP about 3 hours from Arrémoulit, and is also accessible from the Wallon hut in the Marcadau Valley by way of Col de la Fache in about 3½–4 hours. The main route of approach is from the Embalse de La Sarra roadhead above Sallent de Gallego in 2½ hours.

Route 27: Ossau Valley (Caillou de Soques; 1400m) – Refuge d'Arrémoulit (2305m) (via Passage d'Orteig)

Distance:	**5 kilometres**
Height gain:	**960 metres**
Height loss:	**55 metres**
Time:	**3½ hours**

Cars should be left in the Ossau Valley about 9 kilometres south of Gabas at a spot known as Caillou de Soques. This is where the otherwise fairly straight N134 bis road crosses a stream and makes a sudden elbow turn. There is a small cafe/bar on the right, and parking is possible on the left of the road among some large boulders.

Pass an ancient hut and a huge boulder, cross a stream and head up towards the woods on the eastern side of the valley where you soon join a clear path that winds into the Arrious Valley. Emerging from the woods a bridge takes you over the Arrious stream, and you then follow its right bank upvalley for some distance. Behind to the west Pic du Midi looks magnificent, while ahead peaks crowd the horizon.

Gaining height the path climbs in zig-zags, then levels into a narrow false col; an idyllic spot with flat turf, a crystal stream and fine views. At the head of the valley Col d'Arrious (2259m) marks a choice of routes.

Note: If you are heavily laden, or are prone to bouts of vertigo, do not follow the continuing route described here, but use Route 28 outlined below.

Take the path which leads to the right. After about 200 metres come to the narrow Lac d'Arrious. Keep to the eastern (left-hand) side of the lake where the path rises over a low ridge, curves to the right and then narrows as a ledge traversing the North Face of Pic du Lac d'Arrious. This is known as the Passage d'Orteig, exposed but safe-guarded, with Lac d'Artouste 200 metres below to the north and a wall of rock rising steeply on the right. Climbing out of the Passage the path is led by cairns over a very rough landscape of scattered boulders, and eventually down to the hut, seen across the outlet stream at the end of the lake.

Route 28: Ossau Valley (Caillou de Soques; 1400m) – Refuge d'Arrémoulit (2305m) (via Lac d'Artouste)

Distance:	**6 kilometres**
Height gain:	**1074 metres**
Height loss:	**169 meters**
Time:	**4 hours**

This route avoids crossing the airy Passage d'Orteig, but has the disadvantage of losing nearly 200 metres of height after Col d'Arrious, and climbing more than 250 extra to gain the hut.

Follow directions from Caillou de Soques to Col d'Arrious as described in Route 27 above. From the col cross to the north-east and descend a clear path towards the lake. The trail veers right and forks at about 2090 metres. Bear right and climb the steep path which leads directly to the hut.

Route 29: Lac d'Artouste (1989m) – Refuge d'Arrémoulit (2305m)

Distance:	**2.5 kilometres**
Height gain:	**316 metres**
Time:	**1½–2 hours**

A short distance upstream of Gabas in the Ossau Valley lies the dammed lake of Fabrèges with a téléphérique rising on the north side of the valley. At the top station of this téléphérique there's a minia-ture tourist train that winds round the mountainside for 10 kilometres to the northern end of Lac d'Artouste. By use of this mechanical aid a short walk leads to the Arrémoulit hut.

From the Artouste station a good clear path heads up to the lakeside in about 15 minutes, then follows the western shore southward. At the far end the way begins to rise, then forks. Take the left-hand option to climb steeply in a south-easterly direction, coming directly to the hut.

Route 30: Refuge d'Arrémoulit (2305m) – Col du Palas (2517m) – Port du Lavedan (2615m) – Refuge de Larribet (2070m)

Distance:	**5 kilometres**
Height gain:	**310 metres**
Height loss:	**545 metres**
Time:	**3½ hours**

A magnificent crossing of a wild and challenging landscape that demands a good head for heights, clear visibility and a well-fitting rucksack. It cannot be recommended to inexperienced trekkers.

Leave the Arrémoulit hut and enter the hanging valley which rises a little south of east a short distance from it. This valley is gained by crossing some rough granite boulders above the lake. Follow cairns leading beyond a small tarn and up to the obvious saddle of Col du Palas (1 hour from the hut). The view from the col shows the craggy West Ridge of Balaitous, and plunging screes that form a desolate cup to several lakes far below.

Descend a short way below the col to the upper screes, then head left (eastwards), keeping as high as possible. A few vague cairns lead the way towards the steep wall linking Pic Palas with Somet de Batcrabère. Cairns again guide you up to the narrow Port du Lavedan in that ridge, south-east of Pic Palas (45 mins from Col du Palas). The descent on the north-eastern side is, in places, precarious, but waymarks direct you towards the east, now steadily descending over patches of snow, scree blocks and boulders, before the tiny Lacs de Micoulaou (2302m) are reached. From the lower of these a trail heads north-east to the larger of the Lacs de Batcrabère (2180m). This is passed along its right-hand side, climbing and falling until the Brèche de la Garenère brings you into full view of Refuge de Larribet, its soft turf offering welcome respite after the rough boulder country encountered above.

Route 31: Val d'Azun (Porte d'Arrens; 1470m) – Refuge de Larribet (2070m)

Distance:	**4 kilometres**
Height gain:	**600 metres**
Time:	**2½ hours**

At the village of Arrens below Col du Soulor a minor road branches off to the south and goes up the Vallée d'Arrens (Val d'Azun) to the Barrage du Tech where there's a campsite, and continues for another 3.5 kilometres to Porte d'Arrens where there is a large car park and PNP Reception Centre (Maison du Parc).

Cross the bridge and head south on a well-used track that soon comes to Lac de Suyen. Little more than 200 metres later the track forks. Take the right-hand path and, at a shepherd's hut, cross a stream and gain height, now heading west into the Larribet Valley. This wild glen is a delight to walk through with its beautiful natural gardens, pools and polished rocks, and the trail keeps company with the stream for some time. It then crosses a low rock ridge on the left, and bears right to make the final climb to the hut.

Note: Visitors to the hut should consider walking on a little further, over Brèche de la Garenère, to visit the Lacs de Batcrabère. A wild, but fascinating landscape.

Route 32: Val d'Azun (Porte d'Arrens; 1470m) – Refuge Ledormeur (1970m)

Distance:	**4 kilometres**
Height gain:	**500 metres**
Time:	**2 hours**

Take Route 31 from Porte d'Arrens to Lac de Suyen and continue south until the track forks. Take the left branch, in effect continuing deeper into the valley of the Arrens stream for a further two kilometres. Soon after passing a small tarn on your right, cross the stream by way of a footbridge and climb the path which leads up some 150 metres to the hut.

Route 33: Val d'Azun (Pla d'Aste; 1400m) – Refuge Migouélou (2290m)

Distance:	**3 kilometres**
Height gain:	**890 metres**
Time:	**3 hours**

About one kilometre north of the car park and PNP Reception Centre at the roadhead in Val d'Azun, Pla d'Aste, a large meadow, marks the start of this hut approach. A signposted footpath breaks away from the road to the left (west), about 250 metres beyond an electricity works télépherique. The path climbs with the aid of numerous zig-zags up the steep mountainside, the southern flanks of Pique d'Aste (2358m), and enters the National Park. More zig-zags climb on towards the steep walls of Pic Arrouy. Come to a saddle where you view the dam at the end of the sizeable Lac de Migouélou. Bear left along its shore and wander to the hut.

Route 34: Lac d'Artouste (1989m) – Col d'Artouste (2472m) – Refuge Migouélou (2290m)

Distance:	**5 kilometres**
Height gain:	**483 metres**
Height loss:	**182 metres**
Time:	**3 hours**

By use of the Fabrèges télépherique and tourist train (see Route 29) the Migouélou hut is accessible in half a day from the Ossau Valley. Caution is advised where snow is encountered on the descent to the hut.

From the Artouste station take the path up to the barrage at the northern end of the lake, then wander to the eastern end of the dam where a PNP path heads left (north). Make a traverse of the north-west slopes of Pic de la Lie for about 30 minutes, after which the path veers north-eastward and climbs to the Lacs de Carnau (2202m). Above these the route now bears south-east and, by way of zig-zags, reaches Col d'Artouste (2½ hours). Lac de Migouélou lies below and the way descends north-eastward, often over patches of snow, passes round the eastern side and gains the hut.

Route 35: Refuge d'Arrémoulit (2305m) – Refugio Respomuso (2200m)

Distance:	**7.5 kilometres**
Height gain:	**212 metres**
Height loss:	**317 metres**
Time:	**3½–4 hours**

This route between huts is a *variante* of the HRP. It remains south of the Balaitous and passes through some wild and stony country – not always easy to negotiate.

Follow directions to Col du Palas as given in Route 30 above. From the col descend steeply to the northern end of the Lacs d'Arriel and pass along their eastern side. Between the two tarns is a high point (2259m on the map) which you pass on your right, then follow a path descending a little west of south. Walk between two further lakes and follow the stream emanating from them. Keep above a much smaller tarn and veer left (south-east) towards the Respomuso dam in the Circo de Piedrafita. It's a good path which remains high above the stream flowing from the dammed lake (avalanche danger in late spring), and brings you to some ruined huts and a chapel. The last section to the hut climbs in zigzags, then contours to the right before sloping down to softer country, crossing a stream just before the refugio.

Route 36: Sallent de Gallego (Puente de la Fajas; 1445m) – Refugio Respomuso (2200m)

Distance:	**7 kilometres**
Height gain:	**755 metres**
Time:	**2½ hours**

This southern approach to the Respomuso refuge is a very attractive one for it leads through the lovely valley of the Rio Aguas Limpias, at first among meadows and flowers, then through a gorge and along rough mountain slopes below outliers of the Balaïtous massif. The river is a constant companion, but there are also several fine waterfalls that crash down to it. **Note:** In the main summer season there should be no problems, but if the mountains are still coated with

Refugio Respomuso (Routes 35, 36 and High Route 7 Alt.)

snow this route is likely to be threatened by avalanche in several places and therefore must be avoided.

If you have transport drive out of Sallent de Gallego up a minor road at the west end of the village. When it forks at a left-hand hairpin take the right branch signed to La Sarra. Cross to the east side of the La Sarra barrage, ease past the hydro station and park at the road-head at the northern end of the reservoir. This is Puente de las Fajas. (Without transport it will take about an hour to walk from Sallent to this point.)

Cross the bridge to the left-hand side of the Rio Aguas Limpias and wander upvalley along the path of GR11. In the early summer there are many side streams to cross on stepping stones. After 15 mins the path rises above an open meadow (ignore the alternative route branching left), and slants up to cross a bridge above a series of cascades. It then enters woodland on the flank of a deep and narrow gorge. As the gorge begins to curve eastward, a spectacular waterfall pours down from the left, draining the cirque of Laderas de Soba. A bridge crosses the Barranco Garmo Negro beside this waterfall, beyond which the path hugs the rock wall along the last of the gorge. As the valley opens skirt the left-hand edge of a meadow, then cross below an amphitheatre hiding the Arriel lakes and the western crags of Balaïtous. Rising on a stony path now there are more side streams to cross as you climb above another cascade and enter a wild inner section of valley with rocks, slabs and a few stunted trees. Cross below an extensive fan of screes and continue to rise towards the barrage at the western end of the Respomuso reservoir. Just beyond some ruins and a small chapel the path forks. Take the left-hand option which zigzags uphill a short way, then contours to the right before angling downhill to gain the refugio.

Note: This hut makes a fine base for a number of outings, including the ascent of such frontier summits as the Grande Fache (3005m), Pic de Cambales (2965m) and Gavizo-Cristail (Pico de Cristales; 2890m), as well as the Frondella peaks which run along a south-west spur from Balaïtous. Ski ascents of all these mountains are possible when conditions allow in winter. In summer walkers can enjoy wandering from tarn to tarn in the valley-head to the east of the hut, follow the route of GR11 across the mountains to the Baños de Panticosa, or make forays across the frontier into the Marcadau Valley.

PIC PALAS (2974m)

During their survey of 1825, Peytier and Hossard made the first ascent of Pic Palas under the mistaken impression that they were climbing Balaitous. It was not until they were near the summit, gaining a splendid view of its loftier neighbour, that they realised their mistake. Route 37 is thought to be that of the 1825 original; a fine route on a handsome mountain which rises conically from three main ridges, looming over the Arrémoulit hut and offering a pleasant outing.

Route 37: Refuge d'Arrémoulit (2305m) – Pic Palas (2974m)

Grade:	PD inf. (North Ridge route)
Distance:	2 kilometres
Height gain:	669 metres
Time:	3–3½ hours
Equipment:	Rope advised

Bear left out of the hut and aim a little south of east on lakeside boulders for about 200 metres, then cross left to gain the hanging valley which rises to Col du Palas. Cairns guide you to a small tarn. Just beyond this bear left and pass above Lac de Palas (2359m) by its eastern shore, and climb north-east over slopes of granite boulder debris, curving round Pic Palas beneath the West Ridge. Cross also beneath the NNW Ridge, bear to the right (east) and rise towards the North Ridge. The Brèche des Géodésiens is seen as a notch to the south of Pic d'Artouste, and this provides the key to the ascent.

Reach the Brèche (2786m) about two hours from the hut, and turn right to climb along the ridge on rough boulders. The ridge narrows and afterwards begins to steepen. Turn to the right (west) on reaching a gendarme, and find a ledge which facilitates the ascent. Come onto the ridge proper again, and follow this on more large blocks to the summit itself. Views to Balaitous are especially fine, but so too is the scene of lakes and minor peaklets spread below to the west.

Note: The South-East Arête holds a 300 metre AD route, first climbed in 1937, while the South-West Arête provides a challenging AD sup. route (two pitches of IV) from Col du Palas and over Piton Von Martin (2785m) on the frontier ridge. These, however, lie outside the scope of the present guide. Interested climbers should consult *Passages Pyénéens* by Rainier Munsch, Christian Ravier and Rémi Thivel (Éditions du Pin à Crochets) – in French.

BALAITOUS (3144m)

As has already been stated, the attractions of this peak lie in its height and in the savagery of its surroundings. All routes have a degree of seriousness that should not be underestimated; ridges topple to precipices cut by grooves and gullies, and in misted conditions it is easy to become disoriented. However, Balaitous is a big mountain that rewards with some magnificent expeditions. Summit views are extensive, but of more interest than the far distant multitude of peaks is that of the immediate surroundings; the tangled crests and buttresses and hanging valleys devoid of vegetation, 'the vast chaos of bare ridges and mountain heights lying all silent and lifeless in the light of the sun'. From the summit of Balaitous one has a grasp of the size of the range, an impression of an unearthly, unfathomable country, and a profound respect for the pioneers who charted these heavily guarded sanctuaries so long ago.

Route 38: Refuge d'Arrémoulit (2305m) – Balaitous (3144m)

Grade:	F sup. (West Ridge, normal route)
Distance:	4 kilometres
Height gain:	1056 metres
Height loss:	217 metres
Time:	4–4½ hours
Equipment:	Rope, safety helmet advised. Ice axe could be useful.

A superb ascent that will make for a very full day (allow 3½ hours for a return to the hut, thus making 8 hours for the round-trip, plus rests). Without good visibility route finding could be difficult.

On leaving the hut head a little south of east and climb over rough ground into the hanging valley beneath the South-West Face of Pic Palas. Cairns lead beyond a small tarn and guide you up to Col du Palas seen ahead (1 hour). From the col descend diagonally on the Spanish side, keeping eastwards in direction until the Arriel lakes come into view below and the onward route can be assessed. Some way across the bowl of scree and boulders a chute of red dirt and scree fans out of a short gully above, and to the east of, the northern Arriel lake. This chute has to be crossed, after which you climb out of the gully and gain height with the aid of cairns keeping a stream on the right, towards a breach in the rocks through which the stream falls. Cross the breach and pass round the northern edge of a little tarn, Gourg Glacé (2404m). This is a tranquil spot with many flowers; a marked contrast to the chaotic area ahead.

Still following a line a little south of east climb over steepening ground of rocks and patches of snow to the left of a bluff, until cairns lead off the snow towards an easy gully with overhanging cliffs forming its right-hand wall. This is part of the Balaitous's western defences, and marks the start of the climb proper. At the foot of the gully is the Abri Michaud (2698m), an emergency shelter created beneath an overhanging rock.

Climb the gully with caution should another party be above or below, as there is much loose rock. The ascent is made without difficulty. At its head emerge onto the broad sloping West Ridge of Balaitous. Cairns and a vague path lead off to the right (east), gaining height for some distance up this ridge. Then, just as you begin to relax with the ease of progress, alternative routes are offered by a choice of cairns. There is little to choose between them, as each will take you up more gullies (loose stones) and over various rocky spines that now make up this ridge. The cairns are easy to follow, and lead to a final narrow gully, sometimes rimed with ice, which opens just below the domed summit itself.

Grande Diagonale Variante:

On the West Ridge at the top of the gully the Aiguille Lamathe (a rock needle) is seen to the north, on the NW Ridge, with what appears to be a steep ledge rising across the mountain's NW Face; the Grande Diagonale. Despite appearances it makes for an easy route. Turn right and cross to the ledge and climb along it on broken rocks. It is neither as steep nor as narrow as it appeared. When you reach a gendarme on the left of the ledge, about 150 metres from the end, leave the Grande Diagonale (a cairn marks the point of departure) to climb an easy gully in the right-hand wall which leads to the summit.

Caution is advised for the descent, particularly in misty conditions when the cairns and vague trails of the West Ridge may be difficult to follow. Beware too of falling stones in the gullies, and be careful to ascertain the correct route off the lower section of ridge into the gully beneath the overhanging wall. A long and tiring descent.

Route 39: Refuge de Larribet (2070m) – Balaitous (3144m)

Grade:	**D sup. (From the north-east via the Néous Glacier. Includes a pitch of grade III)**
Distance:	**4.5 kilometres**
Height gain:	**1074 metres**
Time:	**4–4½ hours**
Equipment:	**Crampons, ice axe, rope. Safety helmet advised.**

South of the Larribet hut the Pabat Valley rises and narrows with the converging ridges of Garenère to the west and the long Fachon crest to the east. The high point, where the ridges join above the little Glacier du Pabat, is the Cap Peytier-Hossard. About 700 metres north-east of this high point, and some 400 metres lower, Col du Pabat has to be crossed in order to reach the start of the climb.

Descend from the hut a short way, then bear right along a line of cairns heading east, then south-eastwards over rough boulder slopes below the Fachon ridge, to just beyond the rocky spur of Pic Rouge. Veer left and gain Col du Pabat where a steep slope of snow and boulders plunges to a small tarn. Cross the col and traverse this slope to the right (south), keeping well above the tarn, and bear round to the Glacier de la Néous.

The glacier is short but steep. Above and ahead of it runs the long Costerillou ridge supported by pillars and buttresses and seamed with shadowed gullies. To the right rough slopes lead up to the narrowing Cap Peytier-Hossard, and between the Cap and Balaitous itself, the ridge is sliced by Brèche Peytier-Hossard.

Ascend the glacier towards its highest point, and make for the second chimney on the face of Balaitous counting from the Brèche. Crossing the bergschrund may be difficult in some years. The first rock pitch is not long, but is often wet and requires care. Climb the dièdre on the left, then turn the overhang also to the left (III) and continue to a substantial ledge marking the end of the second short pitch. Soon above the ledge the chimney opens as a gully (loose stones) which is climbed without difficulty. It leads almost directly onto the broad summit. (Henry Russell, who made the first ascent of this route, wrote that he was '...half-mad with joy to see the cairn'.)

Other Routes on the Balaitous:

With its bristling ridges Balaitous offers a fine choice of routes of varying degrees of difficulty and commitment. Among the more challenging, mention should be made of the very long traverse of the three main ridges, beginning with the **NW RIDGE**, punctuated by the fine Aiguille Lamathe, and which continues over the summit and along the **CRÊTE DE COSTERILLOU** to the shattered spine of the **CRÊTE DU DIABLE**. This final 'Devil's Ridge' involves much abseil work. The whole round takes a full 12 hours and ranks as one of the most serious expeditions in the Pyrenees.

On the Costerillou Ridge the **TOUR DE COSTERILLOU** is an individual pinnacle of 3049 metres whose North Face rises from the Néous Glacier in a dramatic sweep of granite. A TD- route has been made on this face, with some exposed pitches of IV and V.

The Ollivier *guide succinct* (in French and not easy to find) covering many of the opportunities offered by this fine mountain, is

Groupe Balaitous-Frondella. See also *Passages Pyrénéens* for a selection of the hardest routes.

Route 40: Tour of the Balaitous Region

Start/Finish:	Val d'Azun (Pla d'Aste; 1400m)
Time:	3 days
Accommodation:	Mountain huts

An interesting, and at times a fairly strenuous circuit of the wild Balaitous region may be achieved by linking some of the routes described above. Three manned refuges with meals available make the carrying of camping equipment unnecessary.

It begins in the upper reaches of Vallée d'Arrens (Val d'Azun), south-west of Arrens-Marsous. Car parking is available at the roadhead near the Maison du Parc. From here walk back down the road for about 15 minutes to Pla d'Aste and then head up the western hillside to Refuge de Migouélou on the path described as Route 33 (3 hours).

Head south along the lake shore then veer right, climb to Col d'Artouste (2742m), and descend from there round the Lacs de Carnau and on to the dammed Lac d'Artouste (Route 34 in reverse). From the southern end of Lac d'Artouste ascend steep slopes to Refuge d'Arrémoulit (4 hours from Migouélou).

The next stage is described as Route 35, crossing Col du Palas and making a long journey under the southern flanks of Balaitous as far as Refugio Respomuso. It will take 3½–4 hours for this, and the tour continues to the eastern end of the Campo Plano lake, then climbs northward to the frontier ridge at Port de la Peyre–St-Martin (2295m). Back in France descend through the long valley of the Arrens stream, passing Lac de Suyen and coming to the Maison du Parc and car parking area about 7½ hours from Arrémoulit.

Other Routes:

Many of the peaks in the Balaitous region provide interesting scrambles, often with superb views from their crowns. One such is **PIC D'ARRIEL** (2824m) south of the Arrémoulit hut. By the NE Ridge a PD route of ascent is made in about two hours from the hut via a conspicuous diagonal gully. Another route by the easy NW Ridge, gained from Col d'Arriel, is possible from the western side of Lac d'Arrious (grade F).

East of Balaitous, and reached without difficulty from the upper Arrens Valley, is **PIC DES CRISTAYETS** (2723m) which grants a magnificent grandstand view of the massif. From the southern end of the Lacs de Remoulis a vague trail heads west to a rough shelter and then disappears. But the way heads up towards the Crête du Diable, then north-west and west up to the Brèche de la Néous. The summit is easily reached from here (3½ hours from the car park at Porte d'Arrens).

GAVIZO-CRISTAIL (2890m) rises on the frontier ridge south of Pic des Cristayets. This is another easily accessible peak, gained by way of the Port de la Peyre–St-Martin (2295m) and the Spanish slopes (4 hours from Porte d'Arrens).

A superb seven-hour walking route from Refuge de Larribet to the **MARCADAU VALLEY** is achieved by crossing **COL DE CAMBALES** (2706m), and is described elsewhere in this book as High Route 8.

GOURETTE AND THE EAUX-BONNES MASSIF

Position:	North of the Balaïtous, but south of the Col d'Aubisque road. Situated midway between the Vallée d'Ossau and Val d'Azun. Entirely in France.
Access:	By way of the Col d'Aubisque road
Maps:	IGN Carte de Randonnées No 3 'Béarn' 1:50,000 IGN TOP 25 series no: 1647OT 'Vignemale, Ossau, Arrens, Cauterets' and 1546ET 'Laruns, Gourette' both at 1:25,000
Valley Bases:	Laruns (530m), Eaux-Bonnes (719m), Gourette (1346m)

Too far north of the frontier line of peaks to be numbered among the top-ranking mountains of the Pyrenees, those that form the Eaux-Bonnes massif nevertheless reveal fine, sometimes intimidating, shapes and contain a few challenging limestone walls and ridges for rock climbers. None of their summits reach 2700 metres and several are easily accessible to non-climbers, yet while their north-facing slopes are laced with cable-cars and ski tows, there are some delightful tarn-spattered inner regions that provide rewarding outings for walkers.

The GR10 makes a two-day traverse of the area, but there are other tempting multi-day circuits that also give an opportunity for backpackers to cross little-known cols on an exploration of the outlying valleys. Long views to hard-to-recognise peaks reveal a flavour of the magic such travel offers.

Motorists driving over Col d'Aubisque (1709m) are able to gain a grandstand view by leaving their vehicles at the col and walking a short distance to the south. There, on a grassy hillock, one may gaze without effort at Pic de Ger, Pic de la Latte de Bazen and the two Pics du Gabizos. The rest is a folding contortion of mystery, while northwards green hills plunge to forest and foothill ranges – more delightful walking country.

Valley Bases:

LARUNS (530m) is a large, attractive village situated in the Vallée d'Ossau at the western end of the Col d'Aubisque road. It has a few hotels and a *gîte d'étape* (l'Embarradère, Tel: 05 59 05 41 88), several campsites, tourist information, post office, bank, shops, restaurants and its own *Bureau des Guides* (Place de la Mairie, 64440 Laruns. Tel: 05 59 05 33 04). Because of its position climbers and walkers using Laruns as a base would ideally have their own transport.

EAUX-BONNES (719m) is a spa village whose waters are used in the treatment of rheumatism and respiratory disorders. Situated rather gloomily on the road to the Col d'Aubisque, about six kilometres from Laruns, it has a few hotels (two one-star) and shops, and a campsite just outside, on the road to Aas. Aas itself has a *gîte d'étape*, Auberge du Chemin de Pleysse (40 places, Tel: 05 59 05 42 04).

GOURETTE (1346m) is a purpose-built ski resort, an architectural eye-sore on the edge of some grand mountain country. The Col d'Aubisque road passes through the village on a sharp hairpin bend. For accommodation Gourette has two refuges (see under Mountain Huts below), several hotels (rather more expensive than some of the neighbouring villages) and a campsite a short distance downhill to the west. There are tourist information, shops and cafes.

Mountain Huts:

REFUGE DE GOURETTE (Chalet Pyrénéa Sports) (1350m) is owned by the Pau-based Club Pyrénéa Sport, mainly for use during the ski season. It is, however, open during July and August with a guardian in residence (Tel: 05 59 27 23 11) when meals may be provided. The hut can accommodate 64.

CHALET-REFUGE GOURETTE (Chalet du Club Alpin-Français) (1350m) belongs to the CAF's Section Orthez and is open from the beginning of July to mid-September with a guardian in charge (Tel: 05 59 05 10 56). Meals may be provided, and the hut can sleep 40.

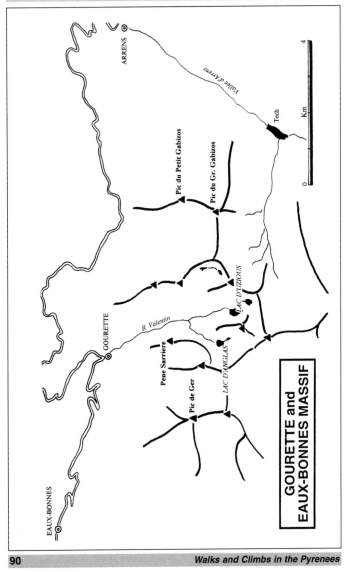

Route 41: Gabas (1027m) – Hourquette d'Arre (2465m) – Gourette (1346m)

Distance:	**22 kilometres**
Height gain:	**1438 metres**
Height loss:	**1119 metres**
Time:	**8 hours**

This long and strenuous walk follows a section of the GR10 and provides an obvious route to Gourette for walkers without transport who have already explored the Pic du Midi region and now need to move further east. Since there are no opportunities to obtain refreshments on the way, it is essential to carry food. Do not set out if the weather is threatening.

From Gabas walk along the road heading east (direction Col du Pourtalet and Spain) for a little over 1.5 kilometres to reach a hydro-electric power station (15 minutes). Join a waymarked path breaking away to the left over the stream. Initially heading back towards Gabas you soon veer right in forest and before long come to a surfaced track which you follow for about 400 metres. The GR10 now continues with a path off to the right; the Corniche des Alhas, an exposed trail carved out of a steep cliff. This impressive section (1 hour from the hydro station) soon ends and you then rise out of the forest of beech and fir, above which the trail relaxes on a long, mostly even contour heading east for about five kilometres. This path was created in order to transport copper ore from a series of mines; from it there are splendid views back to Pic du Midi d'Ossau.

Beyond the mines the path veers south, then swings left (east) to begin climbing towards Hourquette d'Arre. Zig-zags climb first over grass, then on steep screes as you approach the col; a tiring ascent. Reach the col (2465m) about 5½ hours from Gabas.

The descent heads left from the col (north-east), loses height to pass a rough hut, then cuts west of Pic d'Anglas before swinging east then north again on a steep path towards the ruins of mine workings near Lac d'Anglas (6½ hours). Wander along the lake's eastern shore, cross its outlet stream and descend along a narrow valley heading north above the Valentin stream on a clear path that leads directly into Gourette.

Route 42: Gourette (1346m) – Lac d'Anglas (2068m)

Distance:	3.5 kilometres
Height gain:	722 metres
Time:	2–2½ hours

Lac d'Anglas is a popular destination for walkers and anglers alike, and during the main summer weeks it will be rare to have it to yourself. A small tarn above which iron ore was once mined, the remains of former mine workings can be seen close to the lake. From it fine views take account of the ridge of Pene Sarrière to the north (a shark's fin of a ridge) and Pic de la Latte de Bazen to the north-east.

The walk begins in Gourette near the tourist office. Immediately to the south a string of cableways laces the hillside and a signpost directs the path to Lac d'Anglas, Lac d'Uzious etc heading half-left to pass beneath a chairlift. This path is waymarked for the GR10 and climbs steeply at first, then eases into the Valentin Valley to pass below the impressive slabs of Pene Sarrière (1944m). (A number of extreme routes have been achieved on this East Face.)

There is little chance of losing the path. It's well-trodden and clear and rises steadily along the hillside heading south, then veers right (west) to climb more steeply in zig-zags, passes the Cascade d'Anglas and then comes to the lake. (Allow 1½ hours for a return to Gourette by the same path.)

Route 43: Gourette (1346m) – Lac d'Uzious (2115m) – Lac du Lavedan (2179m)

Distance:	4.5 kilometres
Height gain:	833 metres
Time:	2½–3 hours

Set in a high pastureland basin the two small lakes of Uzious and Lavedan provide a more tranquil destination than the more popular Lac d'Anglas described above, and the walk to get there is a little more varied than that previous route.

Initially follow the Lac d'Anglas path (Route 42) from Gourette into the narrow Valentin Valley below Pene Sarrière's East Face. After passing the foot of the slabs you will see a simple shepherd's *cabane* below by the stream (about 2.5 kilometres from Gourette). Soon after this the path begins to zig-zag a little. A single cairn indicates a minor path breaking away left from the main Lac d'Anglas trail; follow this as it heads a little east of south descending slightly. With a few cairns as additional aid the way leads through pastures above the stream aiming towards the head of the valley. (Cascades above to the right.)

Coming to a final bowl of rough pasture punctuated with boulders and the ruins of an old *cabane*, the way becomes more clear and climbs in zig-zags up a stark terrain of rock and scree. The path is another of those used by mine workers in the past, and there are rusting remnants of mine workings lying around. You will come to a large pipe beside which a few steps have been created, and soon above this emerge to a grassy saddle with Lac d'Uzious about five minutes ahead (2½ hours).

Cross the outlet stream and walk along the left-hand side of the lake before climbing on a continuing path which leads in about 15 minutes to Lac du Lavedan. Green pastures slope into the tarn, while off to the west an enticing hanging valley is topped by Hourquette d'Arre by which Gabas and the Vallée d'Ossau may be reached (see Route 41).

Note: For a superb view of the eastern mountains a 20-minute walk above the lake to Col d'Uzious (2236m) is highly recommended.

Multi-Day Tour from Gourette:

As mentioned in the introductory paragraphs to this section, the Eaux-Bonnes/Gourette region lends itself to multi-day walking tours. Not every glen visited, however, has clearly marked footpaths, and some of the cols crossed require a steady head for heights and sound mountain judgement. That being said, experienced mountain trekkers and backpackers used to covering rough ground with a minimum of waymarks to guide them, will find the following suggested route to be very rewarding.

Route 44: The Gourette–Tech Loop

Start/Finish:	**Gourette**
Time:	**2 days**
Accommodation:	**Camping du Tech (Vallée d'Arrens)**

The view east from the Col d'Uzious (Route 44)

A splendid circuit over very mixed terrain: mountain paths, high cols, a descent through a remote glen, a short section of valley road and a return along the GR10; all in all a grand tour. It visits the tarns of Uzious and Lavedan to the south of Gourette, crosses Col d'Uzious and descends to the Vallée d'Arrens. Walking downvalley towards Arrens the way then breaks off on the outskirts of the village to follow the GR10 to Col de Saucède, round the Cirque du Litor and by way of Col de Tortes back to Gourette. Strong walkers could no doubt push the first day as far as Arrens to take advantage of *gîte d'étape* or hotel accommodation, but most (carrying camping equipment) will be content with reaching the dammed Lac du Tech at whose southern end there is a campsite.

Leaving Gourette follow directions for Route 43 to Lac du Lavedan and above the tarn to Col d'Uzious. On the eastern side of the col a path (faint in places) descends into the Labas glen, working a way down the left-hand side (northern slope). The map shows the route curving round a shallow amphitheatre below Pic de Louesque, but it is possible to avoid this by dropping to a stream and following down to the valley bed where there is a simple *cabane* (Cabane de Bouleste) offering emergency shelter. From here a trail continues on the left side of the glen, eventually entering forest and descending among trees and shrubs to the Vallée d'Arrens. Bear right along the road to reach the campsite at the southern end of the lake.

Day two heads downvalley (views back show Balaitous) along the road which, being a dead-end, has little traffic, and passes through pleasant countryside. After nearly six kilometres come to the outskirts of Arrens-Marsous (accommodation available in the *gîte d'étape* La Maison Camélat; Tel: 05 62 97 40 94). Above the road is a large sanatorium building and a GR10 waymark on the left indicates the route heading north-west along a track.

The track steadily gains height through avenues of trees (frequent waymarks), then over more open countryside with views expanding. Eventually a path replaces the track and reaches Col de Saucède (1545m). Descending a broad gully join the road and walk along it round the Cirque du Litor, then leave it on a right-hand bend by taking a footpath which climbs left to gain Col de Tortes (1799m), about an hour from the road. The descent to Gourette is steep in places, but it leads without difficulty back to the village to complete the circuit.

VALLÉE D'ESTAING

Position:	**Wholly in France, the valley reaches south of Val d'Azun and runs east of, and parallel to, the Vallée d'Arrens.**
Access:	**By way of a narrow road from either Arrens-Marsous, St-Savin or Arras-en-Lavedan in the Val d'Azun**
Maps:	**IGN Carte de Randonnées No 3 'Béarn' 1:50,000 IGN TOP 25 series no: 1647OT 'Vignemale, Ossau, Arrens, Cauterets' 1:25,000**
Valley Bases:	**Arrens (877m), Lac d'Estaing (1163m)**

Drained by the Gave de Labat de Bun the Vallée d'Estaing begins among wild, untamed peaks that form a dividing wall between the Balaitous massif and the Vallée du Marcadau; a rocky hinterland brightened by a few small tarns and the remains of stone-walled sheep pens being slowly smothered by tangles of juniper and alpenrose. Its upper reaches lie within the National Park, but north of the PNP boundaries, various minor streams that soak down the hillsides unite to give body to the Gave de Labat de Bun. The valley walls expand a little with forested lower slopes, while its bed is adorned by a glimmering sheen of water that stretches almost the full width of the valley; the Lac d'Estaing. With a restaurant at its southern end the lake is a popular destination for anglers, tourists and dreamers. Most are day visitors, but a campsite behind the restaurant provides an opportunity for a more intimate acquaintance with the valley's many attractive features.

South of Lac d'Estaing rise Pic Maleshores (2703m) and the Grand Barbat (2813m). Barely perceived from the lakeside, on closer scrutiny they supply some fine rock architecture of appeal to experienced scramblers. East of Grand Barbat lies another tarn, Lac d'Ilhéou, with a refuge at its northern end. This is reached by a splendid walk from Lac d'Estaing, by a less-demanding approach from Cauterets or by an interesting cross-country route from the Marcadau.

Downstream of Lac d'Estaing the valley narrows again with rough pastures lower down and boulder-flecked slopes at mid-height. There are no large villages; just a small hamlet or two and a scattering of isolated farms and crumbling barns. But that only adds to its appeal. There are two small campsites, a *gîte d'étape*, Les Viellettes, and a hotel a short distance from the downstream end of the lake.

The 3–4-day Tour du Val d'Azun visits the lower reaches of the Vallée d'Estaing, the GR10 goes upvalley as far as the lake, then climbs to the refuge at Lac d'Ilhéou on its way to Cauterets, while other less-trodden paths explore remote corners of the mountains.

Valley Bases:

ARRENS (877m) lies at the foot of the Col du Soulor/Col d'Aubisque road in level pastures. It has a *gîte d'étape*, La Maison Camélat (Tel: 05 62 97 40 94), hotel accommodation, several campsites, food shops and post office. Walkers and climbers based here would need their own transport though.

LAC D'ESTAING (1163m) offers camping facilities behind the restaurant at the southern end of the lake, and an attractive hotel just beyond the north-eastern end, Hotel-Restaurant du Lac (Tel: 05 62 97 06 25). As mentioned above there is a *gîte d'étape* about 1.5 kilometres downvalley of the lake; Les Viellettes (1070m) – open all-year with places for 20 (Tel: 05 62 97 14 37).

Mountain Huts:

REFUGE D'ILHÉOU (1985m), otherwise known as Refuge Raymond Ritter, this hut enjoys a fine situation overlooking Lac d'Ilhéou. With space for 32 (6 in winter) there is a guardian in residence from mid-June to the end of September, meals provided (Tel: 05 62 92 52 38). Reached by way of Col d'Ilhéou (2242m) in about 4½ hours from Lac d'Estaing, or 1½ hours from the Cambasque roadhead above Cauterets,

---

Route 45: Circuit of Lac d'Estaing (1163m)

Distance:	2.5 kilometres
Height gain/loss:	None worth mentioning
Time:	45 minutes

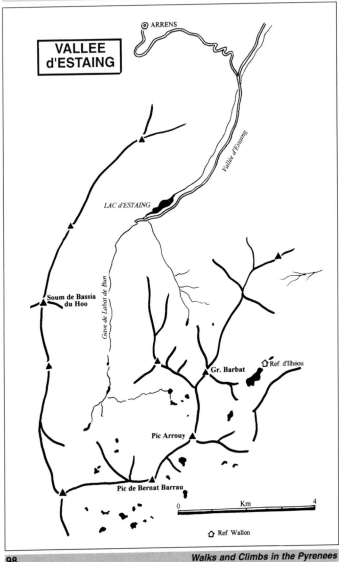

This short and easy circuit needs no description, but is included here to point visitors to the potential for a gentle stroll in idyllic surroundings. Views, especially from the northern shore, are very fine. There are footbridges at both ends giving access to the lakeside path, while the valley road edges part of the southern shoreline.

Route 46: Lac d'Estaing (1163m) – Lac du Plaa de Prat (1656m)

Distance:	6 kilometres
Height gain:	493 metres
Time:	2 hours

Lac du Plaa de Prat is a shallow reedy tarn nestling in a seemingly secretive part of the valley. This walk to it is not unduly arduous, but it does have its strenuous sections.

From the south-western end of Lac d'Estaing cross the Gave de Labat de Bun by way of Pont du Pescadou and walk upvalley along a broad clear track. Ahead the mountains close in, streams glisten on hillsides partly clothed in woods, and the walking is easy. After a little over 2.5 kilometres cross the stream again at Pont de Plasi (1323m), then climb in easy zig-zags through mixed woods of beech and pine. Emerging from the woods a path leads through a rough boulderland with grass patches grazed by sheep (there is a shepherd's *cabane* snug against an overhanging rock), and soon after you pass a very small tarn, Lac de Langle. Boulders give way to an undulating plain where the valley opens, and you come to Lac du Plaa de Prat. (Allow 1½ hours for the return to Lac d'Estaing by the same path.)

Note i: At the far end of the tarn, on the left, is the Cabane de Plaa de Prat (1668m). Sometimes occupied by shepherds it would offer reasonable emergency shelter for four people.

Note ii: Lac de Liantran (1824m) is the next tarn upvalley to the south-west and is reached by a continuing path of about 30–45 minutes, climbing among alpenrose, juniper, bilberries and boulders. This upper lake is a black tarn in a world of grey rocks, but is no less worthy a destination for all that.

Route 47: Lac d'Estaing (1163m) – Col d'Ilhéou (2242m) – Refuge d'Ilhéou (1985m)

Distance:	7 kilometres
Height gain:	1079 metres
Height loss:	257 metres
Time:	4 hours

This is a fine walk with some delightful scenery to enjoy, a high pass to cross and a well-kept hut as the destination. The route follows the GR10 path all the way, and is clear and waymarked throughout. A long haul to the pass, but a short descent to the refuge overlooking a mountain-girt tarn.

The path begins halfway along the lake where a signpost beside the road indicates the way to Cauterets via Col d'Ilhéou. (If you are starting from the campsite or car park by the restaurant at the southern end of the lake, you can take a short-cut on a forest track which eventually brings you to the GR10 footpath.)

The way climbs quite steeply through the Bois de l'Escale (forest), then out to a clearing dotted with holly trees, soon reaching the Cabane d'Arriousec (1400m) about half an hour from the lake. Beyond this join the track which came from the valley, and a few metres later quit this in favour of the continuing path cutting up the hillside to the left. Over open pastures the trail leads up the flanks of a hanging valley topped by the craggy Barbat peaks and the grassy saddle of Col d'Ilhéou seen ahead.

Rising steadily through the valley top a bluff then cross the stream and after climbing a series of zig-zags pass the Cabanes du Barbat off to your right. The path continues and about 3 hours 15 minutes from the lake you come onto Col d'Ilhéou, a broad grassy saddle cutting west to east in a rolling ridge of mountains that grow in stature to the south where Grand Barbat dominates.

Descend on the eastern side of the pass without difficulty but with fine quintessential Pyrenean views ahead. Come to the Cabanes d'Arras (2073m), one of stone, the other of metal (spaces for 6), where a sign gives 30 minutes to Refuge d'Ilhéou. Continuing, the way bears south, crosses a stream, goes over a knoll, makes a traverse of steep mountainside and then descends to Refuge d'Ilhéou (Tel: 05 62 92 52 38). (Allow 3 hours for the return to Lac d'Estaing.)

Lac d'Ilhéou and its refuge

Route 48: Lac d'Estaing (1163m) – Lac du Barbat (1973m)

Distance:	**4 kilometres**
Height gain:	**810 metres**
Time:	**2½ hours**

Lac du Barbat lies trapped in a scoop of rough mountainside north-west of the Grand Barbat, not far from the Cabanes du Barbat, and makes an interesting destination for a walk.

Follow directions to the Cabanes du Barbat as outlined in Route 47, leaving the GR10 just before the huts. Passing the *cabanes* heading south-west the way soon leads over a modest saddle and down to the tarn.

Route 49: Vallée d'Estaing – Marcadau – Vallée d'Estaing Circuit

Start/Finish:	**Lac d'Estaing**
Time:	**3 days**
Accommodation:	**Camping (Lac d'Estaing), Refuge Wallon (Marcadau), Refuge d'Ilhéou**

To link the valleys of Estaing and Marcadau involves crossing some very wild and demanding country. As such this circuit is recommended only to experienced mountain trekkers. Those who tackle it, however, are in for a treat, for there are some magnificent mountain scenes to gaze on, and the contrasts are quite remarkable. A route outline only is given to allow those who are drawn to it to experience the pleasures (and the problems!) of negotiating some of the high country where trails are severely limited.

From Lac d'Estaing head upvalley to the tarns of Lac du Plaa de Prat and Lac de Liantran (already described). Above these the mountainsides grow more wild and uncompromising, but a way leads to the Lacs de Houns de Heche, then south-west where ridges converge on three sides. Skirting Peyregnets de Cambales cross Col de Cambales (2706m) heading east and descend through a tarn and granite wonderland into the soft pastures of the Marcadau to spend a night in Refuge Wallon. (For details see Marcadau section.)

A much shorter stage follows. From the Wallon hut return upvalley a short distance, then veer right and climb to more lakes heading towards Pic d'Arrouy. Coming to Lac du Pourtet (2420m) the way bears right (east), but before dropping to the Lacs de l'Embarrat you leave the main path and traverse below the Aiguilles de Castet Abarca, cross Col de la Haugade (2311m) and descend to Refuge d'Ilhéou.

The final stage of this classic tour reverses Route 47 by crossing Col d'Ilhéou on GR10 and descending to Lac d'Estaing.

Ascent of Grand Barbat:

For its height (2813m) and length of approach from Lac d'Estaing, Grand Barbat provides an ascent of modest proportions by its *voie normale*. This leads via GR10 to Lac du Barbat, then up to the Brèche de Barbat (2643m) found at the foot of the south-west ridge. From the Brèche to the summit involves an easy scramble keeping west of the ridge itself. About 4½–5 hours; allow 3½ hours for the descent by the same route, or make a traverse by descending from the Brèche to Lac Long and the Gave de Labat de Bun. (A much longer route giving a round-trip of about 9–10 hours.)

VALLÉE DU MARCADAU

Position:	**South-west of Cauterets and projecting as far as the Franco/Spanish border**
Access:	**Conveniently reached by road from Cauterets by way of Pont d'Espagne where vehicles should be parked. Cauterets is linked by bus with Lourdes.**
Map:	**IGN Carte de Randonnées No 3 'Béarn' 1:50,000 IGN TOP 25 series no: 1647OT 'Vignemale, Ossau, Arrens, Cauterets' 1:25,000**
Valley Base:	**Cauterets (902m)**

Sandwiched between the rather austere heights of the Balaitous massif to the west and Vignemale to the south-east, the Vallée du Marcadau (see map pp72–3) is an oasis of light, colour and fragrance. Streams come dashing in silver cascades from the surrounding highlands to unite in soft pastures where izard creep in evening shadow. Trout leap from hidden tarns and the hillsides blaze with spring flowers.

It's a walker's paradise with numerous outings of great charm to be exploited. But there are modest ascent routes too on mountains at the head of the valley, and some pleasant, if short, rock scrambles to enjoy on the Arrouy aiguilles that rise as a jagged spine above the waters of Lac du Pourtet. There's no reason for anyone to run short of ideas in the Marcadau and its tributary glens.

From Pont d'Espagne to Refuge Wallon near the head of the valley, the Marcadau is lush with pastures and streaked with streams. There are a few green ponds, stands of pine, rough boulders and the hint of big mountains ahead. But above the hut the valley fans out with short side glens adding their own personality to the overall scene. To the north-west lies a graniteland, unguessed from the low pastures of Wallon. In it lie numerous tarns, either isolated with no apparent outlet, or linked by beautiful meandering streams above which rise rough frontier peaks.

North of Wallon more tarns sparkle among the mountains, while a little south of west from the refuge a charming slope of hillside flows from the valley's highest peak, Grande Fache (3005m), on either side of which trekkers' cols give access to Spain. From Grande Fache the ridge undulates in a south-easterly line to Grand Pic d'Arratille (2900m) before slanting north-eastward at the head of the Spanish valley of the Rio Ara. Below Grand Pic d'Arratille is the dip of Col d'Arratille (2528m), and from it a fine little glen drains northward with yet more tarns to join the Marcadau almost opposite the Wallon hut.

The Marcadau has immense charm and makes one of the finest possible introductions for newcomers to the range, while those who have long succumbed to its beauties find themselves lured back time and again.

Valley Base:

CAUTERETS (902m) began as a spa town and later developed as a winter resort, but it is also very busy in summer, with a wide range of accommodation in hotels, two *gîtes d'étape* (Le Pas de L'Ours; Tel: 05 62 92 58 07; and the Beau Soleil, Tel: 05 62 92 53 52) and several campsites. The town has plenty of shops, banks, restaurants, a tourist information office, PNP office (Maison du Parc) and a mountain guides bureau (Tel: 05 62 92 62 02).

Mountain Huts:

CHALET-REFUGE DU CLOT (1522m) is situated at the entrance to the Marcadau beyond the Pont d'Espagne car park (there is also hotel accommodation at Pont d'Espagne). Open throughout the year, except November, Chalet du Clot has dormitory places for 45, but reservations are essential (Tel: 05 62 92 61 27). There is a full meals service.

REFUGE WALLON (1864m) is a rambling CAF building offering dormitory accommodation (120 places), and with a simple hut adjacent. Open with a guardian in charge from June to the end of September, a full meals service is usually available. (Tel: 05 62 92 64 28) The refuge is invariably very busy during the main season, and is reached in about two hours from Pont d'Espagne. It commands an idyllic position near the head of the valley, with fine views of Grande Fache and its neighbours, and south-east to the topmost snows of the Vignemale's Clot de la Hount face peering above peaks that wall the nearby Arratille glen.

Route 50: Pont d'Espagne (Parking du Puntas; 1465m) – Chalet-Refuge du Clot (1522m)

Distance:	1.5 kilometres
Height gain:	57 metres
Time:	20 minutes

The vast majority of visitors to the Marcadau and parallel Vallée de Gaube journey as far as possible by road. In the past the roadhead was a huge parking area near the Chalet-Refuge du Clot, but vehicles are now restricted to an extensive area just south of Pont d'Espagne, about 7 kilometres from Cauterets – fee payable. The car park is equipped with a PNP information office, public toilets and telephones, while a gondola lift carries those unable to walk the distance from the car park as far as Pont d'Espagne, where there's a chairlift into the Vallée de Gaube.

From the car park walk up the continuing track towards Pont d'Espagne, and when it curves left take the footpath ahead which becomes paved and gives an excellent close view of the scenic arched bridge of Pont d'Espagne itself, then rises to a Hôtellerie/Café/Restaurant. (A path breaks off left to the Lac de Gaube chairlift, and overlooks beautiful waterfalls.) Wander up the track for about 1 minute, then divert onto a footpath heading right (sign to Monument Meillon). This winds easily uphill through sparse pinewoods, goes beneath the Pont d'Espagne gondola lift, and brings you to a stone pillar commemorating Alponse Meillon (1862–1933) – a great Pyrenean enthusiast – from where there's a lovely view across the head of a waterfall to the distant Vignemale. Return to the track and follow this upvalley, soon across open pastures at the far end of which you come to the Chalet-Refuge du Clot.

Route 51: Cauterets (902m) – Pont d'Espagne (1496m) – Refuge Wallon (1864m)

Distance:	12 kilometres
Height gain:	962 metres
Time:	4 hours

As mentioned above, most visitors to the Marcadau travel by road

from Cauterets through the Val de Jeret to the car park below Pont
d'Espagne and walk from there. However, for the benefit of those
without transport and who choose against the option of hiring a taxi
as far as the end of the road, this walk is offered. It is well worth
taking, for the two main sections are quite different yet equally
delightful; the first (to Pont d'Espagne) follows what is known as the
Sentier des Cascades from La Raillère, the second serves as an introduction to the splendours of the Marcadau. Refreshments are available at La Raillère and Pont d'Espagne.

From the southern end of Cauterets (Futaie district) climb steps
on the right of the road to join a footpath adopted as a *variante* of the
GR10. This now goes through beechwoods of the Peguère forest and
in half an hour reaches the abandoned Thermes de la Raillère where
waterfalls come crashing from the woods below the Vallée de Lutour
opposite, and also from the main Val de Jeret – Tennyson's *'stream
that flashest white...'*

The path continues on the north side of the river (true left bank)
climbing past one waterfall after another, forest providing shade all
the way. There are numerous idyllic places to pause to take photographs. In about 1½ hours from La Raillère come to Pont d'Espagne
where you go up onto the road, cross the bridge and walk up the
road to a former car parking area in which is found the Chalet du
Clot refuge. There is now a choice of routes into the Marcadau; the
slightly shorter option being given here, the longer (and perhaps,
preferable) alternative is described below as Route 52.

Cross to the left-hand side of the stream and walk along the
continuing road as it projects into the Marcadau with pastures
spreading across the valley floor. Shortly after you reach the Pont du
Cayan the way narrows to a clear footpath which climbs among trees
and later emerges once more beside the stream to cross by a sturdy
bridge (Pont d'Estaloungue) to the true left bank. The trail delves
deeper into realms of enchantment; across shallow levels, over rocky
bluffs and now and then shaded by pines for a further three kilometres or so until Refuge Wallon is reached standing a little above the
stream to the right of the path.

Route 52: Chalet-Refuge du Clot (1522m) – Refuge Wallon (1864m)

Distance:	4 kilometres
Height gain:	342 metres
Time:	1½ hours

This walk is the preferred route into the Marcadau, and is offered as an alternative to the right bank route described under Route 51.

From Chalet-Refuge du Clot go diagonally across meadowland in which ski-tows stand sentry. A vague path may be detected in the grass, but beyond the first 'meadow' it becomes clearly defined and leads into the Marcadau proper. Remaining on the true left bank (north side) the path maintains a fairly level course and crosses a few minor side streams. Views ahead, and the gentle foreground of winding streams, stands of pine and the smooth pastures of the Plateau du Cayan, make this a truly delightful walk. After almost three kilometres Pont du Cayan is seen crossing the stream on the left. Go over this bridge and join the main route described above as far as Refuge Wallon.

GRANDE FACHE (3005m)

Situated to the south-west of the Wallon hut the Grande Fache rises as a large pyramid; the highest peak in the so-called Marcadau cirque, it makes a pleasing ascent (one of the easiest 3000m summits in the Pyrenees) with very fine views. On 5th August each year it forms the culmination of a pilgrimage in memory of those who have perished in the mountains.

Route 53: Refuge Wallon (1864m) – Grande Fache (3005m)

Grade:	F (*voie normale*)
Distance:	4.5 kilometres
Height gain:	1141 metres
Time:	3–3½ hours

Below the hut cross the bridge to the true right bank of the stream and turn right. Follow the path over pastures to cross tributary streams, then bear left after about 500 metres on a trail which heads west up

Arratille valley from the Wallon Hut

grass slopes, passes above and to the left of a small tarn (2291m) and makes towards Col de la Fache which lies to the right of the peak. This pass forms the frontier and leads to some interesting Spanish valleys and the comfortable Refugio Respomuso. Enriched by views over much fascinating country the col is reached in a little over 2½ hours from the hut.

A clear route with occasional cairns leads south (left) from Col de la Fache to climb the north ridge of the mountain. Without encountering difficulties gain the crest with its little rocky spires and broad gendarmes, which in turn leads easily to the summit in about 40 minutes from the pass. (Allow 2 hours for the descent.)

Other Routes on Grande Fache:

Between Grande Fache and Pic Falisse, its neighbour to the south-east, the ridge dips more than 300 metres to Col Falisse (2685m). An interesting route graded AD climbs from this col up the eastern arête of Grande Fache. Another, graded AD inf., tackles the same arête but on its north-eastern side. The two routes combine some way below the summit.

Route 54: Refuge Wallon (1864m) – Port du Marcadau (2541m)

Distance:	**4 kilometres**
Height gain:	**677 metres**
Time:	**2½ hours**

Below Pic Falisse the Port du Marcadau offers an easy crossing into Spain, and has long been used by travellers bound for Balnerio de Panticosa. Although there is nothing difficult about the walk to the pass, and it lies at a lower altitude than that of Col de la Fache, it has a rather more strenuous approach than its higher neighbour.

The walk begins by following the early stages of the route to Col de la Fache, crossing the Marcadau stream below the hut and heading upvalley over tributary streams. But instead of veering west, as for Col de la Fache, continue heading a little west of south rising over the Pla de Loubosso on a path which follows a stream draining the valley flowing from the Port du Marcadau. The crest of Pic Falisse appears like the huge fin of a dinosaur from here, with the North Face of Muga Nord to its left.

The trail winds its way towards Muga Nord (2676m) before swinging to the right into the wild country between it and Pic Falisse where you come to a small pool known as Hount Frido (2330m). Above this bear left to climb the final steep slopes to reach the Port du Marcadau where views open to the south over a land of lakes and rolling heights dominated by the Picos del Inferno.

Note i: An easy scramble leftwards from the col will take you to the summit of Muga Nord in about 20–30 minutes.

Note ii: Balneario (or Banos) de Panticosa may be reached in a further 2½ hours by way of a fairly easy route among the lakes below, where it joins the path of GR11.

PIC DE CAMBALÈS (2965m)

Pic de Cambalès may not be one of the great peaks of the Pyrenees. It shows no natural elegance of form, offers no challenging rock climbs, has neither glacier nor permanent snowfield on its crown and is rather tucked away from view; out of sight, out of mind. Many wander in the Marcadau without giving it a second glance. Yet its position is such that it commands a truly magnificent panorama and rewards those who are drawn to it, not only with its memorable vistas, but with an ascent that offers surprising variety and no shortage of interest. It rises a little north of west from the hut on the frontier ridge between the rocky pile of Pene d'Aragon and Pic de la Peyre, and the initial approach to it follows a section of trail used on the Pyrenean High Route.

Route 55: Refuge Wallon (1864m) –
Pic de Cambalès (2965m)

Grade:	**F**
Distance:	**6 kilometres**
Height gain:	**1101 metres**
Time:	**4 hours**

Leaving the Wallon refuge take the path which rises among pine trees and alpenroses aiming north-west. Entering a small level area the path divides. That which goes off to the right leads to the lake circuit described below as Route 57. The path for Pic de Cambalès veers leftward, rising still to pass through a false col, beyond which you reach the first of the many Lacs de Cambalès – a string of three to the right of the trail. Ahead, and to the south-west, rises Pic de Cambalès with a long moraine ridge, the Crête de Cambalès, thrusting forward. A cairn by the path indicates the point at which you leave the main trail to break away to the left.

Make towards the Crête de Cambalès following a vague line of cairns and passing to the left of a largish tarn. Reaching the Crête the way initially leads along its northern side, then climbs onto the crest itself. Gaining height without difficulty you overlook a world of grey granite and silent tarns; a naked landscape with its own distinctive charm.

Come off the Crête to enter a hanging valley of moraine boulders and scree, headed by Pene d'Aragon above to the left, and by the steep cliffs of Pic de Cambalès. Between the two is the Col d'Aragon (2808m). Climb to the col, which is gained by a final pyramid of granite blocks (about 3½ hours).

Bear right to climb the broken southern slopes of the mountain which, from the col, appears as a giant slag heap. Cairns lead toward the summit, and as you draw closer to it, so the precipices of the eastern side become impressive and the peak itself improves. The summit is reached in about 30 minutes from the col. Just below it there is a collection of three memorial plaques, but it is the magnificent panorama that will hold your attention. Near at hand to the north-west rises the Balaitous with its bristling ridges and tiny glacier blocked by high protective walls. South are the Picos del Inferno; to the north you can see (on a clear day) far beyond the foothill ranges to the vast plains of south-west France; while to the south-east the Vignemale, Pic du Marboré and distant Maladeta can all be picked out in a vast sea of peaks. (Allow 2½ hours for the descent by the same route.)

Alternative Route to Pic de Cambalès:

Another route (similar grade) leads via Col de la Fache and Pene d'Aragon to join the route described above at Col d'Aragon. 3½ hours from Refuge Wallon.

Route 56: Refuge Wallon (1864m) – Col de Cambalès (2706m)

Distance:	**5 kilometres**
Height gain:	**842 metres**
Time:	**3–3½ hours**

Walkers who might be loath to tackle the ascent of Pic de Cambalès have an opportunity to enjoy the Cambalès tarns and wild views of the Balaitous from Col de Cambalès. It's a strenuous walk, but a rewarding one.

Follow the path described in Route 55 from the Wallon hut to the Lacs de Cambalès. Instead of turning left to climb along the Crête de Cambalès continue on the path heading west among many tarns that lie trapped among granite boulderlands. The way becomes rough as you climb towards the pass. Snow patches often litter the slopes, but it is worth persevering for the view of Balaitous from the col is remarkable, as is the scene below through which you have just wandered.

Route 57: Marcadau Lakes Circuit

Start/Finish:	**Refuge Wallon (1864m)**
Distance:	**10 kilometres**
Height gain/loss:	**799 metres**
Time:	**4–5 hours**

This superb outing is one of the classic walks of the Pyrenees, and one that will demand a full day to tackle, despite the modest walking time quoted above. For there are so many delectable tarns to settle by, so many glorious views to absorb, that progress is frustrated by the need to stop and stare at the wonders of the landscape. And why not? In a previous edition of this guide the circuit was written as an anti-clockwise route. However, having now walked it in both directions (more than once) I believe a clockwise circuit gives the finest views and is a little less demanding for those walkers using Refuge Wallon as a base.

Take the path heading upvalley from the hut, as described at the start of Route 55, through the pines and into the level area where an alternative PNP trail breaks away to the right (north) at a point where a stream issues from an obvious corrie above. This trail is the one to follow; it climbs through a granite bowl and winds up to the open end of a rocky, grassless basin with Lac Nère trapped within.

Continue round the right-hand side of the tarn and at the far end climb to a high valley that leads to Lac du Pourtet above whose northern shore screes are topped by the jagged Aiguilles du Pic Arrouy. Halfway along the eastern shore the path bears right to overlook a steeply-falling valley with yet more tarns lying below. Wander down to these tarns (Lacs de l'Embarrat; 2139m and 2076m) passing below the Aiguilles de Castet Abarca, and continue beyond the lower tarn as the path twists down to the bed of the Marcadau, which you reach at Pont du Cayan. Cross the bridge, bear right and follow the familiar trail upvalley to the Wallon refuge.

Route 58: Refuge Wallon (1864m) – Col d'Arratille (2528m)

Distance:	**5 kilometres**
Height gain:	**664 metres**
Time:	**2½–3 hours**

The walk to Col d'Arratille forms part of a stage on the High Route; a stage which crosses other cols on the way to the Vignemale. It's a fine walk in its own right, and one which could be extended into a long circuit, or a descent through the Spanish valley of the Rio Ara, as an approach to climbs on Grand Pic d'Arratille, or as a variation of Route 59 below.

Leave the Wallon hut and take the main path down-valley heading east, and cross the stream by a footbridge at the mouth of the Arratille glen. A clear path heads south into the glen, soon on the right bank of its stream, the Gave d'Arratille, and gains height without difficulty. Trading grass for glacier-smoothed rocks, then back to grass again, you eventually cross a footbridge just before reaching Lac d'Arratille (1 hour 45 mins).

Walk round the western shore of the lake, then cross the stream again at its southern end. Below a small tarn waymarks lead in a circuitous route up a region of rough broken rocks. In the event of snow covering the way, the general direction to follow is south, keeping to the left of a stream until you gain an upper desolate corrie in which you find Lac du Col d'Arratille. Traverse screes well to the left of this tarn and gain the obvious saddle of Col d'Arratille. Views across the head of the Ara Valley to the Vignemale are delightful. (Allow 2 hours for the return to Wallon.)

Note i: An easy descent into the Ara may be made from here. By following the Rio Ara downvalley on its left bank the hamlet of Bujaruelo may be reached in about 4 hours (6–7 hours to Torla).

Note ii: To continue across to the Vignemale and then to Gavarnie (about 9 hours from here – overnight accommodation in either Refuge des Oulettes de Gaube or Refuge Bayssellance), follow directions for High Route 9.

Note iii: For a long circuit (10 hours in all) cross the head of the Ara, go over Col des Mulets and descend to the Vallée de Gaube, as described under High Route 9, then go north through the Vallée de Gaube to Pont d'Espagne. From there take the path already described (Route 51 or 52) to the Wallon hut.

Route 59: Tarns and Corries of the Arratille Valley

Start/Finish:	**Refuge Wallon (1864m)**
Distance:	**8 kilometres**
Height gain/loss:	**688 metres**
Time:	**4–5 hours**

An exploration of the Arratille glen will provide an entertaining and rewarding day's effort. There are remote tarns, interesting geological formations, a wonderland of alpine plants, bare screes and fine views. The route described below is largely free of paths and, as some of the wild country crossed is rough underfoot and the map not entirely accurate, good visibility will be required.

The author on the Col du Chapeau, with Vignemale as a backdrop

Follow Route 58 as far as Lac d'Arratille. From the southern end of the lake paint flashes and a few cairns direct you away from the main path off to the right (south-west), gaining height easily to top a grassy lip overlooking another tarn, Lac de la Badette (2344m) almost 100 metres above Lac d'Arratille. Lac de la Badette sits in a bowl of rock and grass below the steep crags and screes of the two Pics d'Arratille.

Go down to the lake (a botanist's delight) and wander round its northern shore, then ascend grass slopes to the west in order to reach Col du Chapeau (2552m), below and to the south-west of le Chapeau d'Espagne (2590m). From the col very fine views are to be had of the Vignemale and of the Pics Chabarrou that wall the Arratille glen.

Descend north-west over slopes of diced rock and scree and go round the eastern side of a tarn. Find the unseen line of its outflow stream and follow this roughly northward. Eventually the stream appears and leads among pastures near the junction of the Arratille and Bassia glens. Grass slopes bring you to the Arratille proper where you rejoin the path that leads back to the Marcadau.

VIGNEMALE

Position:	**To the south of Cauterets and west of Gavarnie, on the Franco/Spanish border**
Access:	**From Cauterets by way of Pont d'Espagne and the Vallée de Gaube, or from Gavarnie through the Vallée d'Ossoue**
Maps:	**IGN Carte de Randonnées No 3 'Béarn', or No 4 'Bigorre', both at 1:50,000** **IGN TOP 25 series no: 1647OT 'Vignemale, Ossau, Arrens, Cauterets' and 1748OT 'Gavarnie, Luz St Sauveur' both at 1:25,000**
Valley Bases:	**Cauterets (902m), Gavarnie (1365m)**

Seen from the peaks of Gavarnie, from the Brèche de Roland or Monte Perdido, the Vignemale appears as a large mountain block spawning a broad snowfield below its summit and with a long tongue of glacier draining into the Ossoue Valley. From the south, in the aromatic meadows of the Ara, it rises in terraces and insignificant buttresses, a bewildering structure that has no apparent summit. But approaching from Lac de Gaube one is suddenly struck by the majesty of the valley-head – a tight cirque of grey limestone walls, polished by time here, coarsely-grained there, strutting and straining against each other to attain superiority. Here are north faces that would stand out in any mountain region; defiant walls that are at once superbly attractive and compelling in their challenge.

In 1837 the highest of its summits (Pique Longue, or Grand Vignemale, 3298m) was climbed by Henri Cazaux and Bernard Guillembet, their route of ascent via the Ossoue Glacier. On the way they both fell into a large crevasse, and having extricated themselves, were unwilling to repeat the experience so found a safe, glacier-free descent into the Ara. It was this rather circuitous southern route that was later promoted by Cazaux when he led an English spinster from

Halifax, Miss Anne Lister, on the first tourist ascent in August 1838. The Vignemale has remained a popular mountain ever since, while the Ossoue Glacier, though still the most impressive icefield in the Pyrenees, has shrunk from its former glory and no longer holds the great perils of old. It has therefore become accepted as the easiest route to the summit, while on the North Face there are lines of a very different order.

Seen from Oulettes de Gaube the left-hand peak is the Petit Vignemale. Next to that is Pointe Chausenque, then Piton Carre rising to Pique Longue. Between Piton Carre and Pique Longue the prominent gully is the Couloir de Gaube, a 600-metre seam with a dramatic quality that was first climbed in 1889 by the team of Brulle, Bazillac and de Monts, with the guides Célestin Passet and Bernard Salles. It was a remarkable achievement for the period, and even today is seen as a mixed climb of some consequence (French grade TD), while routes on the faces themselves are exposed throughout and of a severity beyond the scope of the present guidebook. (See *Rock Climbs in the Pyrenees* by Derek L.Walker for a selection of routes. The French guide, *Passages Pyrénéens,* also offers a choice of hard routes.)

Though it may not be easy to reconcile the degree to which Henry Russell's infatuation with the Vignemale was to manifest itself (see the section headed Pioneers in the Introduction), it is not so difficult to understand why it should be this specific mountain that was destined to become the object of his devotion. By any standards it is an impressive peak, and an ascent from any direction will be amply rewarded by the unfolding panorama that its upper reaches display, as well as the ever-varied detail of the mountain itself. The valleys that surround it are equally impressive in their own right too.

Valley Bases:

CAUTERETS (902m) grew from a spa town to an important winter sports resort and mountaineering centre. It has a wide range of accommodation, from campsites to hotels and two *gîtes d'étape* (Le Pas de L'Ours; Tel: 05 62 92 58 07; and the Beau Soleil, Tel: 05 62 92 53 52). There are plenty of shops, banks, restaurants, a tourist information office, National Park office (Maison du Parc) and a mountain guides bureau (Tel: 05 62 92 62 02).

GAVARNIE (1365m) is one of the best-known of all villages in the Pyrenees, by virtue of the magnificent cirque that rises at the head of its valley. An historic place for those with a taste for *Pyrénéisme*, it is, however, architecturally uninspiring with its tacky souvenir kiosks and crowded cafes. It has several hotels, a CAF refuge (Les Granges de Holle), a *gîte d'étape* (Le Gypaëte; Tel: 05 62 92 40 61) and a small campsite at the southern end of the village. Gavarnie has one or two food shops and a tourist information office/Maison du Parc which sometimes organizes local walks. As with Cauterets, it is reached by bus from Lourdes.

Mountain Huts:

REFUGE DES OULETTES DE GAUBE (2151m) is perfectly situated at the head of the Vallée de Gaube with a superb view of the Vignemale's North Face. Owned by the CAF, it can sleep 75. A guardian is in residence from Easter until mid-October when meals may be provided (Tel: 05 62 92 62 97).

REFUGE DE BAYSSELLANCE (2651m) is the highest wardened hut in the Pyrenees. Although old, it has been refurbished without destroying its essential character. The hut can sleep 70, and the guardian provides meals between the beginning of May and late September (Tel: 05 62 92 40 25). As it is convenient for ascents of the Vignemale by the Ossoue Glacier, and is also on the path of the High Route and a *variante* of the GR10, the hut is invariably crowded in summer.

REFUGE LES GRANGES DE HOLLE (1495m) is a little too remote from the Vignemale to be used as a base for an ascent, but could be useful as a walking and or climbing valley base. Owned by the CAF it is located outside Gavarnie on the way to the village ski station. Wardened all year except November, there are places for 48 and meals provision (Tel: 05 62 92 48 77).

Route 60: Pont d'Espagne (1496m) – Refuge des Oulettes de Gaube (2151m)

Distance:	7.5 kilometres
Height gain:	655 metres
Time:	2½–3 hours

A pleasant walk, whether or not you intend to stay at the hut, it provides a dramatic introduction to one of the most spectacular high mountain regions in the Pyrenees. The initial climb through woods from Pont d'Espagne may be avoided by riding the téléphérique.

The footpath begins on the down-valley side of the Pont d'Espagne bridge and is signposted to Lac de Gaube and Refuge des Oulettes. It climbs above the road to the south, snaking among lovely conifer woods until emerging just before Lac de Gaube, a popular picnic site with a small hotellerie above its north-eastern shore (1 hour, *refreshments available*).

Take the path round the northern end of the lake, to join that which leads from the téléphérique, and bear left along the west bank. The path is clearly defined and maintained by the PNP. At the southern end of the lake it reaches the Oulettes stream and crosses by way of a footbridge where a waterfall gushes from the rocks. Nearby is a small unmanned refuge, Cabane du Pinet (1783m), with room for about eight.

Continue through the valley heading south, gaining height without difficulty. As you progress so the valley becomes more barren as first trees, then the lush vegetation of the lower valley, are traded for a wilderness of scattered boulders and patches of old snow. Then you top a rise with the flat glacial plain before you; the Vignemale stands regal ahead, having grown in stature as you drew closer to it. Off to the left is Refuge des Oulettes de Gaube.

Route 61: Refuge des Oulettes de Gaube (2151m) – Refuge de Bayssellance (2651m)

Distance:	3 kilometres
Height gain:	583 metres
Height loss:	83 metres
Time:	2½ hours

In reasonable weather an easy, visually interesting route, this linking of huts across the Hourquette d'Ossoue is adopted by both the Pyrenean High Route and as a *variante* of the GR10. Splendid views of the great walls that overlook the Vallée de Gaube on the way to the pass, and from it the splendour of a new valley system is revealed as you gaze towards the Cirque de Gavarnie. An ascent of Petit Vignemale (3032m) from the Hourquette d'Ossoue is recommended (see Route 64 below).

Refuge de Bayssellance, the highest wardened hut in the Pyrenees
(Routes 61, 62 and 63)

The path to Hourquette d'Ossoue is obvious as it begins at the door of the Oulettes de Gaube hut. It assumes a south-easterly direction, gaining height above the small valley-head plateau which is sliced with streams. A fine view is projected into the Couloir de Gaube from here, but soon the direction changes to head north, then climbs in zig-zags to a trail division. The left-hand path climbs to Col d'Arraille, while the main route continues, now through a region of boulders with the Petit Vignemale seen directly ahead. About 2 hours 15 minutes from the start come onto the col of Hourquette d'Ossoue (2734m). Refuge de Bayssellance is seen a short distance below. The path leads to it in about 10 minutes.

Route 62: Gavarnie (Barrage d'Ossoue) (1834m) – Refuge de Baysellance (2651m)

Distance:	6 kilometres
Height gain:	817 metres
Time:	2½–3 hours

The easiest and most usual way to reach the Bayssellance hut from Gavarnie is to drive eight kilometres of road and track through the Vallée d'Ossoue as far as a small dammed lake, and walk from there. An unmanned, simple refuge, Cabane d'Ossoue, is found near the dam. (If walking all the way from Gavarnie, allow an extra three hours.)

A well-marked path rises up the valley beyond the lake (on its northern shore) and through the Oulettes d'Ossoue, crossing the stream and then climbing above its true right bank. This path was created by Henry Russell's squad of grotto builders over 100 years ago; it skirts a gorge, crosses occasional snow patches, then climbs in zig-zags to reach the three Russell caves in view of the Ossoue Glacier. Leading past the caves the trail climbs leftwards round a spur of mountain, soon after which the hut is suddenly seen above and to the right; a stone beehive on the hillside.

GRAND VIGNEMALE (3298m)

Under standard summer conditions the ascent of the Vignemale by its *voie normale* makes an enjoyable outing for mountaineers accustomed to glacier walking. However, there are plenty of crevasses and no-one should tackle Route 63 without taking normal safety precautions. Check with the hut guardian as to the condition of the glacier. If crevasses are open and dangerous to cross, it is advisable to ascend by the alternative route given below. The final rock scramble has some loose rock to contend with, so take care on this too.

Route 63: Refuge de Bayssellance (2651m) – Vignemale (3298m)

Grade:	F (via the Ossoue Glacier; *voie normale*)
Distance:	3.5 kilometres
Height loss:	232 metres
Height gain:	879 metres
Time:	3 hours
Equipment:	Rope, ice-axe, crampons

Descend from the hut on the path which goes down to Gavarnie. Shortly after passing Russell's grottoes another, more narrow, path continues heading west across the steep slope below the Crête du

The Ossoue Glacier is the main route to the Vignemale's summit

Petit Vignemale. This is the path to take. It leads across scree to a moraine depository at the snout of the glacier. There may well be snow cover here early in the season. Cross below the seracs (caution advised; move fast to avoid danger from falling ice) and then move onto the left-hand (southern) side of the glacier.

Note: If conditions are such that crevasses are dangerously open, do not go onto the icefield, but instead continue to gain the ridge which forms the southern boundary of the glacier. This is the Crête du Montferrat which you climb along its glacier side until the upper basin is reached. Leave the Crête here and join the standard route across the basin.

On the normal route go straight up the glacier, usually a little to the left of centre (true right-hand, southern, side), until the almost level snowfield of the upper basin is gained. Across the basin will be seen Pointe Chausenque and Pique Longue (Grand Vignemale) separated by a saddle where the Couloir de Gaube emerges. Cross to the foot of Pique Longue and choose a line on the final cone of rock that leads to the summit. Although there is plenty of loose rock, a modest scramble is usually all that is required to reach the top.

Views from the summit are magnificent and far-reaching. Perhaps the most dramatic is that which gazes directly down onto the North Face, with the little grassy plain of Oulettes de Gaube appearing like a small green handkerchief far below. Allow 2 hours for the return to Refuge de Baysellance.

PETIT VIGNEMALE (3032m)

Lowest of the four main peaks, the Petit Vignemale provides one of the easiest ascents of a 3000 metre summit in all the Pyrenees; little more than a walk. However, the face which plunges to the Oulettes de Gaube is a very different undertaking and should only be attempted by climbers proficient in ropework.

Route 64: Refuge des Oulettes de Gaube (2151m) – Petit Vignemale (3032m)

Grade:	**F (via the Hourquette d'Ossoue; voie normale)**
Distance:	**3.5 kilometres**
Height gain:	**881 metres**
Time:	**3–3½ hours**

A very easy ascent; no difficulties ought to be experienced by regular mountain walkers – unless vertigo is a problem.

Follow directions as far as the Hourquette d'Ossoue already described as Route 61 (about 2 hours 15 minutes). Bear right (south) and ascend the ridge, keeping a little left of the actual crest. The route is well-trodden and easily followed, and reaches the summit in about an hour from the pass.

Note: Since Hourquette d'Ossoue is only some 80 metres higher than the Bayssellance hut, the ascent of Petit Vignemale from here is even shorter than that from Oulettes de Gaube.

POINTE CHAUSENQUE (3204m)

Named after the man who made its first ascent (in 1822) Pointe Chausenque is the highest Pyrenean summit entirely in France (the Franco/Spanish frontier crosses the Grand Vignemale), and the following route is a popular one with French climbers.

Route 65: Hourquette d'Ossoue (2734m) –
Pointe Chausenque (3204m)

Grade:	**AD inf. (via the Petit Vignemale/ Pointe Chausenque ridge)**
Distance:	**1.5 kilometres**
Height gain:	**470 metres**
Time:	**2½ hours**
Equipment:	**Rope**

Take Route 64 to the summit of the Petit Vignemale. It is advisable to rope-up here before moving left and descending a short gully of only four or five metres. On gaining the ridge proper move along it for a few metres, keeping to the north-west side where there are footholds, then onto the crest itself until you come to a short, very steep descent pitch on the south-eastern side above the Ossoue Glacier. Climb down this pitch and continue along the ridge until you reach another descent pitch (grade III), longer than the last, but also on the south-eastern side. Again follow the ridge until yet another descent has to be made, this time above the seracs of the Petit Vignemale's glacier. The descent of this pitch is rather delicate (III sup.). When the ridge has been regained follow along it with the aid of footholds on the right below the crest (handholds on the ridge), and then by way of brief ledges descend to the Col des Glaciers.

Once at the col difficulties are mostly over. Climb now along the southern slope below the ridge as far as point 3138m where the ridge bears more to the right, just north of west. From here to the summit of Pointe Chausenque, some 250 metres distant and only 65 metres higher, follow along the crest itself.

Note i: To continue to the summit of Pique Longue (Grand Vignemale), descend to the Ossoue Glacier and walk to the final rock cone where a short scramble takes you to the top in a few minutes.

Note ii: To descend, go down onto the Ossoue Glacier and return by the normal Vignemale route (Route 63) to the Bayssellance hut (allow 2 hours).

Other Routes:

A mountain of the calibre of the Vignemale attracts much attention from adventurous climbers. It therefore contains a variety of routes which may be summarised by the following notes.

The original 'tourist' route, known as the **PRINCE DE LA MOSKOWA'S,** is a scramble (AD inf.) following a long approach march into the Ara Valley on the southern flanks. It is a route that has lost its attraction of late, although the Ara is most certainly a valley worth exploring. (See below.)

Two expeditions using the Oulettes de Gaube hut, other than North Face climbs, are: 1) via the couloir of the **CLOT DE LA HOUNT**, a mixed outing with several passages of III and IV that is reached across the Col des Oulettes, and 2) the rather fine ridge climb of the **ARÊTE DE GAUBE**. This too is reached from the Col des Oulettes, is comparatively safe while at the same time giving the impression of a much more serious outing. It involves almost 7 hours from hut to summit and is graded AD.

The **NORTH FACE** did not receive its first ascent until 1933, and all routes (there are a number of lines and variations) are serious undertakings. The original route was made by H Barrio with R Bellocq. It is now graded D sup. and involves some 850 metres of effort. To the right of this is the classic **NORTH BUTTRESS** (ED) which is one of the most advanced climbs on the mountain. Although it has its artificial pitches it is essentially a free line pioneered in 1965 by Patrice de Bellefon.

Wedged between Pique Longue and Pointe Chausenque is the triangular block of **PITON CARRE**. There is a very exposed line (TD) on its North Face, approached up the Couloir de Gaube. Next to it the North-West Buttress of **POINTE CHAUSENQUE** is a serious challenge, while the otherwise modest **PETIT VIGNEMALE** contains a brace of lines on its North Face and N.W. Buttress.

Route 66: Refuge des Oulettes de Gaube (2151m) – Col des Oulettes (2606m) – Torla (1033m)

Distance:	**23 kilometres**
Height gain:	**455 metres**
Height loss:	**1573 metres**
Time:	**8 hours**

This is a superb walk through a delightful, uninhabited Spanish valley – the Ara. Although it is by no means the easiest, quickest or most obvious route from a French centre to the mouth of the Ordesa

National Park, it is a mountain walk of unquestionable character, and one that best displays the contrast between the two sides of the Pyrenees. Although it is long, it could be achieved in one day by fit mountain walkers. However, the Ara is a valley to savour, to wander in at leisure. To enjoy it to the full, take a small tent and provisions for a couple of days and tread the pastures without an eye on the clock. There are campsites at, and below, Bujaruelo, about 5–6 hours from Oulettes de Gaube.

From the hut cross the glacial plain heading south-west towards the jumble of boulders at the base of Pic des Oulettes, and take the path which climbs on the left of the screes. When you come to a stream issuing from the hanging valley on the left, go up the left-hand side of it and soon you will come to cairns and a vague path which leads to the obvious pass of Col des Oulettes (1½–2 hours) with the Arête de Gaube slanting off to the left and grand views in all directions.

Go down to a stream below the pass and pick a route to the right of it as it dances through a narrow gully, the descent of which is not difficult, despite the fact that it is fairly steep in places. At the base of the gully bear left across a field of diced rocks, then onto grass. Heading south now your vision is one of an untracked valley awaiting discovery.

Keep on the left bank of the Rio Ara. For some way a barely perceived trail winds round bluffs and over hillocks above the Ara, and now and then a side stream is crossed where hanging rock gardens flourish in the spray. Then you lose height, descend a step in the valley bed and come to an enclosed area where the stream is diverted into two parts, each with its own character. The 'enclosure' is walled to the south by a natural barricade of rocks and boulders and in the distance is the first hint of Ordesa.

The remainder, and greater, part of the valley is paced still on the left bank, crossing broad pastures below the South-West and South Faces of the Vignemale, climbing and falling over minor hills and traversing the steep edge of a vegetated gorge before the treeline is finally reached.

Some distance before reaching Bujaruelo the path comes onto a track. Wander down the track which crosses to the right bank of the now-swelling stream and comes to the tiny hamlet of San Nicolas de Bujaruelo (1338m; *refreshments, accommodation;* Tel: 974 48 60

60). There is a campsite here, another further down the track. Leave the track, cross to the left bank and follow a path (the GR11) which continues down-valley and takes you through beautiful woods and meadows in a narrowing gorge of steep cliffs. Rejoin the track a little over two kilometres from where the Ara emerges to the open valley of the Arazas at the Puente de los Navarros. Torla (a growing village of hotels, shops and three campsites – see Ordesa National Park chapter below) lies downvalley; the National Park of Ordesa lures off to the left.

Note: To make a magnificent multi-day loop trip, walk up through the Ordesa Canyon to the Goriz hut, and next day pass through the Brèche de Roland and descend from there to Gavarnie. From Gavarnie walk through the Ossoue Valley to the Refuge de Bayssellance, cross Hourquette d'Ossoue and descend to the Oulettes de Gaube hut, and complete the trek by walking from there down to Cauterets. Individual sections of this magnificent trek are described elsewhere in this guide.

Route 67: Refuge des Oulettes de Gaube (2151m) – Col d'Araille (2583m) – Refuge d'Estom (1804m)

Distance:	**5 kilometres**
Height gain:	**432 metres**
Height loss:	**779 metres**
Time:	**2½–3 hours**

The Vallée de Lutour runs parallel to the Vallée de Gaube, its waters bursting free above La Raillère in a superb crash of spray. It's an utterly charming glen, a little less popular than either the Marcadau or Gaube valleys, but no less delightful for that. Near its head there's a small lake, Lac d'Estom, with a privately-owned refuge perched above its northern shore. The hut can sleep 30 in its dormitory; there's a guardian in residence from the beginning of June to the end of September when meals may be provided. For the rest of the valley, see details under the section headed Vallée de Lutour. This walk is an obvious linking of huts and of the two adjacent valleys.

From Refuge des Oulettes de Gaube head towards the Hourquette d'Ossoue following the path described above (Route 61). At the top of the zig-zags where the path divides take the left-hand alternative (cairns), which climbs into a narrow hanging valley with a couple of small tarns in it. The way continues and reaches the stony Col d'Arraille between Pic d'Arraille and a spur jutting from Pic de la Sède. On the way to the col there are fine views back to the Vignemale.

Pass through the col heading north-east on a descending traverse labouring over boulders and scree on a route marked with paint flashes. The path reappears and you lose height with zig-zags before coming into view of the valley proper. Bearing left Lac d'Estom can be seen ahead and the trail leads directly to it, keeping above the western shore among boulder slabs before arriving at Refuge d'Estom (Tel: 05 62 92 74 86).

Note: To descend all the way to Cauterets will take about 3 hours from here. The route is straightforward.

VALLÉE DE LUTOUR

Position:	**South of Cauterets and immediately to the east of Vallée de Gaube**
Access:	**Conveniently reached by road from Cauterets. A minor access road leads into the valley from Val de Jeret above la Raillère (look for sign to la Fruitière).**
Maps:	**IGN Carte de Randonnées No 3 'Béarn', or No 4 'Bigorre', both at 1:50,000**
	IGN TOP 25 series no: 1748OT 'Gavarnie, Luz St Sauveur' 1:25,000
Valley Base:	**Cauterets (902m)**

Travelling out of Cauterets towards Pont d'Espagne one soon arrives at the Thermes de la Raillère and a tight bend in the road. The thunder and spray of waterfalls fill the air; from the right bursts the Gave de Marcadau surging and boiling over its boulder-strewn bed, while ahead from the south the Cascades de Lutour explode from dark woods.

A path climbs alongside these cascades, while a narrow service road snakes back from the main route to Pont d'Espagne and labours into the Vallée de Lutour. Between service road and footpath the Gave de Lutour flows clear among the shadows of pine and fir, but about two kilometres from the cascades the woods recede, the valley opens to a flood of light and the first hint – it's no more than that – of Lutour's gentle charm can be sampled.

This is the end of the road. There's plenty of parking space and a small hotellerie, la Fruitière, offering accommodation and refreshments. Continue upvalley, rising from one level to the next, sometimes among trees, often wandering over open pastures bright with alpenroses and with the stream making its personality felt. For some way it is the Gave de Lutour that gives the valley its special quality of

Trekkers below Col d'Uzious, Route 44

Vignemale North Faces, Routes 60, 61, 64, 66 and 67

The North Face of the Vignemale, seen from the Oulettes de Gaube

magic and at the same time forms the National Park boundary; the quintessential Pyrenean mountain stream, pure and tuneful among the shallows, boisterous as it froths over rocks and minor crags. Some of the loveliest cascades imaginable are to be found here in the Vallée de Lutour.

Near the head of this charming glen a small mountain hut occupies a bluff overlooking Lac d'Estom, while high above, in a rocky cirque of mountains, a collection of tarns lie trapped amid scenes of remote wilderness. In the curving mountain walls that embrace these tarns one or two high cols give access to the upper Vallée d'Ossoue and provide stunning views of the Vignemale. And while the peaks of Lutour may mean nothing to any but the most dedicated of *Pyrénéistes*, several appear graceful and elegant under any conditions, and take on a stature of considerable grandeur under a smattering of late-summer snow.

Valley Base:

CAUTERETS (902m) is conveniently situated for an exploration of the Vallée de Lutour – especially for those with their own transport, for it only takes a few minutes to drive out of town and up into the valley. Cauterets has plenty of accommodation of all standards, including two *gîtes d'étape* (Le Pas de L'Ours, Tel: 05 62 92 58 07) and the Beau Soleil, Tel: 05 62 92 53 52) and campsites. There is a covered market, a good assortment of shops, including mountain equipment suppliers, restaurants, banks, tourist information office, PNP office (Maison du Parc) and a mountain guides bureau (Tel: 05 62 92 62 02).

Mountain Huts:

CABANE DE POUEY CAUT (1540m) is a small refuge found about 45 minutes' walk upstream of la Fruitiere. Basic facilities only, and sleeping spaces for about eight.

REFUGE RUSSELL (1980m) is another non-guarded hut with only basic facilities and room for about 15. Perched high on the eastern hillside on the slopes of Pic d'Ardiden, it is reached by a steeply climbing path which breaks away from the valley trail just south of Cabane de Pouey Caut.

REFUGE D'ESTOM (1804m) is privately owned and with room for 30

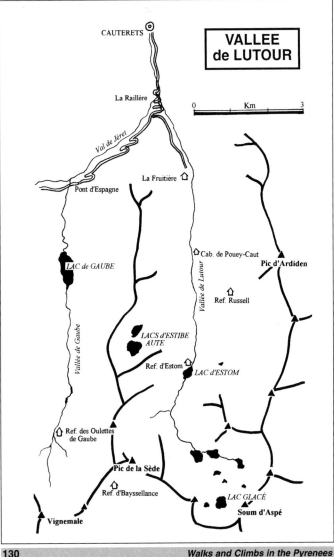

CAUTERETS

VALLEE de LUTOUR

La Raillère

0   Km   3

Val de Jéret

La Fruitière

Pont d'Espagne

Cab. de Pouey-Caut

Pic d'Ardiden

LAC de GAUBE

Vallée de Lutour

Ref. Russell

Vallée de Gaube

LACS d'ESTIBE AUTE

Ref. d'Estom   *LAC d'ESTOM*

Ref. des Oulettes de Gaube

Pic de la Sède

Ref. d'Bayssellance

LAC GLACÉ

Vignemale   **Soum d'Aspé**

in its single dormitory. There is a guardian in summer residence from the beginning of June to the end of September (Tel: 05 62 92 74 86) when meals may be supplied. It is closed for the rest of the year, but there's a simple hut nearby, often used by shepherds, which sleeps about eight, but has minimal facilities.

Route 68: Cauterets (902m) – la Fruitière (1371m)

Distance:	4.5 kilometres
Height gain:	469 metres
Time:	1½ hours

For walkers without their own transport, this is an easy approach to the valley. It begins by sharing the path already described under Route 51 as far as la Raillère (30 minutes). Go over the road towards the prominent Cascades de Lutour where a signposted trail rises into the spray, crosses a footbridge and after climbing a short way, joins another path in the woods. Bear right and wander through woods into the valley to reach la Fruitière on the opposite bank by a bridge.

Route 69: la Fruitière (1371m) – Refuge d'Estom (1804m)

Distance:	5 kilometres
Height gain:	433 metres
Time:	1½ hours

This is a lovely valley walk to be taken at a leisurely pace. It draws you upvalley into a wonderland of streams, cascades, flowers and shrubs, neat woods, open pastures and fine views. If you have time, make a day of it. Spend part of the morning exploring the valley, enjoy lunch at the refuge (*refreshments available*) overlooking the lake, and then wander slowly down again.

From the parking area at la Fruitière cross the bridge over the Gave de Lutour in front of the hotellerie and follow a clear path upvalley. The route needs no detailed description for it is virtually impossible to lose the way. It rises from one level to the next, passes a beautiful cascade, crosses the stream again to the west bank and climbs once more among tall conifers to pass more cascades. The final rise hides the refuge from view until a couple of minutes before you actually reach it. Overlooking the lake from the head of the valley are Pic de la Sède (2976m) and Pic de Labas (2946m).

Allow a little over an hour for the descent to la Fruitière.

Vallée de Lutour (Route 69)

Route 70: Refuge d'Estom (1804m) – Lac Glacé (2571m)

Distance:	5 kilometres
Height gain:	767 metres
Time:	2–2½ hours

A rough granite cirque high above Lac d'Estom to the south-east has captured a number of tarns and transitory ponds; there are more than a dozen of them. This walk is quite demanding and not always with a path to follow, although there are paint flashes and the odd cairn as guidance. Because of this – and because of the nature of the terrain – it is advisable to choose a clear-weather day to tackle it.

To begin with there is a choice of route alongside Lac d'Estom. The east bank option is narrow, and the path grows vague at its southern end, but cairns guide you along the left-hand side of a stream and aim towards the centre of the valley. The west bank alternative is clearer, but make sure you take the lower of two paths alongside the lake. At the southern end the path crosses towards the centre of the valley and joins the east bank option.

Towards the head of the glen veer left (waymarks) to cross the stream issuing from cascades that spray down the slabs ahead. A path now climbs in a circuitous route up broken slopes at the south-eastern end of the valley. Beware of snow patches in early summer. Soon traverse right beneath a large overhang, then beyond this rise over increasingly rough countryside, led by clear waymarks throughout.

In about 1½ hours from the refuge you will come to the first of the tarns, Lac de Labas (2281m) nestling among raw stony scoops and hollows. Go round the left-hand side of this and rise up a spur above Lac des Oulettes d'Estom Soubiran heading south-east. Passing to the right of more tarns and ponds follow a stream up to Lac Glacé nestling beneath Soum d'Aspe (2968m).

Note: It might be worth scrambling up to Col des Gentianes, seen above the tarn to the south-west, for a view of the Vignemale.

Route 71: la Fruitière (1371m) – Refuge Russell (1980m)

Distance:	4.5 kilometres
Height gain:	609 metres
Time:	2 hours

This is a steep walk, mostly in forest shade. As outlined above the hut has only very basic facilities, so if your intention is to spend a night there you will need to carry food and cooking equipment.

Wander upvalley along the main path which leads along the eastern side of the Gave de Lutour. In about 45 minutes pass Cabane de Pouey Caut seen to the left of the path, and soon after the way crosses a side stream, the Lanusse. A signpost here directs you left onto a narrow trail known as the Sentier Falisse. Follow this in its steep climb, eased in places with zig-zags among much vegetation, so to gain Refuge Russell.

Note: Above the hut rises Pic d'Ardiden (2988m), a noted view-point. This may be reached in about three strenuous hours from the refuge. (Allow 3½ hours for the descent to la Fruitiere from the summit.)

Other Routes:

Another tarn walk in the Vallée de Lutour leads steeply up the western hillside from a point just south of the bridge which takes the main path over to the true left bank of the Gave de Lutour. A cairn marks the point where you leave the main path. The two **LACS D'ESTIBE AUTE** are found high above the valley at an altitude of 2324 and 2328 metres, and are reached in about 3½ hours from la Fruitière.

A rewarding two-day circuit, beginning and ending in Cauterets, could be achieved by linking **VALLÉE DE LUTOUR** with **VALLÉE DE GAUBE** by way of the 1583 metre **COL D'ARRAILLE**. Follow routes already described as far as Refuge d'Estom, and continue upvalley on the upper of two paths leading above the western shore of the lake. This climbs along the flanks of Pic de l'Estibet d'Estom and Pic d'Arraille and eventually crosses Col d'Arraille. Descend on the western side of the col to Refuge des Oulettes de Gaube and continue heading north through Vallée de Gaube to Pont d'Espagne, and from there down to Cauterets. Overnight possibilities in either Refuge d'Estom or Refuge des Oulettes de Gaube. The crossing of Col d'Arraille is given (in reverse order) as Route 67.

GAVARNIE

Position:	South of Lourdes, at the headwaters of the Gave de Pau
Access:	By road (bus link) from Lourdes via Argeles-Gazost and Luz
Maps:	IGN Carte de Randonnées No 4 'Bigorre' 1:50,000 IGN TOP 25 series no: 1748OT 'Gavarnie, Luz St Sauveur' 1:25,000
Valley Base:	Gavarnie (1365m)

The Cirque de Gavarnie is the best known feature of the Pyrenees, Gavarnie the most-visited village. Throughout the summer it receives a touristic pilgrimage of quite considerable proportions and, standing at the road-head, is geared to cater for the transient visitor with locals cajoling every new coach-load into hiring donkeys, ponies or mules to transport them to the end of the track for a closer look at the cirque and its waterfall.

Gavarnie's fame is justified by the impressive amphitheatre walls which rise in a sweep of over 1300 metres from the green valley floor. Walls which consist of three bands of cliffs broken by two horizontal tiers of snow and ice; walls on which there is much climbing activity during the drier months of the year (July to September), and which now attract attention during the winter too. The crowning ridge forms the frontier and bears a number of summits in excess of 3000 metres. From left to right as seen from Gavarnie, these are: the twin Astazou summits (3071m and 3012m), Pic du Marboré (3248m), the three Pics de la Cascade (3161m, 3095m and 3073m) above a 423 metre ribbon of waterfall (Grande Cascade) that has its source beyond the frontier. Then comes a fairly level section broken by the lump of the Tour du Marboré (3009m), and to the west of that, Casque du Marboré (3006m) buttresses the great cleft of the Brèche de Roland

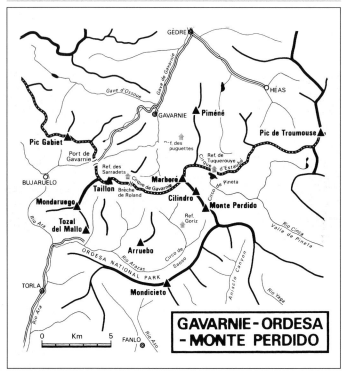

GAVARNIE - ORDESA - MONTE PERDIDO

(hidden from Gavarnie) which stands as a gateway to Spain and a convenient route to many of the summits of the cirque. Beyond and above the Brèche the frontier rises in the pyramid-shaped Taillon (3144m). After that there's just the Pics des Gabietous (3031m and 3034m) before the ridge dips to the Port de Gavarnie – approached by road from the village.

Gavarnie competed with Luchon for the favours of the pioneers in the early days of *Pyrénéisme*, but with so many fine peaks on its doorstep Gavarnie clearly had the edge over its rival, and the visitor's book at the *Hotel des Voyageurs* is rich with names of the greatest of these pioneers. Henry Russell obviously features, and at the entrance

The Cirque de Gavarnie

to the village a statue of this splendidly eccentric mountaineer gazes wistfully through the Vallée d'Ossoue towards the Vignemale.

This is a region well-suited to mountain enthusiasts of all degrees of commitment. The hard rock-and-ice man has the walls of the cirque; the general mountaineer, to whom summits are the aim rather than specific problems of ascent, has a variety of peaks offering worthwhile expeditions; the walker may content himself with side valleys or a traverse of the frontier in a choice of routes leading to pastures of another order, while the indolent lover of fine scenery whose ambitions are easily satisfied by a glass of beer, a marble-topped table shaded by a large umbrella and a dramatic view that does not require effort to enjoy, will find in the bars of Gavarnie sufficient to make the trip one of value.

Valley Base:

GAVARNIE (1365m), despite its historic associations and its century and more of tourist focus, has little in the way of architectural elegance. However, for the indiscriminate mountain lover whose interests lie in the grace of landscapes rather than urban development, it will do as a holiday base. There are several hotels, a CAF refuge (Les Granges de Holle) on the outskirts, a *gîte d'étape* (Le Gypaëte; Tel: 05 62 92 40 61), and a small campsite at its southern end. There are a few food stores and a tourist information office/Maison du Parc which sometimes organizes local walks. Though it is crowded by day, once the cars and coaches have left, its charm is substantially enhanced.

Mountain Huts:

REFUGE LES GRANGES DE HOLLE (1495m) is found west of the village on the road leading to the Port de Gavarnie. Owned by the Lourdes section of the CAF it is open throughout the year, except November, and has a guardian in residence (Tel: 05 62 92 48 77). There are dormitory places for 48 and meals provision.

REFUGE DES ESPUGUETTES (2027m) is a PNP hut about two hours' walk above Gavarnie on the hillside to the south-east. Open with a guardian in occupation from the beginning of July until mid-September (Tel: 05 62 92 40 63), it can sleep 60, but with room for just 15 at other times. Meals may be provided when the guardian is in residence.

REFUGE DE LA BRÈCHE (2587m), also known as Refuge des Sarradets, is owned by the Tarbes section of the CAF. As its name suggests, it is based just below the Brèche de Roland and is very heavily used throughout the summer. There is a guardian in charge from the beginning of May until the end of September (Tel: 05 62 92 40 41). During summer the hut can sleep 60; winter quarters hold 30.

Route 72: Gavarnie (1365m) – Refuge des Espuguettes (2027m)

Distance:	**4 kilometres**
Height gain:	**662 metres**
Time:	**2 hours**

Views of the Cirque de Gavarnie from the Espuguettes hut are delightful, and contrast with those from the valley itself. The walk to it is steep in places, but not overly demanding.

Evening clouds over the Cirque de Gavarnie –
from the Refuge des Espuguettes

Leave Gavarnie heading south towards the cirque. Cross to the eastern side of the Gave de Pau at the campsite. About 500m beyond this a path (signpost) heads off to the left, climbing the hillside in a rough south-easterly direction. It rises without difficulty, and with good views to the cirque off to your right, and comes to the green pastures of the Plateau de Pailla in which there is a simple hut (Cabane de Pailla, 1800m). The path does not go to the cabane, but swings left in a northerly sweep, gains more height and then heads back to the south-east to reach the Refuge des Espuguettes, from which there is a fine panorama.

Route 73: Gavarnie (Col de Tentes; 2208m) – Pic de Tentes (2322m)

Distance:	1 kilometre
Height gain:	114 metres
Time:	30 minutes

This short and easy walk leads to an acclaimed panoramic view of the Cirque de Gavarnie, Vignemale and the distant Néouvielle massif.

Drive (or walk) up the road leading to the Port de Gavarnie, passing through the Gavarnie-Gèdre ski station of Les Espécières, and park at Col de Tentes. There you will find a path heading north-east over a series of humps to gain the summit of Pic de Tentes across which runs the National Park boundary. The view is magnificent.

Note: another classic viewpoint on the same ridge as Pic de Tentes is Pic Mourgat (2101m) east of Les Espécières from which it is gained in about 1 hour.

Route 74: Gavarnie (1365m) –
Refuge de la Brèche (2587m)

Distance:	**6 kilometres (via the Vallée de Pouey Aspe)**
Height gain:	**1222 metres**
Time:	**3½ hours**

Before the opening of the road to the Port de Gavarnie, this was the normal route of approach to the Refuge de la Brèche – the ascent of the so-called Echelle des Sarradets (Route 76) being rather more demanding than this. Even so, the climb out of the Vallée de Pouey Aspe is a strenuous one that demands a little care.

The path begins by the village church and leads towards the cirque gaining height along the western hillside. With increasingly fine views it leads onto the Terrace des Entortes, a sloping pasture at the mouth of the valley cut by the Tourettes stream. Take the path into this valley, heading south-west. Just beyond a point where a side stream emerges from the southern side of the valley, descend to the Gave des Tourettes, cross it and climb the zig-zags on the far side. In places the path fades. It swings to the east and crosses a stream, then climbs steeply once more.

Having gained about 450 metres of height from the Vallée de Pouey Aspe you join a crossing path and turn left to pass below the Taillon Glacier (snow patches and glacial debris), through a rocky area and round to the Col des Sarradets from which the strange folds of the cirque walls are clearly displayed. The hut is seen a short distance below the col.

Route 75: Port de Gavarnie (2270m) – Refuge de la Brèche (2587m)

Distance:	**4 kilometres**
Height gain:	**317 metres**
Time:	**1½ hours**

For those with their own transport this is the most convenient route to the hut. Leave your vehicle at the Col de Tentes and walk up the continuing road to the Port de Gavarnie (Port de Boucharo), and follow the obvious path heading a little south of east from the pass. It cuts below the Taillon on an unmistakable course, rising gradually above the valley for about two kilometres, then climbs more steeply and is joined by the trail from the Vallée de Pouey Aspe (see Route 74). The refuge is reached soon after.

Route 76: Gavarnie (1365m) – Refuge de la Brèche (2587m)

Distance:	**7 kilometres (via Échelle des Sarradets)**
Height gain:	**1222 metres**
Time:	**4 hours**

Although this is the longest approach to the hut from Gavarnie, in many ways it is also the finest, for it allows a close inspection of the cirque walls and is more typical of an Alpine hut approach than a Pyrenean one. A disadvantage is that for the first hour or so the way is shared with the mounted procession, a carnival that will either amuse or appal (Packe described those who rode to the cirque as having 'indolence and bad taste'). The 'échelle' is also rather steep and exposed and this route is therefore not recommended for walkers of limited experience.

Take the track which leaves Gavarnie heading south towards the cirque. It is impossible to lose the way for it is well-cairned with mule-dung and even an unguided blind person could find the way by smell alone! That being said, it is a scenically delightful walk; the track bordered at first by meadows rich in wild flowers early in summer, then across the stream-washed Plateau de la Prade, the towering walls of the cirque growing more dramatic by the minute.

The track goes as far as the Hotellerie du Cirque (1 hour, *refresh-*

ments), beyond which a path leads on, crosses a stream by a foot-bridge and curves south-west towards the western base of the cirque wall. The climb begins soon after and is guided by paint flashes; a series of steps have been cut in places to facilitate the ascent (caution when wet) up rocky terraces. These lead to grass slopes, and before heading through the steep little Vallon des Sarradets, walled to the north by the cliffs of Pic des Sarradets, pause to admire the view across the cirque to Marboré and the sparkling ribbon of the Grande Cascade. Without difficulty the path now rises westward through the valley, bears left to pass through a 'gateway' of rock and continues to the hut over low stony terraces.

BRÈCHE DE ROLAND (2807m)

This notable gap in the frontier ridge, measuring about 40 metres across, and with walls 100 metres high, is the key to many climbs and trans-frontier walking routes. Legend has it that the hero Roland, nephew of the great Charlemagne, attempted to break his sword on the rock rather than have it fall into the hands of the 'Saracen' army in 788; but instead of the sword breaking, the rock wall split, thus enabling Roland to escape. Geological fact is more prosaic. A section of this thin, heavily-eroded ridge simply collapsed – without the assistance of Roland or his sword.

Between the hut and the brèche is a steep snow-slope topped by a little glacier which, in the summer, is grooved with deep trenches cut by hundreds of boots that have gone up or down it day after day, week after week. It is not a difficult or dangerous glacier to tackle, except for those without the means for protecting themselves in the event of a slip. The 'path' can be either very slippery from hard ice, or from watery slush late in the day. Caution is therefore always advised when tackling it, whether in ascent or descent. (About 40 minutes from the hut to the Brèche de Roland.)

The brèche itself is remarkable, not only for its curiosity value, but for the astonishing scenic contrasts displayed. Gazing north the mountains are full of drama as they stretch off towards the foothills. There is vegetation in the valleys and on the hillsides; the peaks are rugged and dashed with snow. But turning to the south, one is confronted by a foreground of decay, a desert of barren rock and scree. The middle ground provides a hint of Ordesa, for the bald-topped hills are cleft with the lip of Europe's answer to the Grand

Canyon. Yet far-off, sun-baked sierras recede into the haze of main-land Spain, confused and bewildering.

Pic Bazillac (2972m) walls the brèche to the west and offers some short, sharp rock climbs, particularly from the south. At its Spanish base a low cave offers emergency shelter. About a kilometre away to the south-east is the entrance to a fabulous ice world, the Grotte Casteret, named after the man who discovered this complex of high ice caves in 1926. (See the classic *Ten Years Under the Earth* by Norbert Casteret, which describes this, and many other cave discoveries in the Pyrenees.) No-one should attempt to explore Grotte Casteret without full caving equipment.

PIC DU MARBORÉ (3248m)

Pic du Marboré is the highest peak around the Cirque de Gavarnie. The following route is a scenically dramatic one whilst still being comparatively easy.

Route 77: Refuge de la Brèche (2587m) – Pic du Marboré (3248m)

Grade:	**F sup. (*voie normale*)**
Distance:	**6 kilometres**
Height gain:	**661 metres**
Time:	**3½–4 hours**

From the hut wander up to the Brèche de Roland and pass through to the Spanish side. Bear left and descend below le Casque on a path that hugs the mountain wall. It is very narrow in places, but is safe-guarded by a fixed handrail. Continue down until you see an obvious saddle (Col des Isards) to the right. At the end of the wall bear left and begin to climb, sometimes on snow, following a path to a wide terrace shelving the southern slopes of Tour de Marboré, and continue until a short chimney is reached on the left, indicated by a cairn. Climb the chimney up its left-hand wall. Above it opens onto an upper terrace level. Turn right along this, heading eastwards, then go left to the edge of the Cirque de Gavarnie which you then follow, with suitably dramatic views, as far as Col de la Cascade, immediately in front of l'Epaule.

Cairns mark a path continuing eastward, moving away from the

Pic du Marboré seen from the Refuge de la Brèche (Route 77)

lip of the cirque towards the huge lump of Cilindro. Follow the cairns until you reach a point about half-way between the Col and Cilindro. Leave the path and bear left along the slope which is broken by boulders and patches of snow, then mount the bald southern slopes of Pic du Marboré heading a little west of north. The summit is gained without difficulty. (Allow 2½–3 hours for the return to the hut.)

TOUR DU MARBORÉ (3009m)
The Tour is not so much a peak as a lump along the cirque's skyline. Its North Face provides an exhilerating route for rock climbers (ED inf; 400 metres) while the following suggestion offers an easy but popular excursion from the hut.

Route 78: Refuge de la Brèche (2587m) – Tour du Marboré (3009m)

Grade:	**F** (*voie normale*)
Distance:	**3 kilometres**
Height gain:	**422 metres**
Time:	**2½ hours**

Follow directions as for Route 77, but when you reach the lip of the cirque east of the Tour, turn left and head westward along the cliff edge. The way rises steadily to ascend the Tour's unimpressive slopes, the summit being reached with ease.

CASQUE DU MARBORÉ (3006m)

The Casque du Marboré guards the cleft of the Brèche de Roland forming its left-hand (eastern) wall. Its ascent by this route makes it one of the easiest 3000 metre summits accessible from the refuge, and could easily be combined with ascents of both the Tour and Pic du Marboré.

Route 79: Refuge de la Brèche (2587m) – Casque du Marboré (3006m)

Grade:	**F** (*voie normale*)
Distance:	**2 kilometres**
Height gain:	**419 metres**
Time:	**2 hours**

Follow Route 77 through the Brèche and traverse round the southern wall of the Casque into the slopes sweeping between it and the Tour. Turn left and scramble over rough, mixed slopes of snow and jumbled boulders a little below the summit of the Casque. Rocks then lead up to the summit to your right from where views are among the finest of all the Cirque de Gavarnie.

PIC DU TAILLON (3144m)

Le Taillon has the reputation of being the easiest 3000-metre peak in the Pyrenees. The ascent by this route is little more demanding than a high mountain walk, yet is recommended for the splendour of its summit views, which are among the best in this part of the range and challenge those from the Casque. Unimpeded by crowding mountains, the Vignemale dominates the scene to the north-west. Eastward, most of the summits of the cirque are clearly defined, and both Cilindro and Monte Perdido look grand.

Route 80: Refuge de la Brèche (2587m) – Pic du Taillon (3144m)

Grade:	**F (*voie normale*)**
Distance:	**2 kilometres**
Height gain:	**557 metres**
Time:	**2 hours**

Climb through the Brèche de Roland and take a little path that skirts to the right, heading west towards the False Brèche, an obvious cleft in the wall bordered by a single rock pillar known as the Doigt. Pass through the cleft to the northern side and resume a westerly direction. The way rises along the uncomplicated east ridge of the Taillon to the summit itself.

Note: The 700 metre high triangular North Face is a very different challenge. First climbed by Henri Brulle and Célestin Passet in 1895, it received its first winter ascent from Bernard Clos of Bagnères de Bigorre and his partners P.Sauton and E.Escalona in December 1954. It's now seen as one of Gavarnie's classic winter climbs.

Route 81: Refuge de la Brèche (2587m) – Refugio de Goriz (2170m)

Distance:	**7 kilometres**
Height gain:	**220 metres**
Height loss:	**637 metres**
Time:	**2½–3 hours**

This hut to hut route is justifiably popular with mountain walkers, for it forms part of a grand circuit of the Gavarnie/Ordesa regions. Despite the rather barren, desolate scenery (particularly just south of the Brèche de Roland), there is plenty of landscape interest.

Go up to the Brèche de Roland and cross into Spain. Heading south descend through a jumble of boulders and scree and then, having lost a little over 100 metres of height, veer left (south-west) to pass through the saddle of Cuello del Descargador (2495m). The cuello, or col, lies to the north of the bare domed 'hill' of El Descargador (2622m) and the continuing route takes you down into the flat wastes of the Plana de San Ferlus, whose streams flow off to the Cotatuero cirque and thence into Ordesa.

Crossing streams traverse this plain heading south-east, and rise again on the far side to gain the Cuello (or Collado) de Millaris (2467m). Now walk down the path which heads below white lime-stone cliffs on the Faja Luenga, coming to the slopes of Cilindro and Perdido, soon with the Goriz hut appearing below.

The Goriz hut can accommodate 100 in its dormitories. Open throughout the year, meals provided (Tel: 974 341 201). For routes on from here please refer to the Ordesa National Park section below.

PIMÉNÉ (2801m)

An ascent of Piméné on a fine-weather day will almost always be worth tackling for the delightful panorama its summit affords. An insignificant peak, so far as altitude is concerned, it is nevertheless ideally situated on the ridge separating Gavarnie's valley from that of Estaubé to show not only the Cirque de Gavarnie, but also Cirque d'Estaubé and Monte Perdido.

Route 82: Gavarnie (1365m) – Piméné (2801m)

Grade:	**F**
Distance:	**7 kilometres**
Height gain:	**1416 metres**
Time:	**4 hours**

Follow Route 72 as far as Refuge des Espuguettes and continue beyond it on the path which climbs eastward with the ridge linking Piméné with Pic Rouge de Pailla forming a barrier ahead. The path divides at about 2260 metres. Take the left-hand option (the alterna-tive crosses Hourquette d'Alans), now heading roughly north, then by zig-zags gain the ridge at Col de Piméné (2522m) and cross to the eastern side. Continue in a northerly direction to regain the ridge near the top of Petit Piméné, and follow the crest to the main summit. (Allow 3 hours for the descent to Gavarnie.)

Route 83: Gavarnie (1365m) – Hotellerie du Cirque (1570m) – Plateau de Pailla (1748m) – Gavarnie

Distance:	**8 kilometres**
Height gain/loss:	**383 metres**
Time:	**4 hours**

This circuit makes good use of a day. Although the first part, to the Hotellerie du Cirque, is inevitably shared with the procession of horse-riding tourists, views of the cirque make it a visually exciting walk. The return along the eastern hillside restores a degree of solitude.

From the village head south along the main track (Route 76) to the hotellerie, which sits in the mouth of the Cirque de Gavarnie (1 hour, *refreshments*). The return path begins on the east side of the building and is signposted. Follow this on a long traverse of hillside heading north-east. Just beyond a holiday chalet come to a junction of paths (1742m) below the Plateau de Pailla. Turn left and descend to Gavarnie.

Route 84: A Frontier Crossing from Gavarnie to the Pineta Valley

Start:	**Gavarnie (France)**
Finish:	**Bielsa (Spain)**
Time:	**2–3 days**
High point:	**Brèche de Tuquerouye (2666m)**
Accommodation:	**Mountain huts (Espuguettes & Tuquerouye in France, Pineta in Spain), hotels in Bielsa & Pineta Valley**
Equipment:	**Ice axe, crampons useful**

The route outlined below may be used as an expedition in its own right, as part of a circumnavigation of the Gavarnie region, or of a lengthy Pyrenean trek. It explores some outstanding mountain scenery, has moments of hard exercise, gains and loses much height, but rewards with stunning panoramas. The route may conveniently be broken with overnights spent in Refuge des Espuguettes, Refuge de Tuquerouye (oldest of all Pyrenean huts; spartan and with only basic facilities) or either the Parador hotel at the head of Valle de Pineta or Refugio Pineta further down-valley. Please note that the climb to Brèche de Tuquerouye is not for the inexperienced and may be subject to stonefall danger.

The first part, from Gavarnie to Refuge des Espuguettes is described above as Route 72. Continue beyond the hut to cross Hourquette d'Alans in the ridge north of Pic Rouge de Pailla. Descend towards the Cirque d'Estaubé, then break away from the main path heading south-east to the base of an obvious gully which you climb (crampons often useful) for about 300 metres to Brèche de Tuquerouye and the hut. (Superb view of the North Face of Monte Perdido.)

Go down on the south side of the brèche to Lac Glace (Lago de Pineta) and walk round its western shore. Bear left on a line of cairns to gain the Balcon de Pineta, and descend in numerous zig-zags to the Valle de Pineta. The Parador Nacional de Monte Perdido (Tel: 974 50 10 11) sits on the left bank of the Pineta stream. A little over 1 kilometre further south, and just below the road, stands Refugio de Pineta (open all year, 73 places; Tel: 974 341 147). Walk down the valley all the way to Bielsa. (Hotels, camping, restaurants, shops. It might be possible to hitch back to France through the Bielsa Tunnel.)

ORDESA NATIONAL PARK

Position:	In Spain, south of the Cirques de Gavarnie and Estaubé. The National Park comprises the canyons of Ordesa, Anisclo and Escuain, and the upper reaches of the Valle de Pineta.
Access:	By road to Ordesa: from France via Col du Pourtalet to Biescas, then east to Torla; or via the Bielsa Tunnel to Ainsa and north-west from there. Access to Anisclo is south from the Bielsa Tunnel to Escalona and north-west from there on a dramatic minor road. For the Gargantas de Escuain take a narrow road signed to Escuain from a little west of Escalona. Valle de Pineta is easily accessible from Bielsa. Public transport through Spain is by bus from Sabiñanigo to Torla for Ordesa; Sabiñanigo being on the Zaragoza–Canfranc railway line. There is no public transport serving Anisclo, Escuain or Bielsa.
Maps:	Editorial Alpina 'Ordesa' 1:40,000. Editorial Pirineo 'Ordesa and Monte Perdido National Park' 1:40,000 – comes with useful booklet with English text. The IGN Carte de Randonnées No 4 'Bigorre' 1:50,000 slightly overlaps to include the Park's northern rim.
Valley Bases:	Torla (1033m) for Ordesa; Bielsa (1024m) for Valle de Pineta. Camping at Puyarruego (680m) west of Escalona for Anisclo and Escuain.

The neighbouring canyons of Ordesa and Anisclo, that together comprise a major part of the *Parque Nacional de Ordesa y Monte Perdido*, form one of the most spectacular regions in Europe; a remarkable series of landscapes of equal appeal to walkers, climbers, artists and naturalists.

Monte Perdido forms a partial hub to the park, with Ordesa and Anisclo radiating spoke-like from it to west and south. Added to these canyons is the narrow gash of the Gargantas de Escuain which cuts into the high country south-east of Perdido, and the beautiful Valle de Pineta whose headwall lies immediately below Perdido's east flank. The park's northern border traces the frontier ridge from Pic des Gabiétous at the western end of the Cirque de Gavarnie as far east as the Circo de Pineta, then runs south along the west wall of the Pineta valley. It then traces a ragged arthritic route westward to enclose the canyons that are the main focus of attention here.

Ordesa's canyon has been cut by the Rio Arazas which drains the western flanks of Monte Perdido, and is geologically unusual in that it lies roughly parallel to the frontier crest. Anisclo, on the other hand, is more conventional in its north–south flow with the Rio Vellos rising on the southern slopes of the Perdido massif.

Seen from the summit of Monte Perdido the curious plateau-like highlands spread out below seem to have been sliced by a great knife, and it was this that first attracted Ramond de Carbonnières when he stood on Perdido's crown in 1802, and there determined to make an exploration – his discoveries were later published in *Voyages au Mont Perdu*. But it was Charles Packe whose visits in the early 1860s led to a broader publicity for both Ordesa and Anisclo through his writings. Not known for extravagant descriptions, his enthusiasm for Ordesa is obvious: 'Truly grand is the walk down the valley,' he wrote. 'First we have a series of cascades... then come the magnificent walls...rising above the forest zone, the ruddy pinnacles and bastions towering above the trees for a thousand metres and then capped with snow.' Of Anisclo he later wrote: 'In places the walls of rock so overhang the stream as all but to bar passage; in others they recede in terraces, rising one above the other, and supporting on their ledges impossible fir-trees.'

Ordesa is the more open canyon of the two, and its wildly-coloured castellated rocks form an indelible impression; soaring faces, shadowed ravines, seductive amphitheatres of an ochre hue, and vast slab pinnacles seemingly transported from the Dolomites. 'If Arazas were in the Alps its peculiar and contrasted beauty of trees and rocks and the facilities for climbing would have made it a centre.'

So wrote a leading member of the Alpine Club after his visit in 1913. Now, with ease of access by road, the canyon walls and the great foaming waterfalls of the Arazas are regularly admired by crowds of visitors each summer. But only the more adventurous stray much farther than a viewpoint overlooking the first of these waterfalls.

By contrast Anisclo is much more narrow and mysterious and requires more effort to discover. Although there is minor road access to its lower reaches the compelling beauty that is a hallmark of Ordesa is missing at this point, and only those who penetrate on foot to the deep heart of the canyon may absorb its true majesty. Then it's very much a case of 'once seen, never forgotten'.

As for the Gargantas de Escuain between Anisclo and the Valle de Pineta, this is probably the least-known section of the National Park. The Rio Yaga and its cascades have cut an unbelievably narrow slice in the wooded limestone plateau to create the Valle de Escuain (a popular venue for canyoning). On its south-west lip at the end of a tortuous 15 kilometre road huddles the tiny, all-but-abandoned hamlet from which the valley takes its name. In 1850 Escuain (1215m) had a population of 138. By 1960 it had been abandoned. In 1981 there was a single inhabitant, and three lived there in 1991. In the early summer of 2000 a lone goatherder had the place to himself. Two long distance trails pass through: GR15, the *Sendero Prepirenaico,* and GR19, *Sendero del Sobrarbe*, and there's a pleasant 2 hour walk from Escuain to the Puente de los Mallos near the head of the gorge. GR15 links Escuain with the hamlet of Estaronilla (4 inhabitants) beside the Yaga, and on this eastern side of the gorge there are other tiny hamlets, including Revilla (1220m), as remote as Escuain. Another minor road snakes into this forgotten corner by way of Tella, which has a National Park information office.

The Valle de Pineta is a charming U-shaped valley which reveals its glacial origin. At its head the Circo de Pineta supports a high sub-valley, the Balcon de Pineta, which looks directly onto the North-East Face of Monte Perdido and its impressive tiers of ice cliffs. These are all that remains of the glacier responsible for carving the Valle de Pineta, and the beauty that is left behind in the semi-frozen tarns, waterfalls and clear streams. Above it all Monte Perdido reigns supreme.

The *Parque Nacional de Ordesa y Monte Perdido* is a fabulous region not only for its scenery, but also for its wildlife, which numbers some 171 bird species, 32 mammals, eight reptiles and five species of amphibia. As for plantlife, the most obvious are the trees – beech, silver fir, box and mountain pine – but masses of flowers carpet the low meadows and high grasslands alike, and adorn rock faces too. Edelweiss and the endemic *Ramonda myconi*, which can be found among the cliffs of Ansiclo and the Circo de Pineta, are merely two of the more spectacular, but alpenrose, gentian and orchid, and swathes of crocus are also there in season among many other species to delight all who visit.

Rock Climbing in Ordesa:

One only need peer up at the great vertical cliffs that wall the canyon to realise that rock climbing here is a serious affair. Major cliffs are those of Mondarruego, Tozal del Mallo, Gallinero and the Fraucata face of Monte Arruebo upon which there is still scope for creating new routes. Lines already developed fall outside the scope of this book, but readers with an interest in the climbing potential of the area should consult Derek L.Walker's *Rock Climbs in the Pyrenees* (Cicerone Press, 1990).

Valley Bases:

TORLA (1033m) is situated about four kilometres south of the entrance to the Ordesa canyon. It has several hotels, two *albergues* (the Lucien Briet, Tel: 974 48 62 61; and smaller L'Atalaya, Tel: 974 48 60 22) and three campsites; bars, restaurants, shops, a bank and a post office. The village is often filled to capacity in high summer, despite expanding to cater for increased numbers of tourists. Happily the heart of Torla retains some of its former charm with narrow alleys climbing between old stone buildings. Upvalley there's a Parque Nacional information office housed in a former Parador, with interesting exhibitions. Note that in the high summer a shuttle bus service transports visitors from Torla to the roadhead car park inside the National Park boundary.

BIELSA (1024m) sits at the entrance to the Valle de Pineta, with an attractive central square. The village boasts several hotels, restaurants and shops, and there's a tourist information office open summer only (Tel: 974 50 07 67). A well-equipped campsite is located about 8 kilometres upvalley, and near the head of the valley there's an approved camping area with basic facilities on the south side of the river. On the north side, about 14 kilometres from Bielsa, stands a Parador (National Park hotel).

Mountain Huts:

REFUGIO DE GORIZ (2170m), otherwise known as Refugio Delgado Ubeda, is the only mountain hut, as such, within the National Park. Open all year, and with a guardian in residence, there are dormitory places for 100 and a full meals service. The hut is owned by the *Federación Española de Montanismo* (FEM) and is reached by a fine walk through the canyon. It stands in somewhat barren country on the south-west slopes of Monte Perdido. (See Route 76 for an approach from France via the Brèche de Roland.)

Note: Wild camping is officially forbidden in the Valle de Ordesa below 2200 metres (but allowed on terraces near the Goriz hut), and in Anisclo below 1400 metres.

REFUGIO DE PINETA (1240m) was built in 1997 and is easily accessible by vehicle. It stands just below the valley road near the head of the Valle de Pineta, and has its own climbing wall. Open all year with places for 73 and meals provision (Tel: 974 341 201).

Route 85: Torla (1033m) – Ordesa (roadhead) (1320m)

Distance:	**6 kilometres**
Height gain:	**287 metres**
Time:	**2 hours**

The vast majority of visitors to Ordesa either travel by car (outside the main summer season) and fill the large parking area at the roadhead, or use the shuttle bus service from Torla. For those using Torla as a base, this walk is a much-to-be-preferred option.

This walk begins beside Hostal Bellavista on the road which bypasses Torla, where a signed path descends to the river. Cross the Rio Ara on a hump-backed bridge, and follow the track of the Camino de Turieto on the east bank curving into the canyon, and rising above several waterfalls on the way. Finally cross one of two bridges that will take you to the roadhead on the opposite bank. Near the car park there is a restaurant, La Pradera de Ordesa, and public toilet.

Route 86: Ordesa (1320m) – Refugio de Goriz (2170m)

Distance:	**9.5 kilometres**
Height gain:	**850 metres**
Time:	**4 hours**

At the eastern end of the roadhead car park a clear signposted trail leads through shrubbery across grass neat as a Surrey lawn keeping some way from the river, and rises through woods towards a gorge. On the left is the towering Fraucata face of Monte Arruebo at the entrance to the Circo de Cotatuero. Behind you will be seen the flake of Tozal del Mallo in profile and across the canyon the long wall of the Sierra de las Cutas extends flat-topped in both directions.

Continue along the path which climbs through the woods in a south-easterly direction within earshot of the falls. These are mostly unseen, but at the top of a steep section of path you come into view of the top fall, Cascada Frachinal, a dramatic plunge of water whose bore is in part responsible for much of the mountain architecture spread out below to the west. The view over forest and lower valley is ample reward for the walk to this point, and is as far as most visitors stray. The path climbs a little farther, then emerges from forest into the valley's upper level. Along this stretch there are one or two rough shelters intended for use only in emergency.

Crossing pastures you will reach a rocky section which the path ascends to the left of a delightful series of cascades known as Las Gradas, where the stream falls over broad steps bordered by cushions of moss and miniature pines. At the top of this you enter the final meadows below the Circo de Soaso, with the great bulk of Monte Perdido and Sum de Ramond above, and the lovely waterfall of Cola de Caballo tumbling down the left-hand side of the cirque walls. At the head of the valley the path crosses the stream and then climbs in steep zig-zags up the face of the cirque. Having gained height the path then takes a northerly course, waymarked with paint flashes, and rises steadily to gain the hut (about 1 hour from Circo de Soaso).

Route 87: Ordesa (1320m) – Circo de Soaso (1880m) – Faja de Pelay – Ordesa

Distance:	12 kilometres
Height gain/loss:	580 metres
Time:	6 hours

This circuit is one of the great walks of the region. Indeed, it stands as one of the classic walks of the Pyrenees and one that ought to be on the list of all walkers visiting the Ordesa National Park. Although the trail along the airy belvedere of the Faja de Pelay is exceedingly dramatic and with a great sense of exposure, under normal summer conditions there is nothing difficult or dangerous about it. The final descent to the valley via the so-called Senda de los Cazadores is, however, a knee-straining plunge amid forest.

Follow directions given under Route 86 as far as the Circo de Soaso (about 3 hours). Crossing the stream by the Puente de Soaso bear right along an obvious path that rises easily, then levels among shrubs and dwarf pine and with magnificent views growing as you progress along it. The Faja de Pelay follows along the 1900 metre contour and maintains interest all the way. A short distance beyond the Refugio y Mirador de Calcilarruego (a small shelter with a projecting walled bay providing a stunning view over the valley) you will come to a path junction; the Senda de los Cazadores. Bear right and descend very steeply through forest for almost 600 metres to reach the bed of the valley. Cross the Rio Arazas to the car park by way of a wooden bridge.

Route 88: Ordesa (1320m) – Circo de Cotatuero – Faja los Canarellos (1775m) – Ordesa

Distance:	9 kilometres
Height gain/loss:	455 metres
Time:	4–5 hours

Another exciting high-level route, the Faja los Canarellos is a little more exposed even than the Faja de Pelay described in Route 87. This route tackles the steep walls that guard the east side of the Circo de Cotatuero just beyond the Ordesa car park, and provides lots of splendid views, but is not suitable for anyone with a history of vertigo.

From the parking area take the main track upvalley signed to the Cascadas. After about 8 minutes the way forks. Take the left-hand option, a well-made path that weaves through woodland, then winds up the left side of the Barranco de Cotatuero. After about 1 hour come to a small wooden shelter beside the trail (1630m). A few paces beyond this bear right where the path divides, and cross a footbridge just below a waterfall that pours from the upper cirque. It's a wonderful situation, with soaring ochre-coloured walls and feathery cascades in view. Over the bridge the path zig-zags to gain more height, then at about 1725 metres it eases to the right among a few pines. Beyond the trees cross an open sloping sill of rock and scree, and gain a fine aerial view onto the Ordesa forest.

Reaching a high point the path eventually turns the south spur of the Circo de Cotatuero then slopes down a little among pine, silver birch and boxwood. Coming to a shallow indent on the Fraucata face the path teeters along a narrow shelf – exposed but safeguarded with a sturdy chain – after which you cross a stream on stepping stones and soon begin the descent through the Bosque de la Hayas. In places a trail of cairns guides the way down through the woodland, bringing you onto the main valley track. (To visit the Gradas de Soaso waterfalls, bear left and walk upvalley for about 40 minutes.) To complete the circuit turn right and follow the track downhill, with opportunities to study the impressive Arazas waterfalls on the way to the car park.

Outline Routes:

The following suggestions are given with basic outline details to encourage walkers to explore for themselves. There will, of course, be other possibilities not listed here. Study the map to conjure ideas of your own.

Route 89: Ordesa (1320m) – Circo de Cotatuero – Faja de las Flores (2400m) – Circo de Carriata – Ordesa

Like the Faja los Canarellos (Route 88), Faja de las Flores edges the northern canyon walls but west of the Cotatuero cirque; it offers tremendous views and with an awesome sense of exposure – definitely not for those who suffer from vertigo. The way uses a series of iron pegs (*clavijas*) made by a Torla blacksmith in the 1880s on behalf of the English ibex hunter, Edward North Buxton, who tracked his prey onto the remote walls of the canyon. The *clavijas* take the route onto very steep and exposed ground – be warned. Follow directions for Route 88 as far as the path division near the small wooden shelter (1 hour). Continue to rise on the left of the stream and come to the start of the Faja Racún which cuts left. Ignore this and soon come to the first of the *clavijas* that enable you to reach a horizontal ledge with more safeguards leading to easier ground. The way reaches the head of the Cotatuero cirque, then swings left on the long traverse round to Circo de Carriata, with an option of going up onto Pico de Salarons (2752m). Descend through the Circo de Carriata by path which eventually leads onto the Ordesa road below the parking area (about 6–6½ hours in all).

Note: A less demanding, but still dramatic, route traces the same wall as that of the Faja de las Flores, but some way below it. This is the Faja Racún and it too leads into the Carriata cirque.

ANISCLO

The annexing of the Anisclo Canyon to the *Parque Nacional de Ordesa* came as a great relief to all who feared the flooding of this glorious valley for hydro purposes in the 1970s. Protected by its National Park status it is a sheer delight to descend through the canyon and to absorb its unique atmosphere, its peaceful tranquillity, its dappled light and spray-dampened vegetation that was so beloved by the pioneers.

Route 90: Refugio de Goriz (2170m) – Collado de Arrablo (2329m) – Anisclo Canyon – Puente de San Urbano (Rio Aso junction) (980m)

Distance:	**16 kilometres**
Height gain:	**159 metres**
Height loss:	**1349 metres**
Time:	**6–6½ hours**

This route is one to remember, for it leads through almost the complete length of the canyon, from top to bottom; a fabulous walk with plenty of opportunities to laze by the stream or to bathe in one of its many beautiful deep pools. Note that initially the descent of the Barranco Arrablo, by which Anisclo is reached, requires caution, and it is essential to locate the correct point at which to leave its upper rim.

In order to reach the head of the Anisclo Canyon from the Goriz hut it is necessary to cross the easy low-slung saddle of Collado de Arrablo (or Collado Superior de Goriz). This lies to the south-east of the hut and a path leads to it, rising steadily. On the final climb to the col red–white waymarks appear as a guide (30 minutes). From the col one gains a first hint of the canyon ahead, while behind the scene is one of a bleak dry wilderness.

Descend from the col into a soft pastureland basin with a stream flowing through it, the Barranco Arrablo (also known as Barranco Fon Blanca) dropping away ahead. Wander along the south-west edge of the Arrablo gorge following a line of cairns for about 400 metres. Still led by cairns, now descend into the gorge down a broken line of cliffs to reach a grassy terrace about 50 metres below. Bear right along the terrace on a faint path to another rock band. The route is well-cairned and obvious as you descend several terraces broken by more rock bands. Finally go down a boulder slope to a mixture of grit, grass, thistles and scree, at the bottom of which you come to the stream flowing through the gorge. Cross the stream to a continuing path, now on the north-eastern side of Barranco Arrablo, rise a little, then begin to lose height with a series of zig-zags on grit and scree (caution advised). The path works its way down to pass near a fine waterfall (Fon Blanca) and among fragrant box trees to reach the bed of the Valle de Anisclo (small hut nearby) where the Rio Vellos cascades down a series of natural rock steps and through deep green pools; a beautiful sight (2½–3 hours from Refugio de Goriz).

Bear right and wander downvalley (there is another path on the left bank by which Collado de Anisclo at the head of the valley is reached). Soon come to a bridge, cross to the left bank and continue downvalley, and before long you will enter the canyon proper where the towering walls lean closer to each other. A good path, it climbs among trees and shrubs, then levels with the Vellos stream far below.

After almost an hour from the foot of Barranco Arrablo the path forks (signpost). Take the right-hand option (the left-hand path climbs to Cuello Vicento) and descend in long, well-made zig-zags to recross the Vellos again by a bridge. Now on the right bank the path continues on an undulating course, and about ten minutes later divides again. Take the left-hand path and wander through beautiful beechwoods.

Further detailed instructions are unnecessary. Once across the mouth of the Barranco de Pardina continue downvalley on the right bank all the way for nearly two more hours until you reach another bridge and cross to the left bank. Pass the shrine of San Urbano (San Urbez) and cross to the right bank once more, this time on a bridge built above the medieval hump-backed Puente de San Urbano. Here you come upon a tarmac road (parking area nearby) which leads for 12.5 kilometres down to Escalona. If, however, you head into the Valle de Vió (the valley of the Rio Aso) through which the road climbs, you can get to the hamlet of Nerín (1281m), eight kilometres away, where basic accommodation and refreshments may be had (see details under Route 91).

Note: The Spanish coast to coast traverse GR11 uses the first section of the above route, then climbs out of the head of the Anisclo Canyon at the 2440m Collado de Anisclo (4 hours from Goriz), before descending steeply on a fairly difficult path into the Valle de Pineta. (7–7½ hours to Refugio de Pineta.)

Route 91: The Spanish Canyons Tour

Start/Finish:	**Ordesa**
Time:	**3 days**
Accommodation:	**Refugio de Goriz, Albergue and Pension in Nerín**

This three-day circuit, which entails wandering through both the Ordesa and Anisclo canyons, makes quite a demanding tour, and the heat of summer may add to those demands – particularly on the final stage from Nerín where there is little shade. But it is unquestionably one of great beauty that will appeal to experienced wild-country trekkers.

The first stage goes from the Ordesa car park to Refugio de Goriz and is described as Route 86. The second day's walk crosses Collado de Arrablo and descends through the Anisclo Canyon (Route 90), then heads up the Valle de Vió along the road, and takes a side road

The daily mounted procession from Gavarnie to the Cirque, Routes 76, 83

up to Nerín (1270m), a small medieval-like hamlet perched on the hillside with a view east to the Peña Montañesa. Accommodation is available here in both the Anisclo Albergue (Tel: 974 48 90 10) and Pension El Turista (Tel: 974 48 90 16). In the summer of 2000 a hotel was being built here.

In the past it was necessary to descend to the main road and walk up it to a saddle north of Fanlo, and there find a bulldozed track/path leading to the Cuello de Diazas (2093m). There is now a rough track/road leading north-west out of Nerín into remote, open and shadeless country – take plenty of water with you. The dirt road cuts along the south-west flank of Mondicieta and continues to the upper slopes of the Sierra de las Cutas. Along here a grass track diverts to the right to the Brecha de Arazas with spectacular views into the Ordesa Canyon and across to Monte Perdido. The dusty dirt track pushes on to the Cuello de Diazas, beyond which you break away on a clear path which climbs a grass slope ahead and then forks. Take the right-hand option and you will come to the lip of the canyon. The path then descends (at first it seems impossible that it could) all the way to the bed of the valley, which it reaches near the Puente de Cazadores. Needless to say, it is a very steep descent.

MONTE PERDIDO (3355m)

Third highest mountain in the Pyrenees, Monte Perdido (Mont Perdu to the French) is the 'lost mountain'; a great limestone hulk that towers over the head of the Ordesa Canyon. From this view, it must be admitted, Perdido appears singularly unimpressive, but its North-East Face above the Valle de Pineta is a very different story. From the Balcon de Pineta the huge mass is seen to best advantage; a scene of glacial tiers undercut by banks of gleaming seracs and ribs of seamed rock leading to a hint of the distant summit. An ascent from the north seldom betrays the promise such a scene offers.

Ramond de Carbonnières first caught sight of Perdido during his explorations of 1787. Ten years later he led two attempts to climb it by way of the Vallée d'Estaubé and the Brèche de Tuquerouye. Both attempts failed. When he returned again in 1802 he sent ahead two local men, Laurens and Rondau, to reconnoitre a route. With the help of a Spanish shepherd they reached the summit itself, and returned a few days later to guide Ramond on his ascent.

Route 92: Refugio de Goriz (2170m) – Monte Perdido (3355m)

Grade:	F (*voie normale*)
Distance:	3.5 kilometres
Height gain:	1185 metres
Time:	3½–4 hours
Equipment:	Ice axe, crampons

Leave the hut climbing north, well to the east of the Goriz stream, on a route that is abundantly cairned and with traces of path ascending grassy terraces and rock bands. Higher there may be patches of snow early in the season. Without difficulty you should reach a small tarn, Lago Helado (3000m), below the Cuello del Cilindro and with the steep wall of Cilindro rising on your left. From here Monte Perdido assumes a very different appearance and at last admits superiority over its neighbours.

Turn right (south-east) away from the tarn and tackle the steep slope (often snow-covered) towards a broad open gully which climbs under the obvious summit. (In times of minimal snow-cover a more apparent route is a path going well to the right of the tarn.) The gully steepens towards the top and emerges onto a broad saddle with a steep snow ridge (sometimes barred by easy boulders) climbing to the right. Climb this snow ridge and so gain the summit, which is adorned by a large cross.

Summit views are immense and varied. Immediately to the south-east the crags of Sum de Ramond fall to the depths of the beautiful Valle de Pineta while far-off shine the distant snows of the Posets. Anisclo's canyon carves away to the south, and the upper reaches of Ordesa are clearly visible below to the south-west. The limestone desert of highlands between Ordesa and the frontier peaks appears depressingly unattractive, yet French mountains (particularly the distant Vignemale) are very fine.

Note: For a much longer but more inspiring ascent, see Route 93 below, from the Valle de Pineta.

VALLE DE PINETA

Draining south-east from Monte Perdido, this lovely U-shaped valley is easily accessible by road, but although its upper reaches are only

Bergschrund at the foot of Perdido's north-east face

separated from the headwaters of the Ordesa Canyon by the bulk of Monte Perdido, it's a very long way from one to the other by motor vehicle. The Valle de Pineta has a number of idyllic aspects: the dappled trees beside the river, parkland-like meadows, waterfalls that cascade from many different directions, abrupt limestone walls, the wild but majestic view from the Balcon de Pineta, and the charming tributary glen of La Larri.

Route 93: Valle de Pineta (1300m) – Monte Perdido (3355m)

Grade:	**P**
Distance:	**8 kilometres**
Height gain:	**2055 metres**
Time:	**7 hours**
Equipment:	**Ice axe, crampons, rope advised**

This long expedition (allow 5 hours for descent by the same route) gives a challenging but very rewarding day out. Note that an overnight's camping is allowed on the Balcon de Pineta near the partly-frozen Lago Helado de Marmoré (Lago de Pineta on the IGN map), thus providing options for a two-day ascent. Alternatively, you could make use of Refuge de Tuquerouye in the frontier ridge above Lago Helado. This hut has only basic facilities and all food and cooking equipment will need to be carried.

From the unsurfaced parking area on the opposite side of the river to the Parador, follow a stony track upvalley, soon curving to the foot of cliffs that form the steep walls of Circo de Pineta. After about 40 minutes the track crosses a bridge beside the Cascada del Cinca (1435m). A few paces beyond this take a footpath on the left. It's a steep trail, yet it makes numerous zig-zags to ease the gradient where possible, first over grass, then on narrow terraces until you emerge thankfully on the Balcon de Pineta, an area of desolation with the debris of Perdido's former glaciers strewn in a wilderness of lime-stone boulders and ancient moraines. But the view of Perdido's North-East Face impresses with its ice barriers and snowfields.

Follow cairns north-west towards the head of the hanging valley. When you reach the ruins of a hut below Lago Helado (unseen from here) whose stream gushes beyond to the right, turn to face Perdido and study the line of cliffs which support its lower glacier. At the right extremity of the glacial seracs you will recognise the line of a left-sloping gully at almost the narrowest point of the cliffs. Cross the snow slope and climb this narrow gully with ease, then up steep snow to the next band of cliffs where a straight gully (almost a chimney) is climbed also without difficulty. The only problem could be in climbing out of this if the snow and ice are out of condition. Above this gully the snowfield rises towards the saddle of Cuello del Cilindro which is finally reached across a large patch of scree.

Descend from the col heading south-west over scree, then slabs with scree ledges, towards the tarn of Lago Helado (not to be confused with the other Lago Helado below Brèche de Tuquerouye). At the first opportunity leave rocks for snow, losing as little height as possible, and head left towards slopes leading to the obvious summit of the mountain, and there join the route from the Goriz hut (Route 92).

Route 94: Valle de Pineta (1300m) – Llanos de La Larri (1600m)

Distance:	**4 kilometres**
Height gain:	**300 metres**
Time:	**1½ hours**

This easy but enjoyable walk visits a remote pastureland in a hanging valley headed by frontier mountains that also form part of the Cirque de Troumouse, with cracking views across the Circo de Pineta to Monte Perdido and Cilindro, and of the great south wall of the Valle de Pineta.

From the parking area on the south side of the river near the head of the valley (Parking Pineta), take the stony track at the north-west end where a sign indicates the route to Llanos de Larri and Cascada del Cinca. This track takes you through groups of trees and swings round the head of the valley. Gently rising you have an early view to the east where the Rio Lalarri crashes down the hillside in a series of waterfalls. Cross a bridge beside the Cascada del Cinca (40 minutes)

Llanos de La Larri, a tributary of the Valle de Pineta (Route 94)

and continue along the track for a further 25 minutes or so to reach the Lalarri waterfall. (Note that just before this is reached there is a path on the right which makes a direct descent to the valley – worth taking on the way down.)

Remain with the track as it loops easily up the hillside – there is a waymarked path which short-cuts these loops, but it's a steep one better saved for the descent. Eventually, about 1½ hours after setting out, the track brings you to the entrance of the Llanos (pastures) of La Larri which stretch ahead to the Circo de La Larri. To the right of the track stands a small cabane used by a local shepherd, the hillside above it is starred with gentians in spring, and it makes a splendid vantage point from which to study the Circo de Pineta, Monte Perdido and the La Larri glen.

Note: There are various possible extensions to this walk. One would be to follow GR11 south-east for exceptional views on the way to Collado de Pietramula (the Collado is another 2 hours or so from here); another works its way upvalley to the Cuello de las Puertas (2575m), while a third goes a little north of this to pass between the two Lagos de la Munia.

ESTAUBÉ, TROUMOUSE AND BARROUDE

Position:	East of Gavarnie along the frontier ridge, and spreading north from it. The cirques of Estaubé and Troumouse drain via the Gave de Héas into the Gave de Pau at Gèdre, while the Cirque de Barroude forms the eastern wall of the Cirque de Troumouse above the Vallon de la Géla.
Access:	By road from Gèdre for Estaubé and Troumouse. No road access to Barroude. This is reached by a long approach march from either Aragnouet in the Vallée d'Aure or from Héas, above Gèdre.
Maps:	IGN Carte de Randonnées No 4 'Bigorre' 1:50,000 IGN TOP 25 series nos: 1748OOT 'Gavarnie, Luz St Sauveur' and 1748ET 'Néouvielle, Vallée d'Aure' 1:25,000
Valley Base:	Gèdre (1071m) and Héas (1500m) for Estaubé and Troumouse. None for Barroude.

East of the Cirque de Gavarnie on the northern side of the watershed two other fine amphitheatres are worthy of a visit. The first is that of Estaubé at the head of its quiet glen, the second is Troumouse, the largest of the three and with a toll road providing partial access above the hamlet of Héas. Neither receive as much publicity as their more illustrious neighbour and are therefore shunned by the vast majority of Gavarnie's visitors – which is unquestionably to their advantage. However, they are both worth exploring.

The Cirque de Estaubé encloses the head of a relatively short glen partially hidden from general view behind the barrage that holds back Lac des Gloriettes halfway along the Vallée de Héas. But the Cirque de Troumouse is much more open, and lying south-east of the little hamlet of Héas is the largest true cirque in the Pyrenees – 10 kilometres from end to end – a wild place of rough pastures, tiny pools, streams and rock walls.

But there is yet another cirque that is less-known even than these; a small amphitheatre, remote and secluded and with a charm all its own. Barroude is visited by trekkers on the Pyrenean High Route, and by rock climbers attracted to its dominant wall. Otherwise it is largely ignored.

The major feature is the vast Barroude Wall which is, effectively, the eastern side of the Cirque de Troumouse. Under a bright summer sun the whole area smiles with benevolence; the lake stretching below the rock face, an ancient glacial tongue projecting towards it from Pic de Troumouse, the grassy mound upon which sits a hut with another tarn cradled behind. Beyond to the north-east valleys yawn amongst a welter of converging ridges dipping and rising with great appeal. South, over the shale hump of Port de Barroude, is the Cirque de Barrosa in Spain, below which seemingly impenetrable depths contain the snaking Barrosa Valley which flows out to join the Cinca and a Spain far removed from these enchanted uplands.

This is trekkers' country. It also holds challenge for the rock man. It's a dreamer's landscape too; a corner of high country where time may be held immobile; a place to sit and become absorbed by the isolation and untarnished simplicity of the mountain world.

Valley Bases:

GÈDRE (1071m) is the last village in the valley of the Gave de Pau before reaching Gavarnie, 9 kilometres away. It squats below the entrance to the Vallée de Héas and is served by bus from Lourdes. There is a choice of hotel accommodation, a *gîte d'étape* (Granges de Saugué, Tel: 05 62 92 48 73) and three campsites. The village has a restaurant, few shops and a summer-only tourist information office.

HÉAS (1500m) is little more than a collection of farmhouses and a small chapel 8 kilometres from Gèdre. Accommodation is available at La Chaumière – also camping – (Tel: 05 62 92 48 66), at Auberge de la Munia (Tel: 05 62 92 48 39) and the *gîte d'étape* Auberge Le Refuge (Tel: 05 62 92 47 74). Beyond the hamlet the road curves south to a toll booth, then twists up the hillside to Chalet-hôtellerie Le Maillet (Tel: 05 62 92 48 97) on the way to the Cirque de Troumouse.

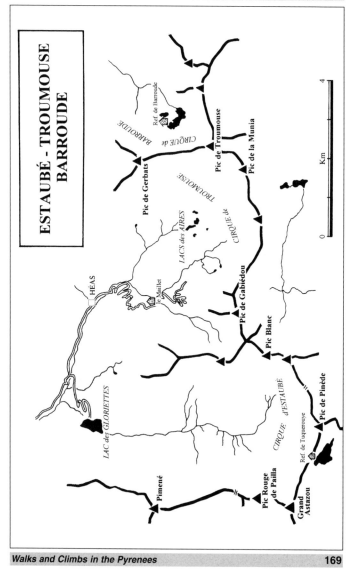

ESTAUBÉ - TROUMOUSE
BARROUDE

No habitation is really close enough to form an effective valley base for the Cirque de Barroude. The nearest villages are those of the Vallée d'Aure, north of the Bielsa Tunnel. Of these, St-Lary is the largest, but then motor transport would be required to reach Aragnouet-le-Plan for a three-hour walk through the Vallon de la Gela as far as the Barroude refuge.

Mountain Hut:

REFUGE DE BARROUDE (2373m) was built by the PNP authorities in 1974. A comfortable, tent-shaped hut with room for 20 in its single dormitory, plus ten in a tent annexe, there is a guardian in charge from the beginning of July until mid-September when meals may be provided. It stands on a grassy bluff between tarns overlooking the Barroude Wall (Tel: 05 62 39 61 10).

Route 95: Barrage des Gloriettes (1667m) – Cirque de Estaubé (1819m)

Distance:	**5 kilometres**
Height gain:	**152 metres**
Time:	**1½ hours**

This short and easy walk is suggested as a means of introduction to the Estaubé glen. In order to get to the barrage (dam) at the northern end of Lac des Gloriettes take the narrow side road which breaks away south of the Gèdre to Héas road at Pont de l'Arraillé (1459m) about 2 kilometres below Héas. There's parking space at the dam. If you have no transport, it will take about an hour to walk there from Héas.

From the car park walk up to the top of the dam, cross to the north-west corner of the lake, and follow the lakeside footpath heading south. The cirque walls, seemingly topped by Monte Perdido, enclose the head of the valley at the end of rough, boulder-littered pastures. The path, which is adopted by the Pyrenean High Route, keeps to the true left bank of the Estaubé stream (west side) and soon begins to slant up the hillside on the way to Hourquette d'Alans and Gavarnie. However, for the present walk you are advised to stay in the valley bed and cross a footbridge to the east side of the stream and wander as far as you feel comfortable before turning back.

Note i: The way across Hourquette d'Alans (2430m) is uncomplicated, following a good path all the way. When it forks take the right-
hand option. Close views of the cirque headwall are very fine. The
path leads over the western ridge to Gavarnie by way of Refuge des
Espuguettes.

Note ii: Instead of crossing Hourquette d'Alans to Gavarnie, a
crossing of the frontier ridge can be made at the 2666 metre Brèche
de Tuquerouye (see Route 84), or by way of the Port Neuf de Pinède
further east. Both crossings give access to the Valle de Pineta in Spain.

Route 96: Héas (1500m) – Cirque de Troumouse – Lacs des Aires (2099m)

Distance:	**5 kilometres**
Height gain:	**599 metres**
Time:	**2–2½ hours**

The easiest way to get into the heart of the vast Cirque de Troumouse
is to take the toll road which climbs beyond Héas and ends at a
parking area at 2090 metres. A 15 minute stroll north-east of the car
park leads onto a bluff topped by a statue of the Virgin, a magnificent
viewpoint being almost in the centre of the cirque. Another 15
minutes from there will bring you to the Lacs des Aires, a collection
of tarns and pools below Pic de Troumouse. The walk offered here,
however, is longer and more rewarding since it keeps you away from
tarmac and enters the cirque by an alternative route.

From Héas walk along a signed footpath cutting south-east
towards a narrow groove between rock walls, the groove carrying the
Gave des Touyères. Keep to the left of the stream, rising steadily, then
more steeply towards the upper end of the groove where you climb
up to the Cabane des Aires. Another path cuts in from the left (an
alternative route from Héas via the Vallon de l'Aguila), but we swing
right (south) with the limestone cirque walls stetching ahead, above
and behind, and soon come to the Lacs des Aires.

Either return by the same path, or walk across to the statue of the
Virgin and take the path to the roadhead car park, then walk down
the road (there are shortcuts) back to Héas via the Chalet-hôtellerie
Le Maillet. (Allow another 1½–2 hours for this.)

Route 97: Héas (1500m) – Hourquette d'Héas (2608m) – Hourquette de Chermentas (2439m) – Refuge de Barroude (2373m)

Distance:	**10 kilometres**
Height gain:	**1227 metres**
Height loss:	**354 metres**
Time:	**6 hours**

This approach, used by trekkers on the High Route, is the most obvious for walkers coming from the west. A fine walk with a variety of scenic interest, caution is however required early in the season when snow may be lying on the approach to the two pass crossings. A full description of the route will be found below, under High Route 12.

Route 98: Aragnouet-le-Plan (1337m) – Refuge de Barroude (2373m)

Distance:	**7.5 kilometres**
Height gain:	**1036 metres**
Time:	**3–3½ hours**

The shortest, and most usual approach to Barroude, involves a walk through the pleasant Vallon de la Gela.

About two kilometres west of Aragnouet village in the Vallée d'Aure, on the approach to the Bielsa Tunnel, a short distance beyond the Chapelle des Hospitaliers, a PNP footpath branches away from the road at a sharp hairpin bend (1380m). This path climbs into the Vallon de la Gela heading south-west on the left-hand side (true right bank) of the Gela stream. There are no difficulties or complications, but at a bridge over the stream about three kilometres into the valley another trail heads off to the right, aiming for Hourquette de Chermentas. Ignore this and remain on the left of the stream, now heading south.

Shortly afterwards the path again divides near Cabane de la Gela, a shepherd's hut (1720m; 1 hour 15 mins). That which continues south aims for Port Vieux; ours goes south-west. Bear right, cross the stream and climb along the path until you reach a trail junction below

The long Barroude Wall forms the eastern side of Cirque de Troumouse (Routes 97–99)

Pic de Gerbats. Now join the route from Héas, bear left and follow the path which goes directly to the Refuge de Barroude.

Route 99: Refuge de Barroude (2373m) – Pic de Port-Vieux (2723m) – Port Vieux (2378m) – Refuge de Barroude

Distance:	**8 kilometres**
Height gain/loss:	**663 metres**
Time:	**5 hours**

This circuit makes an interesting, scenic day without any great difficulties involved. It passes over a couple of summits (Soum de Barroude 2674m; and Pic de Port-Vieux 2723m), follows the frontier ridge and affords some lovely views.

From the hut go down to the stream issuing from the eastern extremity of Lac de Barroude and take the path heading south up to the obvious saddle of Port de Barroude (2534m; 40 minutes). From here a spectacular view north-west looks over the Barroude cirque, and south to the western limits of the Cirque de Barrosa in Spain.

The broad frontier ridge heading east is followed round to the bald summit of Soum de Barroude; more fine views. Now head north to gain Pic de Port-Vieux, and descend from its summit on the steep grass of the Spanish side as the ridge itself becomes potentially dangerous. Having descended about 200 metres head once more towards the ridge, but keeping on a horizontal course. Once back on the ridge follow it as far as Port Vieux.

Turn left and descend the steep path on the French side until it divides. Go left (south-west) to traverse uncomfortable slopes of rough boulders led by a line of cairns and paint flashes, steadily gaining height to reach a grassy spur known as Pène Male to the north of Pic de Port-Vieux. The way now goes south-westwards along the western slopes of the mountain. It's an invigorating trail; narrow and exposed in places as it picks a way along narrow terraces, and leads directly to the stream flowing from Lac de Barroude. Follow the stream up towards the lake, and then cut off to the right to regain the hut.

Other Routes:

From Pic de Troumouse in the south to Pic des Aiguillous at its northern extremity, the Barroude Wall stretches almost four kilometres. Along it the main summits are Pic de Troumouse (3085m), Point 3028m, Pic Heid (3022m), Petit Pic Blanc (2957m), Pic de Gerbats (2904m) and Pic des Aiguillous (otherwise known as Pic de la Gela; 2851m).

PIC DE TROUMOUSE received its first ascent from survey officers in 1825. The *voie normale* from Port de Barroude is a PD outing of about three hours. Elsewhere along the wall the Ravier twins, Jean and Pierre, were responsible for taking the lion's share of pioneering during the fifties and sixties. Their routes range from the Central Buttress (Petit Pic Blanc) graded AD sup., to Lake Wall (Point 3028m) which is ED with passages of V and VI.

For a two-day walk across the mountains to Viados in the shadow of Pico de Posets, it would be possible for experienced backpackers to cross **PORT DE BARROUDE**, descend the Cirque de Barrosa and follow the Barrosa stream down to **PARZAN** in the valley of the Cinca above Bielsa. From there a route heads east up the Barranco de Ordiceto, crosses **COLLADO DE ORDICETO** (2326m) and eventually descends to **VIADOS**. Food would need to be carried for this two-day trek.

RÉSERVE NATURELLE DE NÉOUVIELLE

Position:	Wholly in France, to the north of both Gavarnie and Barroude regions. Bordered on the west by the valley of the Gave de Pau, to the north by the Tourmalet road, and to the east by the Vallée d'Aure.
Access:	The only proper vehicular access is from the south-east where a service road climbs out of the Vallée d'Aure at Fabian and goes as far as the dammed lakes of Cap de Long, Oredon, Aubert and Aumar. Footpath access is best from the north via Pont de la Gaubie above Barèges, which is served by bus from Lourdes, or from the service road mentioned above.
Maps:	IGN Carte de Randonnées No 4 'Bigorre' 1:50,000 IGN TOP 25 series no: 1748OT 'Gavarnie, Luz St Sauveur' and 1748ET 'Néouvielle, Vallée d'Aure' both at 1:25,000
Valley Bases:	Barèges (1247m), St-Lary (810m)

The Réserve Naturelle de Néouvielle forms an adjunct to the Parc National des Pyrénées; a large area of granite upland liberally spattered with tarns of varying size. It holds a number of attractive peaks, boasts several lovely valleys and with a good collection of mountain huts linked by trails to lure the lover of fine scenery into its heartland.

Hydro engineers have dammed many of the lakes and are responsible for pushing the road from Fabian deep into the heart of the region. But elsewhere one gains a sense of remoteness when exploring from valley to valley. From lofty cols prospects of grandeur greet the eye; grey peaks jut dramatically from extensive ridge systems, the glint of a tarn dazzles from a far-off valley and glorious stands of mountain pine throw pockets of shade on otherwise raw hillsides.

As early as 1787 the geographers, Vidal and Reboul, climbed Turon de Néouvielle; first of the 3000-metre summits in the Pyrenees to be won. Ramond de Carbonnières explored parts of the region during his self-imposed exile at Barèges, and made an attempt on Pic de Néouvielle. In 1847 de Chausenque succeeded where Ramond had failed, while nearby Pic Long (3192m) received an early ascent from the Duc de Nemours with Marc Sesquet as his guide. During two centuries of activity the Néouvielle has attracted the attention of numerous *Pyrénéistes* with some difficult climbs being achieved. But the modest scrambler and the valley walker will also find an abundance of outings to suit, for which this guide and the map serve merely as brief introductions and a spur to dreams.

Valley Bases:

BARÈGES (1247m) is situated about eight kilometres north-east of Luz on the road to Col du Tourmalet on the northern edge of the region. It makes a good centre for mountain-based activities; walking, climbing, parapenting and skiing. That one or two British adventure-holiday companies use this village as their Pyrenean centre is an endorsement of its pedigree. There are several modest-priced hotels, a *gîte d'étape* (l'Oasis; Tel: 05 62 92 69 47) and a campsite; plenty of shops, bars, restaurants, PTT and tourist information. The village is served by bus from Lourdes.

ST-LARY (810m) is an expanding resort in the Vallée d'Aure. Served by bus from Tarbes via Arreau, it provides access to the eastern side of the Néouvielle by way of the GR10 which passes nearby, or for those with their own transport, the possibility of driving into the region on the service road to the dammed lakes. St-Lary offers hotel accommodation (several campsites nearby), a *gîte d'étape*, Le Refuge (Tel: 05 62 39 46 81), plenty of shops, restaurants, bank, PTT, tourist information, guides' bureau and a Maison du Parc.

Mountain Huts:

CHALET-HOTEL DE LA GLÈRE (2103m) is a large stone-built refuge on the edge of some wild country. It has places for 90 and is open with a guardian in charge from the beginning of July to the end of

September, when meals are available. Accessed by a rough dirt road from Barèges, it will otherwise take about 3½ hours to reach on foot (Tel: 05 62 92 69 47).

REFUGE PACKE (2509m) offers only the most basic facilities and can sleep about eight. Named after Charles Packe, who in 1893 presented the CAF with 1000 francs as a contribution towards the construction and upkeep of refuges, it is found about 2.5 kilometres west of Pic de Néouvielle and is reached in about 2½ hours from la Glère.

CABANE DU RABIET (2199m) lies just to the south of Refuge Packe, and about 100 metres to the east of Lac de Rabiet. This too is a simple, but solid little shelter that can accommodate about half a dozen. More useful as an emergency shelter on a long trek than as a planned base. Reached in about 30 minutes from Refuge Packe.

CABANE DETS COUBOUS (2041m) stands above the little dammed Lac dets Coubous, about 1½ hours walk from Pont de la Gaubie. Permanently open, but offering just basic shelter, it can sleep about six.

CABANE D'AYGUES-CLUSES (2150m) is also reached from Pont de la Gaubie in about two hours. It stands in pleasant open pastureland south-west of Pic des Quatre Termes and offers emergency accommodation for half a dozen.

REFUGE CAMPANA DE CLOUTOU (2220m) was built in 1971 by the CAF to the east of Lac du Campana and has a guardian from June to the end of September. The refuge can sleep 25 and is reached from Artigues in the Vallée de Gripp in about 3½ hours, or in about two hours from Refuge du Bastanet (Tel: 05 62 91 87 47).

REFUGE DU BASTANET (2250m) is the property of the PTT. With a guardian in residence between the beginning of July and mid-September, when meals may be available, the hut can accommodate 20. It stands in splendid country among tarns and clumps of pine north-east of Lac de l'Oule, from whose southern limit it is reached in about 1½–2 hours (Tel: 05 62 98 48 80).

CHALET-HOTEL DE L'OULE (1819m) is owned by the Commune of St-Lary and stands by the dam at the southern end of Lac de l'Oule. There is a guardian in occupation through the main summer season when meals are available. The building can sleep 30 in bedrooms and dormitory (Tel: 05 62 98 48 62). Access is by road from Fabian, followed by a walk of about 45 minutes.

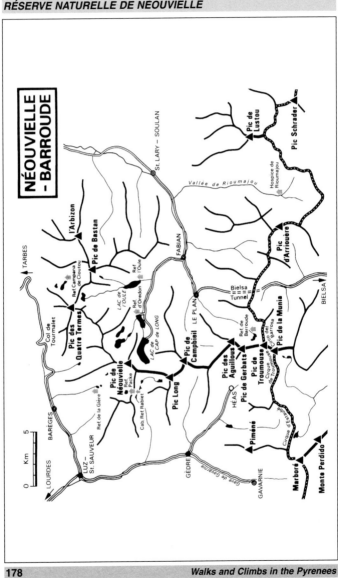

CHALET-HOTEL D'OREDON (1852m) can sleep 40 in its dormitory and bedrooms. Situated at the eastern end of Lac d'Oredon, and accessible by car, restaurant service is available. The chalet-hotel is open mid-June to mid-September (Tel: 05 62 39 63 33).

Route 100: Barèges (1247m) – Chalet-Hotel de la Glère (2103m)

Distance:	**7 kilometres**
Height gain:	**856 metres**
Time:	**3½ hours**

Visitors with their own transport might choose to drive at least part of the way to this hut. If so, it is advisable to park with care in one of a few rough 'lay-by' areas along the dirt road. To drive all the way is to risk damage to your vehicle, unless you have four-wheel drive. From Barèges drive upvalley towards the Col du Tourmalet. Take the second turning on the right after the sign announcing that you've left Barèges. This narrow road cuts back sharply and is signposted Restaurant le Lienz. The road becomes a track after Chez Louisette and twists into the Vallée de la Glère proper.

The walker's route begins behind the thermal baths in Barèges itself, where a track zig-zags up through beechwoods, goes beneath a funicular and in about an hour comes to an open clearing of pastureland where you'll find the restaurant of Chez Louisette. Head across the pastures (signpost) to enter the Vallée de la Glère, which is green and pastoral in its lower reaches, but wild and austere as you go deeper into it. The way follows the dirt road, but towards the head of the valley when the road begins to climb in tight bends, footpath short-cuts allow you to gain height directly to the hut. There is plenty of wild country to explore from it.

Route 101: Barèges (Pont de la Gaubie) (1538m) – Cabane dets Coubous (2041m)

Distance:	**2.5 kilometres**
Height gain:	**503 metres**
Time:	**1½ hours**

About 3.5 kilometres north-east of Barèges on the way to Col du Tourmalet, the N618 road makes a deep curve to the south into the mouth of the Coubous glen. The road crosses a stream at a left-hand hairpin bend by a small cafe. There is plenty of car parking space opposite. This is Pont de la Gaubie, starting point for several walks into the northern edge of the Néouvielle massif.

Just beyond the cafe a path heads into the Coubous glen (signposted Étangs de Coubous) and soon joins a major track that has its beginnings 150 metres from the cafe. Walk along the track (GR10) heading south. When it eases leftwards at the mouth of a side valley cross a stream and come to a junction of paths. Ignore that which heads left (the continuing GR10 which goes off to the Aygues-Cluses) and continue ahead, soon rising in zig-zags over increasingly stony terrain. The path reaches another trail (a horizontal one) where you bear left, and soon after come to the Lac dets Coubous with the hut perched above it.

Note: There are several attractive tarns a short walk beyond Lac dets Coubous – the path goes round the left-hand (east) shore – and make a worthwhile visit. Beyond them the path climbs to Hourquette d'Aubert and descends on the far side to the Lacs d'Aumar and Aubert. This route is described in reverse as part of the Néouvielle Lakes Circuit (Route 110), a splendid two-day trek.

Route 102: Barèges (Pont de la Gaubie) (1538m) – Cabane d'Aygues-Cluses (2150m)

Distance:	**5 kilometres**
Height gain:	**612 metres**
Time:	**2 hours**

The Aygues-Cluses glen is a delight of clear streams, tarns, fine views and lots of marmots. Although the hut is suitable only as an emergency shelter, it is worth wandering to it in order to have an excuse to explore its lovely situation.

Follow Route 101 as far as the junction of paths at the entrance to the side glen near the head of the Coubous glen. Bear left and follow the GR10 path as it works its way through the glen by way of a series of soft-turf steps, or minor plateaux, adorned with stunted pines, the stream tumbling over modest cascades. Without any difficulties the waymarked path leads directly to the hut, which overlooks a tarn set within a large bowl of grassland.

Route 103: Barèges (Pont de la Gaubie) (1538m) – Col de Madaméte (2509m) – Lac dets Coubous (2041m) – Pont de la Gaubie

Distance:	**14 kilometres**
Height gain/loss:	**1039 metres**
Time:	**5–5½ hours**

A splendid circuit with lots of variety and good views nearly every step of the way. It begins by following Route 102 as far as the Cabane d'Aygues-Cluses, and continues on the GR10 heading south, climbing to pass a string of tarns, then over boulders to gain Col de Madaméte (3 hours). Views from the col are sufficient to make you want to sit and absorb them for a while before continuing with the circuit.

Bear right on a narrow trail that climbs towards Pic de Madaméte, but then passes below the peak on its northern side. Descend on another path towards Col de Tracens (north of Pic de Madaméte), then veer left on a cairned route that leads to Lac de Tracens, one of several tarns in the glen below. Work round the north side of the tarn and join a clear path alongside Lac Blanc. Follow this path as it heads to the right, soon coming to the dammed Lac dets Coubous. Cross the dam to the cabane and descend into the valley below where the GR10 leads back to Pont de la Gaubie.

Route 104: Barèges (Pont de la Gaubie) (1538m) – Col de Madaméte (2509m) – Chalet-Hôtel de l'Oule (1819m)

Distance:	**15 kilometres**
Height gain:	**1101 metres**
Height loss:	**820 metres**
Time:	**6½–7 hours**

This challenging walk forms one of the best sections of the GR10 long distance trans-Pyrenean trail. It crosses two cols and is therefore quite demanding, but it makes an ideal introduction to the Néouvielle region.

Follow directions for Route 103 as far as Col de Madamete (3 hours). The path descends into the Réserve Naturelle, skirts the left-hand edge of a tarn, Gourg de Rabas, and goes down to meet a road by Lac d'Aumar. Bear left and walk along this to the far end of the lake where the GR10 breaks away and strikes off ahead, going south-eastward while the road snakes down to Lac d'Oredon. The path takes you among trees and rises to the saddle of Col d'Estoudou (5½ hours), crosses over and then drops steeply to the west bank of Lac de l'Oule. Leaving GR10 bear right and walk along the lakeside to reach the dam at its southern end, where you will find the Chalet-Hôtel de l'Oule.

Route 105: Barèges (Pont de la Gaubie) (1538m) – Hourquette Nère (2465m) – Refuge du Bastanet (2250m)

Distance:	12 kilometres
Height gain:	927 metres
Height loss:	215 metres
Time:	4–5 hours

Follow Route 102 as far as Cabane d'Aygues-Cluses, then take either a faint path leading round the northern end of the Lac de Coueyla-Gran, or that which skirts the southern side. If you take the southern option veer left round the lake and when the path disappears, go up onto a broad sloping 'ridge' adorned with pine trees and boulders to a view overlooking Lac d'Agalops, there to join the path which came round the north side of the earlier tarn. Follow this path to the right (east) as it climbs nearly 300 metres to reach Hourquette Nère. The route grows steeper towards the top.

From the bald saddle you can see several more tarns below. The continuing path descends to Lac de Port-Bielh (2285m). Halfway along the southern side of this tarn the route heads down the left-hand side of a stream flowing south-eastwards. A clear path takes you above a string of small tarns, then up a slope to a minor ridge where you find Lac de Bastan (2247m) whose northern shore is rock-strewn and whose southern bank is marked by a pine-topped hillock. Pass the tarn at its south-eastern end and descend to another, but much smaller, tarn (2197m) with a stream flowing from it.

Cross the stream and go up a smooth grass slope towards an

obvious ridge with a number of pines upon it. Towards the top the path loops to and fro to ease the ascent. More fine views from this broad crest. Go down the eastern side to the edge of Lac Superior, pass along the southern side of this lake and soon you will come to Refuge du Bastanet at the northern edge of yet another tarn.

Route 106: Refuge du Bastanet (2250m) – Col de Bastanet (2607m) – Refuge de Campana de Cloutou (2220m)

Distance:	**4 kilometres**
Height gain:	**267 metres**
Height loss:	**297 metres**
Time:	**2 hours**

A variante of the GR10 (GR10C) links these two huts by way of Col de Bastanet, and continues down to Artigues in the Vallée de Gripp on the eastern side of Col du Tourmalet. The route between the huts is not difficult, although there are some steep and rough sections.

On leaving the Bastanet hut follow the path north to reach in ten minutes Lac Superior. The path branches away from the tarn to the left and then divides. Bear right (north) to climb to Col de Bastanet which is found midway between Pic de Bastan and Pic de Portarras. Drop down on the northern side of the ridge and continue north to pass a number of pools and tarns set in a rugged landscape. The hut is found to the east of Lac du Campana.

Note: Artigue is reached in a further three hours from here by following the GR10C on its continuing northbound course.

Route 107: Chalet-Hôtel de l'Oule (1819m) – Refuge du Bastanet (2250m)

Distance:	**5 kilometres**
Height gain:	**431 metres**
Time:	**1½–2 hours**

From the Chalet-Hôtel below the dam head north along either shore of Lac de l'Oule to reach the basic shelter of Cabane de la Lude. Soon after this bear right on a track which winds up the hillside and, about 20 minutes from the end of the lake, comes to the Cabane de

Bastan. The GR10 then breaks off to the right. Ignore that turn-off and head north to enter a hanging valley in which you come to the lovely Lac Inferieur (2141m). The path leads along its eastern shore, swings right and climbs to a second, smaller tarn, beyond which you come to Lac Milieu. Refuge du Bastanet is found at its northern end.

Route 108: Vallée de Couplan (1591m) –
Chalet-Hôtel de l'Oule (1819m)

Distance:	**2 kilometres**
Height gain:	**228 metres**
Time:	**45 minutes**

The shortest and most obvious approach to the Chalet-Hôtel de l'Oule is by road from Fabian in the Vallée d'Aure, then by this easy path. The road was built by the electricity authority for the construction of various dams, and leaves the Vallée d'Aure at Fabian, upvalley of St-Lary. About six kilometres along this service road there is a sharp hairpin bend, the second such since Fabian. Shortly beyond it, and where the road bends to the left, a flat grassy area is seen on the right by a bridge. A PNP notice board stands here, and cars may conveniently be parked at this point.

Cross the bridge and follow the path which bears right and steadily slopes above the valley heading east. As you rise so you gain views ahead with flowers clustered on the rocks that wall the path on your left. Through pines the way swings left to enter the lower reaches of the valley in which lies Lac de l'Oule. The huge dam which is responsible for the lake is seen ahead. The path rises to the dam, which you then cross to its eastern side. The Chalet-Hôtel is located below.

Route 109: A Walking Circuit of Lac de l'Oule

Distance:	**7 kilometres**
Height gain/loss:	**228 metres**
Time:	**2–2½ hours**

This easy walk is popular with French picnic parties, and is recommended for families with young children. Choose a bright summer's day when views are a delight.

Follow Route 108 from the parking area as far as the lake. Stroll along the western shore on a clear, well-made path with fine views to the north. At the lake's northern extremity you'll curve round to the right and pass Cabane de la Lude. Walk along the eastern shore as far as the dam, then cross to the western side and return down the valley-bound path. (Refreshments are available at Chalet-Hôtel de l'Oule.)

Route 110: A Néouvielle Lakes Circuit

Start/Finish:	**Barèges (Pont de la Gaubie)**
Time:	**2 days**
Accommodation:	**Mountain hut (Refuge du Bastanet)**

Several magnificent walking circuits could be created within the Néouvielle region. A study of the map will reveal a variety of possibilities. The following is just one, and is highly recommended.

The first section has already been described from Pont de la Gaubie to Refuge du Bastanet (Route 105). This takes between four and five hours, without rests, but is likely to demand much longer on account of the glorious scenery through which you pass. Taken at a leisurely pace this should be enough for the first day.

Day two heads south along the eastern side of Lac du Milieu and alongside another, much smaller tarn, before the path swings right and descends to the east bank of the lovely Lac Inferieur – one of the finest on this circuit. The continuing path goes down to Lac de l'Oule where you pass along its right-hand (western) shore until, about halfway down the length of the lake, another trail breaks off to the right (GR10). This climbs among trees, steeply at times, to Col d'Estoudou (2260m). Fine views from this saddle, where Pic de Néouvielle is the dominant mountain to the west.

From the col descend westwards for about five minutes and come to a trail division. Take the right-hand option (straight ahead), a lovely mid-level traverse among pinewoods, heading north-west. Crossing small streams and dodging in and out of tree shade you reach a gentle grassy crest with splendid views. Continuing, come to an open, moorland-like patch and wander down to Lac d'Aumar.

Walk along the road as far as a car park by Lac d'Aubert, and continue ahead from this on a track rising among rough granite boulders towards the pass of Hourquette d'Aubert. When the track ends a path continues, steeply in places but more easily-angled near the top, and finally brings you onto the pass at 2498 metres. Yet more fine views.

Go down the northern side on a steep stony path that eases lower down and passes several tarns. The small, dammed Lac dets Coubous is the last of these. Beyond it the trail descends to the Coubous glen along which the GR10 path leads directly to Pont de la Gaubie.

PIC LONG (3192m)

Highest of the Néouvielle peaks, Pic Long rises from sharp ridge systems to the south-west of Lac de Cap de Long, and was first climbed in 1856 by the Duc de Nemours (son of King Louis Phillippe) and his guide, Marc Sesquet. The *voie normale* is a modest yet interesting route, but both the East and North faces have somewhat challenging lines on them.

Route 111: Lac de Cap de Long (2161m) – Pic Long (3192m)

Grade:	**AD+ (*voie normale* via Hourquette du Pic Long)**
Distance:	**7 kilometres**
Height gain:	**1031 metres**
Time:	**4½–5 hours**
Equipment:	**Rope, ice axe, crampons useful**

This standard route provides an interesting, but long day (allow 3 hours for the descent, making 8 hours in all). Follow the road along the southern shore of Lac de Cap de Long at the head of the Vallée de Couplan. At the end of the road take the PNP path which continues to skirt the lake towards the south-west, but keeping some way above it. The path descends to meet a stream flowing from a valley to the south. Enter this valley following a path and, later on the left bank of the stream, along a line of cairns that direct the route over boulders and several rock terraces.

On reaching the snout of a long moraine work a way up to the little Glacier de Pays Bache which hangs under the East Face of Pic Long. Above this runs the ridge linking Pic Long with Pic Badet. In this ridge, left of Pic Long's rising cone, a cleft is seen. This is

Hourquette du Pic Long, the point to make for across the glacier. Due to glacier shrinkage the chimney providing access to the hourquette (3099m) is becoming more serious. The first pitch is now probably Severe/HS, while the remainder of the climb becomes becomes progressively easier.

Head to the right at the top of the chimney to find a ledge which goes left onto the South Face. From the ledge an obvious, easy gully leads for a little under 100 metres onto the summit itself.

Note: The East Face, rising out of the glacier to the right of the above route, has a couple of lines on it; one graded AD sup., the other D. On the North Face, which rises steeply from Lac Tourrat, several hard routes have been forced on the 600 metres of mixed rock and ice which combine to make this one of the most challenging of faces in the Pyrenees. The 'direct' here is graded TD inf. and involves between 7 and 8 hours of climbing.

PIC BADET (3160m)

Joined to Pic Long by a short dipping ridge running south-east, Pic Badet may conveniently be included in the above outing, or as a day's scramble in its own right.

Route 112: Lac de Cap de Long (2161m) – Pic Badet (3160m)

Grade:	**PD (via the North-west Arête)**
Distance:	**7 kilometres**
Height gain:	**999 metres**
Time:	**4–4½ hours**
Equipment:	**Rope, ice axe, crampons useful**

Take Route 111 to the top of the chimney leading from the Glacier de Pays Bache; Hourquette du Pic Long. Bear left and follow the ridge, which is broken here and there and notched with several minor gendarmes, to reach the summit. (Allow 30 minutes from Hourquette du Pic Long.)

Note: The *voie normale*, graded F, passes below the summit to attack it by way of the South-east ridge.

PIC DE CAMPBIEIL (3173m)

This large mountain, south-east of Pic Long, boasts a panorama from its summit that is both vast and impressive, and is noted for the ease of its ascent. In fact Pic de Campbieil compares with le Taillon as one of the easiest 3000-metre summits in the Pyrenees.

Route 113: Lac de Cap de Long (2161m) – Pic de Campbieil (3173m)

Grade:	**F** (*voie normale* via **Hourquette de Cap de Long**)
Distance:	**6.5 kilometres**
Height gain:	**1012 metres**
Time:	**5 hours**

Take Route 111 into the valley walled by the lengthy Arête de Cap de Long to the west and the Crête des Alharisses to the east. Continue beyond the Glacier de Pays Bache and mount towards the cirque above a small tarn, Gourg de Cap de Long, where cairns lead up to the broad saddle shown as Hourquette de Cap de Long (2902m) on the map, but also known as Hourquette Badet. Bear left here and rise over boulders to Point 3157m where the ridge makes a north–south turn. Follow along the left-hand side of the ridge, now heading north, to reach the summit of Pic de Campbieil. By virtue of its position and height, summit vistas include not only the immediate countryside, but practically all the High Pyrenees region, from Pic d'Anie in the west to the heights of Andorra in the east.

Other Routes:

With the Lacs de Long, Oredon, Aumar and Aubert being accessible by road, a number of modest peaks are within reach without the necessity of staying overnight in the wild inner regions of the Néouvielle. **PIC DE NÉOUVIELLE** (3091m) has a couple of *Facile* routes beginning at Lac d'Aubert, in addition to a fair choice of more difficult scrambles and climbs. (Via Hourquette d'Aubert a popular ascent will take 3½ hours from the parking area at Lac d'Aubert.) **PIC DES TROIS CONSEILLERS** (3039m) provides some interesting routes on its northern arête, and an AD climb on its South Face which rises from the waters of Lac de Cap de Long.

Turon de Néouvielle (left), Pic des Trois Conseillers and Pic de Néouvielle

TURON DE NÉOUVIELLE (3035m) rises at a junction of ridges above the western end of Lac de Cap de Long, but is often climbed from the Chalet-Hotel de la Glère by an easy, but interesting route, of about three hours.

POSETS

Position:	**In Spain; east of the Rio Cinca and west of the Esera**
Access:	**Approach routes from the west are long; 24kms by road and track from Salinas in the valley of the Cinca as far as Viados, via Plan. From the east access is by way of the Esera Valley; on foot through either the Estos or Eriste Valleys. Eriste and Benasque may be reached by bus from Huesca via Barbastro.**
Map:	**Editorial Alpina 'Posets' and 'Bachimala' both at 1:25,000**
Valley Bases:	**Benasque (1138m), Eriste (1118m)**

The Posets massif covers a large area of delightful country; a region of high ridges and wild cupped hollows, of cradled snowfields and sharp jutting aiguilles protected by the *Parque Natural Posets-Maladeta*. Like a fortress, bare crests cut by crumbling gullies top buttresses that rise from beautiful pinewoods; a swollen upland whose moated valleys are among the most attractive in all the Pyrenees. To the north runs the Valle de Estos, to the west that of the Cinqueta de Añes Cruces, while the major valley of the Esera marks the eastern limit of the massif. Dozens of sparkling tarns add a dimension of tranquillity to a serene mountain wilderness.

The culminating point is Pico de Posets, at 3375 metres the second highest in the range. South-west of this rise the Picos de Eriste, while above the Batisielles glen (a charming corrie draining into the Estos) the Agujas de Perramo appear tantalising to rock climbers. But throughout the massif there are so many possibilities for climbing and scrambling of an exploratory nature, that a party concentrating on this region would find ample rewards for their single-minded dedication. Walkers have valleys and hidden glens to explore, passes to cross and an opportunity to make a very fine three- or four-day circuit of the massif, while botanists will be well pleased with an impressive local flora.

On 6th August 1856 Pico de Posets (Punta de Llardana) received its first ascent from the little-known pioneer H. Halkett with the guides, Redonnet and Barrau. Redonnet, incidentally, was also a member of the party that made the first ascent of Aneto 14 years earlier, while Pierre Barrau was one of a distinguished family of guides active in the Pyrenees during the middle years of the 19th century, especially in the Posets and Maladeta regions. A decade later saw the emergence of Russell, whose energies found expression in several new routes in the massif; either alone or with Firmin Barrau. The 'majestic desert of huge boulders, eternal snow, and frozen ponds' also attracted Packe, who spent many days and nights basking in their solitudes, and having made the third ascent of Posets, later created a new route of his own – the route now adopted as the *voie normale*.

Valley Bases:

BENASQUE (1138m) is the northern-most village in the long Valle del Esera. An historic place with a medieval heart of cobbled streets and alleys running between stone-built houses, some of which were once used by the nobility of Aragon, it has become a major resort town with a number of hotels, apartment blocks, shops and restaurants. Among the shops several stock mountaineering equipment, butane gas cartridges and the full range of Editorial Alpina maps. Benasque also boasts a Visitor Centre for the *Parque Natural Posets-Maladeta*, a tourist office, banks and a post office. There are several official campsites nearby.

ERISTE (1118m) lies about three kilometres downvalley from Benasque. Smaller than its neighbour and with less immediate appeal, it is overlooked by an ugly electricity works, while the Esera has been dammed on the outskirts of the village to create a small lake. There is, however, a fine glen behind the village that leads into the heart of the massif. Eriste offers accommodation with three one-star hotels.

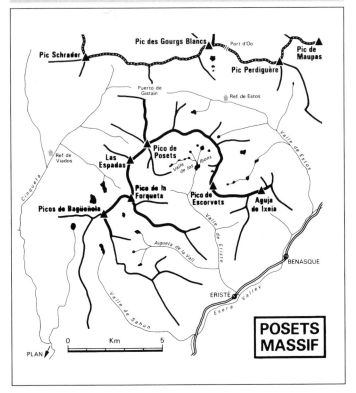

Mountain Huts:

REFUGIO ANGEL ORUS (2100m) (also known as EL FORCAU) was built in 1981 by the FEM. It can sleep about 30, is permanently open but with a guardian from July to end-September (Tel: 974 34 40 44), and is situated in a fine position on the western hillside above the Valle de Eriste, about 3½ hours walk from Eriste. It is also possible to drive part of the way on first road, then track, as far as the Puente de Espiantosa. The hut is reached in about 1½ hours from the roadhead.

REFUGIO CLOT DE CHIL (2000m) is also accessible from Eriste, but is found in the Valle de Chil, an eastern tributary of the Valle de Eriste.

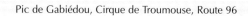

Pic de Gabiédou, Cirque de Troumouse, Route 96

A small, unguarded hut, it can sleep 16. About one hour from Puente de Espiantosa.

REFUGIO DE VIADOS (1810m) in the valley of the Cinqueta de Añes Cruces, is privately owned, can accommodate 40 in the main building and six in an annexe. Camping is also allowed on neighbouring ground. The guardian is in residence from the beginning of July until late September, when meals are provided. Some provisions may also be available for self-cookers (Tel: 974 50 60 82). Viados is a charming hamlet of small summer-only farm buildings with a magnificent view of the vast western face of the Posets massif. A rough track leads to Viados from Plan, which has road access from Salinas in the valley of the Cinca. A classic walk over Puerto de Gistain links Refugio de Viados with the Estos hut.

REFUGIO DE ESTOS (1835m) is a very fine three-storey building that can accommodate 180 people. Owned by the FEM it is open all year and the guardian and his staff provide a full meals service. There is also a well-equipped kitchen for self-caterers. The hut stands on a bluff above the north bank of the Rio de Estos, about 3½–4 hours walk from the entrance to the Valle de Estos, a short distance upvalley of Benasque (Tel: 974 55 14 83).

Route 114: Eriste (1118m) – Refugio Angel Orus (2100m)

Distance:	**7 kilometres**
Height gain:	**982 metres**
Time:	**3½ hours**

As mentioned above, it is possible to drive on a combination of road and track from Eriste to the Puente de Espiantosa, thereby reducing the walk to about 1½ hours. This road is joined a little upvalley of the village, where it winds above the true left bank of the Eriste stream. The alternative, footpath walk, however, climbs out of Eriste above the village church and heads into a ravine on the west bank. In about one hour cross to the east bank at the humpbacked Puente de Tramarrius, go onto the track and continue upvalley until you reach the roadhead at Puente de Espiantosa. Off to the left there is a fine waterfall.

Cross the concrete bridge to the west bank again and follow a clear path among trees and shrubs parallel to the stream at first, then break away left at Pleta de los Riberes near a simple domed shepherd's hut, where the path climbs steeply to Refugio Angel Orus. The hut has a splendid wild outlook, an enticing landscape to explore.

Route 115: Eriste (1118m) – Refugio Clot de Chil (2000m)

Distance:	**6 kilometres**
Height gain:	**882 metres**
Time:	**3 hours**

Follow directions as for Refugio Angel Orus (Route 114) as far as Puente de Espiantosa (2 hours). A signpost here directs the path, which climbs steeply a little north of east, for about one more hour, at first among trees, to gain this small unguarded refugio. A good base for climbs on the Tucas de Ixea, Aguja del Xinebra and assorted peaklets guarding the Valle de Perramo to the north.

Route 116: Benasque (1138m) – Refugio de Estos (1835m)

Distance:	**12 kilometres**
Height gain:	**697 metres**
Time:	**4–4½ hours**

About 3.5 kilometres upvalley from Benasque the Rio Estos emerges through a short rocky defile to the north, obscuring any hint of the splendours to be found deep within that glen. An official campsite (Camping Chuise) is located at the entrance to the Estos.

Leaving Benasque walk upvalley along the tarmac road. (It is possible to drive to the entrance to the Estos glen and leave cars there.) The road crosses to the true right bank of the Esera at Puente de Cuera (San Chaime), and just beyond the bridge a service road cuts away to the left and winds a short way up towards the Estos defile.

Walk through the brief gorge on its eastern side, and soon after cross to the west bank and wander into the valley along a dirt track. This leads easily upstream, sometimes among trees, often over open pastures, and eventually veers right to reach the Cabane de Turmo beside the Estos stream. There are two ways from here to the hut. The original route crosses the bridge, bears left and follows the stream north-westward all the way to the hut. But an alternative path (waymarked) leads from the Turmo cabane along the true right bank of the stream (south bank) a short distance, then crosses to the opposite bank to join the original trail. Either route will be easy to follow, and both have plenty to commend them. Refugio de Estos is gained about 3½–4 hours from the entrance to the valley.

Route 117: Granges d'Astau (1139m) – Refuge d'Espingo (1967m) – Port d'Oo (2908m) – Refugio de Estos (1835m)

Distance:	**12 kilometres**
Height gain:	**1769 metres**
Height loss:	**1073 metres**
Time:	**2 days**
Accommodation:	**Refuge d'Espingo**
Additional map:	**IGN Carte de Randonnées No 5 'Luchon' 1:50,000**

This long, strenuous northerly approach is best suited to experienced mountain walkers and climbers who have travelled to the Pyrenees by train. The nearest railhead is Bagnères de Luchon, from where the Granges d'Astau (*gîte d'étape*) may be reached by taxi (or hitch-hike) via the village of Oo, just south of the Col de Peyresourde road.

A distinctive path (GR10) which needs no description leaves the Granges for Lac d'Oo, about two kilometres to the south. The lake is understandably popular with tourists. A cafe is situated on its northern shore, while a long waterfall cascades into the lake at the southern end.

The continuing path climbs above the eastern shore, sometimes in the shade of trees, sometimes in the open, and eventually passes through a shallow 'corridor' below the slopes of Cap des Hounts-Secs to mount a saddle with the Refuge d'Espingo seen lying about 200 metres off to the right. (About 2½–3 hours from Granges d'Astau.)

Note: Refuge d'Espingo (1955m) is owned by the CAF, can accommodate about 70, has a guardian in residence from May to October (Tel: 05 61 79 20 01) when meals are available. Winter quarters can sleep 20. Views overlook Lac d'Espingo, Val d'Arrouye and an assortment of rocky peaks.

Continue on the path heading south. Come to Lac Saussat and

Refuge d'Espingo

pass along its western side. The path is well-engineered (it goes to a dam at Lac du Portillon), and leads easily up towards a wilderness of mountains. About 20 metres before the path crosses a bridge to the east side of a stream, leave the trail at a cairn on the right and climb grass slopes to reach another path which leads round rock bands then, higher, among a boulder field following a line of cairns.

Topping a rock barrier you come to a small tarn overlooking Lac Glace. Ahead can be seen the Seil de la Baque icefield. More cairns lead over rocky terraces and up shallow gullies to gain a high rolling wilderness of barren rocks with the frontier ridge in full view. Cross the glacial scarf of Seil de la Baque to the foot of screes which guard the approach to the Port d'Oo, then work a way up the scree slope to reach the pass.

Magnificent views from Port d'Oo show across the depths of the Estos Valley to Pico de Posets; along the frontier ridge to the southeast where French slopes are draped with an icy apron and those of Spain are just bare rocks; and north-east to the handsome form of the Grand Quayrat next to Pic Lezat.

The descent to the Estos Valley is steep and tiring, and passes through some wild, desolate country. Bear leftwards below the Port down scree-covered rocks, then through a boulder-field before easing towards Lago de Gias seen ahead to the right. Before reaching this tarn, however, bear left to follow a line of cairns that lead all the way down to the Estos hut. The route descends through gullies, over rough terrain and down a stream bed before a proper path emerges beside the stream and takes you round a bluff to find Refugio de Estos a short distance away. (Allow 6–7 hours from Refuge d'Espingo; 9–10 hours from Granges d'Astau.)

Route 118: Refugio de Estos (1835m) –
Puerto de Gistain (2603m) – Refugio de Viados (1810m)

Distance:	**11 kilometres**
Height gain:	**768 metres**
Height loss:	**793 metres**
Time:	**4–4½ hours**

This linking route between huts makes a classic crossing, a very fine day's walk. The route is not overly demanding, under normal summer conditions, and may be enjoyed at a leisurely pace with the temptation of a short diversion from the pass itself to a bare minor summit with long views.

From the bluff crowned by the Estos hut, descend to stream level upvalley and continue along the path that remains on the north bank of the Rio de Estos, steadily gaining height towards the obvious saddle of Puerto de Gistain. The path is easy, and when it fades across grassland cairns take over. Beyond the tributary stream of the Barranco de Clarabide, cross to the south side of the Estos stream. The final ascent to the pass is over rock and scree. From the pass views back to the east show the great lump of the Maladeta dominating the horizon. (Allow about 2 hours from the hut.)

Note: Given time, energy and inclination, it might be worth wandering up the steepish slopes to the north in order to gain an insignificant bald summit from which you will enjoy long views to Monte Perdido and Pic du Marboré in the west, and an unusual view south to the Posets. (Allow about 45 minutes in all for this diversion.)

The Puerto de Gistain is a scoop of rock and grass, and the descent to the valley of the Cinqueta de Añes Cruces is again led by cairns, veering a little left of the drainage stream. A more obvious path is joined lower down towards an open bowl of grassland where the Barranco de Gistain feeds into the Añes Cruces. Contrary to indications on the Editorial Alpina map, you must cross to the right bank of the Añes Cruces here, then bear left and follow the downward trail all the way to Viados. It's a lovely walk.

Route 119: Refugio de Viados (1810m) – Collado de Eriste (2970m) – Refugio Angel Orus (2100m)

Distance:	9 kilometres
Height gain:	1160 metres
Height loss:	870 metres
Time:	5 hours

This fairly strenuous route should be avoided if there is any expectation of inclement weather, and ought in any case to be tackled only by experienced mountain trekkers. The crossing of Collado de Eriste is not unduly difficult, but the route is not always clearly defined.

Opposite, and to the south-east of Viados, stretches Valle de Millares. At its head, between the crest of Picos de Eriste and the South-West ridge of Pico de Posets, the dip of Collado de Eriste can virtually be seen from the refugio.

From the hut go down to the barns (or granges) of Viados, then break away right from the main valley path onto a trail that leads to a wooden footbridge over the Añes Cruces stream. From the left bank the path now winds among pine trees, enters the Millares Valley, then becomes somewhat indistinct. Remain well to the left of the stream (Barranco de la Ribereta) heading south-east where the path gradually becomes more clear.

The trail climbs in zig-zags up the left-hand hillside, at first on slopes of scree and rock (cairns and paint flashes), then in and out of pines. On occasion there are rocks bearing the words 'Collado de Eriste'. Approaching the head of the valley towards a prominent rocky crown (unshown on the Editorial Alpina map), the path veers right towards a stream. (This path leads to Lago and Collado de Millares.) About 150 metres before reaching the stream, however, a waymark directs you away from the path, climbing steeply now to the left of the rocky crown.

Gaining height with the aid of cairns, paint flashes and, later, a twist of path, enter a small hanging valley littered with boulders. The way again divides. A large boulder bears a marker directing you half-left towards Collado de Eriste. (The alternative route goes to Collado de Sahun.) Cairns lead through a stony wilderness to gain the obvious saddle of Collado de Eriste. (About 3–3½ hours from Viados.)

From the pass a ridge of jagged teeth forms one wall of a deep hanging valley, while far-off the snows of the Maladeta can be seen.

Below to the north-east lies Lago Llardaneta; the way descends a steep slope of scree and grit, then near the foot of the slope veers left towards the lake, passing a small black tarn on the way. Pass round the left-hand (western) side of Lago Llardaneta (2680m) and at the far end go through a narrow gap which looks down onto a small gorge. Cross a stream issuing from the left and, keeping well to the right of the gorge, cross a rocky barrier to make a descending traverse of grass slopes where you locate a clear path heading down-valley. (Fine view of the Aguja del Forcau.)

Descending still, come to a stream where the path forks. Cross to the right bank and follow a line of cairns over a rough terrain of rocks, boulders and slabs to pass round the base of Aguja del Forcau; the valley a very long way below and the Esera hinting far ahead. Cairns continue to lead down, steeply in places, and eventually bring you to Refugio Angel Orus (about 1½ hours from the pass).

Route 120: Tour of the Posets Massif

Start/Finish:	**Benasque**
Time:	**3–4 days**
Accommodation:	**Mountain huts**

On this short tour mountain walkers have an opportunity to discover the many different faces of the massif without having to resort to climbing. That being said, the section which crosses the mountains from Viados to Refugio Angel Orus and on to Eriste, should not be attempted by those inexperienced in wild-country travel unless accompanied by someone who is. Each stage is fairly short, thereby leaving plenty of time to explore the valleys through which you wander.

Day One: This stage leads from Benasque to Refugio de Estos and is described as Route 116. Allow 4–4½ hours.

Day Two: Crossing Puerto de Gistain (2603m) the route goes from the Estos hut on the northern side of the Posets, to Viados in the valley of the Cinqueta de Añes Cruces which flows down its western side. Allow 4–4½ hours for this stage, details of which are given as Route 118.

Day Three: The hardest section of the tour, this crosses Collado de Eriste (2970m) to link Viados with Refugio Angel Orus for a five-hour day. See Route 119 for a full route description. Strong walkers could combine this stage with the following short section to Eriste and Benasque.

Day Four: An easy, mostly downhill stage completes the circuit. Descend from the Angel Orus hut into the bed of Valle de Eriste on a clear path, and join the dirt track at Puente de Espiantosa. Walk down the track to Puente de Tramarrius where you leave it, cross the bridge and then take a footpath on the right bank of the valley stream down to Eriste in the Valle del Esera. Cross the Esera by a bridge just upstream of Eriste and walk into the village of Anciles, and from there on a minor road to Benasque (about 3 hours in all).

PICO DE POSETS (3375m)

By reputation the summit of Posets has the finest view of the Pyrenees by virtue of its great height and central position in the chain. The big sprawling mass of the Maladeta certainly looks very fine to the east, while numerous peaks jostling for superiority to the west are dominated by Monte Perdido and beyond, more to the north, the Vignemale. Immediately below lies an area of great charm offering a taste of rewarding exploration.

Route 121: Refugio de Estos (1835m) – Pico de Posets (3375m)

Grade:	**F** (*voie normale* via the Coma de la Paúl)
Distance:	**6 kilometres**
Height gain:	**1540 metres**
Time:	**5½–6 hours**
Equipment:	**Rope, ice-axe, crampons useful. Safety helmet advised.**

The lovely Estos Valley on the north side of the Posets massif

This, the standard route to the second highest summit in the Pyrenees is not difficult, but because of loose rock there are potential dangers to beware of. On leaving the hut descend to the Estos stream, cross on a makeshift log bridge and follow a path leading off to the right. About one kilometre from the hut the path branches left to gain height up the hillside towards an obvious glen opening to the west. The path winds below the twin peaks of Aguja de La Paúl and Tuca de La Paúl, then enters the lower reaches of the glen known as Coma de La Paúl.

Rise through this short valley, keeping to the centre to reach the clear saddle of Collado de La Paúl at its head. The steep little glacier that once led to the pass has almost completely disappeared; when Packe first came here it extended right down the glen.

Having gained the pass cross through to the south side onto the shrinking Glacier de Posets and bear right to reach the East Face of the mountain. This is climbed by way of an obvious chimney, or narrow gully and, as with many similar features of these mountains, is not so much difficult as threatened by stonefall. (There are several possible gullies of ascent, all with the same danger.) Beware of parties above you, and also of dislodging stones onto those below. The chimney opens onto the North Ridge. Turn left and scramble along the ridge to the summit.

Route 122: Refugio de Estos (1835m) – Pico de Posets (3375m)

Grade:	**AD inf. (by the South-East Arête)**
Distance:	**6 kilometres**
Height gain:	**1540 metres**
Time:	**6 hours**
Equipment:	**Rope, ice axe, crampons useful. Safety helmet advised.**

The South-East Arête is the short ridge which faces the climber emerging through the Collado de La Paúl. An interesting route, it offers a pleasing alternative to the standard East Face chimney ascent above. It also makes a viable descent route which, when taken following the *voie normale*, concludes an interesting traverse of the peak.

From Collado de La Paúl (Route 121) cross the glacier to find a steep and obvious gully of ascent which leads directly from the ice onto the ridge itself. Turn right at the top of the gully to climb a couple of initial pitches that require some delicate moves (two belay pegs in situ). Above these the ridge holds no real problems, other than that caused by the loose rock typical of the mountain, and leads without incident to the summit.

Other Routes:

The Ollivier guide (now hard to find) details more than twenty routes of ascent on Pico de Posets alone, which gives an idea of the tremendous possibilities that exist here. In addition there are plenty of other summits, faces and sharp aiguilles *(agujas)* within the massif that would keep an active climber or scrambler happy for a couple of weeks or more. And there are some interesting wild-country traverses that could be created by experienced mountain walkers.

Please note that the Editorial Alpina map cannot always be trusted to show the correct route of some trails, and an ability to 'read' the country will be a distinct advantage to anyone exploring this region.

The **VALLE DE BATISIELLES** and neighbouring **VALLE DE PERRAMO** are certainly worth exploring, as is the tarn-dashed **VALLE DE LOS IBONS** on the western side of the Batisielles ridge. It is possible to link these glens in one traverse, best started from **ERISTE**. This will take two days and you must be self-sufficient with food and tent. First go up the Valle de Eriste to the Pleta de Sallent (beyond the turn-off for Refugio Angel Orus described above), then climb roughly northwards to Lago de las Alforjas (2401m) high on the Valle de los Ibons. From here head eastwards over **COLLADO DE LA PIANA** (2660m) which gives access to the Valle de Perramo, then down to the lakes in Valle de Batisielles before dropping steeply to the Estos Valley.

Another interesting traverse of the massif could be made by following Route 121 from Refugio de Estos to **COLLADO DE LA PAÚL**, then breaking away from the Posets ascent route below the Glacier de La Paúl and descending to the **VALLE DE LOS IBONS**, and from there into the main **VALLE DE ERISTE**, which in turn leads to the Esera at Eriste village.

And there are, of course, many other options available. Each little sub-region of the massif has its own appeal and will demand more than a single visit.

MALADETA

Position:	Central Pyrenees, in Spain. East of the Posets massif and separated from it by the Valle del Esera.
Access:	By rail to Luchon (in France), then on foot via Hospice de France. By road via the Viella Tunnel, Vilaller, Castejon-de-Sos and Benasque. Benasque is reached by bus from Huesca via Barbastro.
Map:	Editorial Alpina 'Maladeta-Aneto' 1:25,000
Valley Base:	Benasque (1138m)

All our attention was taken up by a very majestic summit,' wrote Ramond de Carbonnières of his visit to the upper reaches of the Esera in 1787; '...seen in all its grandeur, covered with eternal snows, surrounded with large bands of ice, and overtopping every thing. It is the Maladetta, a mountain reputed inaccessible.'

The Maladeta is, however, far from inaccessible, and its considerable size contains a wide variety of routes. It's a splendid region of streams, cascades, glistening tarns and glacial pavements. In its hanging valleys there are nurseries of flowering plants, while the upper moat of the Esera was, until comparatively recent years, a valley of rare perfection.

The north-eastern slopes of the massif are dressed with four glacial remnants of the large bands of ice noted by Ramond over two hundred years ago. But shrunken though they may be, their drapery adds contrast to the rich vegetation of the lower slopes, while their icy ramps aid approach to the granite spine that forms the very backbone of the massif. This spine maintains an elevation of more than 3000 metres, culminating in Pico de Aneto, at 3404 metres the highest in the Pyrenees. On the south-western flanks the Maladeta is broken into a series of corries containing lakes, or lesser tarns, and the topmost slopes adorned with tiny icefields.

On 20th July 1842 a Russian officer, Platon de Tchihatcheff, succeeded in making the first ascent of Aneto with Albert de Francqueville and the guides Argarot, Redonnet and Ursule. Their route was a complicated one from the south-west, but Tchihatcheff made a second ascent four days later, this time across the Aneto Glacier; the route now adopted as the *voie normale*.

Road access has given the upper Esera increased popularity, but the effect has been to devalue its former pristine grandeur. Hopefully the designation of the *Parque Natural Posets-Maladeta* in 1994 will give the area the protection it needs. Private vehicular access is now restricted in the high summer season from a point about six kilometres above Benasque, with a shuttle bus service in operation as far as the roadhead just beyond the Plan d'Estan. Away from the road it is still possible for climbers and walkers to enjoy corners of solitude in and around the Maladeta massif. Routes offered below merely scratch the surface of possibilities, and those with an eye for the country will seize every opportunity to explore further.

Valley Base:

BENASQUE (1138m) lies some 18 kilometres downvalley from the Renclusa hut and is the nearest village for supplies. A road links it with the upper Esera on the northern side of the Maladeta, but note private vehicle restrictions in place during the main summer period. Benasque is the most important mountain centre in the Spanish Pyrenees with several hotels, apartment blocks, restaurants, shops, banks and post office. It has a tourist office and a Visitor Centre for the *Parque Natural Posets-Maladeta*. Some of its shops stock mountaineering equipment, maps, guidebooks and butane gas cartridges. A number of official campsites are dotted along the valley above the town.

Mountain Huts:

REFUGIO DE LA RENCLUSA (2140m) is a large, barn-like building on the northern slopes of the Maladeta not far from the original stone shelter used by 19th century pioneers. Owned by the CEC it can sleep 150 (14 in winter) and is open with a guardian from July until late September, during which time a full meals service is offered (Tel: 974 55 21 06). From the roadhead near Plan d'Estan a short walk of about

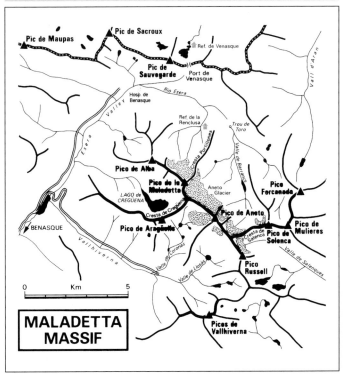

MALADETTA MASSIF

40 minutes leads to the hut. From the Hospice de France via Port de Venasque allow 5 hours.

REFUGIO FORESTAL DEL PUENTE DE CORONAS (1990m) is an unguarded shelter with room for about 20 people. Situated to the south of the Maladeta, below the Coronas corrie in the Vallhiverna, a dirt road leads directly to it.

Other Accommodation:

HOSPITAL DE BENASQUE (1750m) stands on the true left bank of the Esera where the upper valley makes a pronounced bend to the south-west. Served by road, this former pilgrims' hospice has been rebuilt and opened as a hotel-refuge with different grades of accommodation on offer. Open all year, meals provided (Tel: 974 55 10 52).

Route 123: Hospital de Benasque (1750m) – Ibon de Gorgutes (2313m)

Distance:	**3 kilometres**
Height gain:	**563 metres**
Time:	**1½–2 hours**

Ibon de Gorgutes is a moderate-sized tarn caught in a hollow under the frontier ridge by the Puerto de la Glera north of the Hospital de Besaque. The walk to it is popular with day visitors to the valley.

Cross the bridge over the Esera just below the Hospital and go up the hillside opposite to the roadhead (there are several minor streams to cross on the way). The path to Ibon de Gorgutes is signed from the end of the road. It twists uphill guided by green waymarks, crosses a stream and climbs among dwarf pine and alpine flowers. Though faint in places there are sufficient cairns and waymarks to keep you on route. About 20 minutes or so from the roadhead come onto a gently sloping shelf of hillside that provides an aerial view onto the Esera pastures and the Hospital de Benasque. Slanting across this shelf, now above the treeline, you gain a first view of the Maladeta's summit and glacier, as well as the double-pronged Forcanada at the head of the valley. To the north rocky bluffs hide from view a section of the frontier ridge, and it is behind these bluffs that the Ibon de Gorgutes is concealed.

After twisting uphill for a while the path then cuts straight up the left-hand side of a torrent which it eventually crosses on stepping stones. (At this crossing point an alternative path breaks left for the Puerto Viell, beyond which lies the Vallée du Lis in France.) On the east side of the stream the way angles across a grass-covered hillside, then along a natural line below the band of rocks. This long eastward slant is eventually checked with a cut back to the north-west, rising above two small tarns. You then climb a minor ridge that rims the rock bands previously skirted, followed by edging round the left side of a rocky dome to find the Ibon de Gorgutes, with the saddle of Puerto de la Glera just above.

Route 124: Hospital de Benasque (1750m) –
Forau dels Aigualluts (1990m)

Distance:	**6 kilometres**
Height gain:	**240 metres**
Time:	**2 hours**

At the eastern end of the upper Esera valley lies a delightful open plain with splendid views of Pico de Aneto – the Plan dels Aigualluts. Several streams flow into this plain, the most notable being that which drains the Aneto glacier. These streams unite at the northern end of the plain, then cascade into a large pit known as the Forau dels Aigualluts (or Trou de Toro) – see Norbert Casteret's classic *Ten Years Under the Earth*. Here the waters disappear, but instead of reappearing further down-valley, they actually tunnel north-eastward through the limestone Tuca Blanca de Pomero, and have their resurgence in the Vall de l'Artiga de Lin as the infant Garonne, one of the major rivers of south-west France which enters the Atlantic near Bordeaux.

From the Hospital de Benasque go down to the Esera stream but instead of crossing the bridge turn right and walk upstream on a narrow but waymarked path. After about 3 minutes cross on a log footbridge and continue upvalley. Soon come to a second log bridge and recross to the right-hand side of the Esera where the path rises up a grass slope between streams. In 10 minutes take the right branch where the path forks. (The left branch goes to the Port de Venasque/Portillon de Banos.) Cross a pine-topped bluff, beyond which you edge two or three shallow marshy troughs to reach the Plan d'Estan, literally the 'Plain of the Lake'. In the spring and early summer there may be a sizeable sheet of water here, but by mid-summer this has invariably disappeared without trace.

The path skirts the left-hand edge of the Plan with lovely views up to the cockscomb Cresta de los Portillones which separates the Maladeta and Aneto glaciers. Now curve right to join the unmetalled road from the Hospital de Benasque and follow it a short distance upvalley. It ends at a rough parking area known as Besurta (1915m), about 1 hour 15 mins from the start.

Cross the stream to the end of the track where the Renclusa path rises as a partially-paved trail and forks about 10 minutes later. Ignore

*Pico de Aneto, above
the Plan dels Aigualluts
(Route 124)*

the right-hand option (to the Renclusa – Route 125) and take the alternative path which rises gently for a few minutes, then more steeply with zigzags to gain a minor ridge. From this point a lovely view down the Esera can be enjoyed, while up-valley the twin peaks of the Forcanada look especially fine. The 'ridge' in fact serves as a ramp to gain a higher level of valley, and from it you then go down to another pastureland leading directly to the Forau dels Aigualluts. At the right-hand edge of the Plan dels Aigualluts stands a metal refuge (Cabane del Aigualluts) with room for about 8 – it is for emergency use only.

Route 125: Hospital de Benasque (1750m) – Refugio de la Renclusa (2140m)

Distance:	5 kilometres
Height gain:	390 metres
Time:	2 hours

An easy route to the Renclusa, this approach explores the mid-valley pastures of the Upper Esera before making the final ascent to the hut from the roadhead.

Follow Route 124 as far as the fork in the path 10 minutes beyond the Besurta roadhead. Take the right-hand option which twists easily in loops to gain the rocky basin in which sits the Refugio de la Renclusa, base for numerous climbs on the Maladeta massif.

Route 126: Hospice de France (1385m) – Port de Venasque (2444m) – Refugio de la Renclusa (2140m)

Distance:	**8 kilometres**
Height gain:	**1289 metres**
Height loss:	**534 metres**
Time:	**5 hours**
Additional map:	**IGN Carte de Randonnées No 5 'Luchon' 1:50,000**

The Port de Venasque (Portillon de Benasque) was used for hundreds of years for cross-border trade, by invading armies and, in the last century and more, by adventurous tourists making the classic outing from Luchon. Today holiday makers still drive to the Hospice de France and wander up to the Port to gain a view of the Maladeta before returning to Luchon; a worthwhile excursion for its own sake, as well as being the most obvious northerly route of approach to the Maladeta for climbers and walkers.

Note: The northern slopes below Port de Venasque are threatened by avalanche in spring and should not be tackled when there is any likelihood of unstable snow conditions in the narrow section of the valley leading to the Boums de Port, or between the refuge at the tarns and the pass itself. Under summer conditions, however, this approach demands little more than a steep walk.

The D125 road heads south from Luchon and winds for about 11 kilometres through the wooded Vallée de la Pique as far as the historic Hospice de France (large car park at the roadhead). Taxis are available for hire from Luchon and, unless you plan to hitch-hike, will probably be worth taking for this journey.

From the Hospice de France a path leads south-west across a stream and climbs, easily at first, then in zig-zags, through a narrow valley towards the frontier ridge. This ancient mule path needs no detailed description. It mounts to a high stony corrie in which three tarns are cradled (the Boums du Port). Beside one of these stands Refuge du Port de Venasque (2–2½ hours from Hospice de France).

Refuge du Port de Venasque (2249m): owned by the CAF, can sleep 16 and has a guardian from June to September when meals may be provided (Tel: 05 61 79 26 46).

Keeping well to the left of the tarns and the hut, the path skirts the base of Pic de la Mine, then gains height in zig-zags up scree to find the narrow cleft of Port de Venasque wedged between Pic de la Mine and Pic de Sauvegarde (3 hours). Across the depths of the upper Esera rises the Maladeta, while to the south-east the Mulleres group forms a barrier of peaks subordinate to the double-toothed Forconada.

Descend on a path that soon bears left to follow the lip of a grassy terrace, then zig-zags down into the valley a little beyond a shallow pool. The way is clearly defined and height lost quickly. At a fork in the path turn left and descend less steeply towards another pool (Lago de Villamorta on the map), then bear right to cross an idyllic area of dwarf pines and shrubs in the general direction of the Maladeta's northern corrie in which the Renclusa is to be found. A major path coming from the valley roadhead off to the right is soon reached. Follow this as it climbs in zig-zags directly to the hut.

Route 127: Hospice de France (1385m) – Pas de la Montjoie (2069m) – Puerto de la Picada (2470m) – Refugio de la Renclusa (2140m)

Distance:	**10 kilometres**
Height gain:	**1315 metres**
Height loss:	**560 metres**
Time:	**5½–6 hours**
Additional map:	**IGN Carte de Randonnées No 5 'Luchon' 1:50,000**

This route offers a longer alternative to Route 126. Should snow conditions prevent a crossing of Port de Venasque, it may be possible to use this option. However, avalanche is also a possibility on sections of this route.

Leave the Hospice de France on a broad path that leads upvalley towards woods at the entrance to the Vallée de la Freche. In the woods fork left where the path divides, and climb in zig-zags until you emerge from the trees onto a rolling pasture. Turn right at the junction with another path and continue round, climbing gradually on grass slopes above the valley. (Drifts of narcissi here in spring.)

Eventually Pas de la Montjoie is reached, marked with a frontier stone. Do not cross the pass, but bear right along the rising path which now assumes a southerly course towards the head of the valley. It crosses the frontier and descends on the south side of crags at the end of the west ridge of Pico de la Escaleta (Soum de l'Escalette), to join another path just below Port de la Escaleta. Bear right and traverse the southern slopes of Cap de la Picada, rising to the saddle of Puerto de la Picada (4 hours).

Cross the pass and lose height in an enclosed bowl until the full sweep of the Esera is seen below. Bear left, descending to the zig-zag path used on the descent from Port de Venasque. The final section of the route is the same as that described in Route 126 above.

PICO DE ANETO (3404m)

As the highest mountain in the Pyrenees Aneto is understandably popular. The *voie normale* makes an interesting ascent and summit views are immense. But lacking any distinctive peaks they are not as spectacular as some from lesser mountains. Yet the curving valleys with their glistening tarns look fine, and there are plenty of barely-seen ridges and spires as a backcloth to inspire dreams.

Route 128: Refugio de la Renclusa (2140m) – Pico de Aneto (3404m)

Grade:	**PD** (*voie normale*)
Distance:	**5 kilometres**
Height gain:	**1264 metres**
Time:	**5–5½ hours**
Equipment:	**Rope, ice axe, crampons**

The standard route to Aneto (Néthou to the French) crosses the rocky spine of Cresta de los Portillones to the Aneto Glacier. Of no great width, this spine forms a watershed, for the stream which drains the Maladeta Glacier on its western side flows through the Esera to the Ebro basin, and eastward to the Mediterranean. On the eastern side,

Aneto's glacier is a major source of the Garonne, the great French river that waters the vineyards of Bordeaux on its journey to the Atlantic.

Follow the path which leads from the Renclusa for about 100 metres before climbing steeply southwards up to the crest of the Portillon ridge. It is a well-marked route which rises to the ridge at a significant saddle, Portillon Inferior (2745m), from where you have a first sighting of Aneto's cone across the glacier. (In snow conditions, the route ascends south-south-westwards from the Renclusa to gain a snow saddle at about 2800m, then turns left to reach Portillon Superior.)

Although it is possible to descend from Portillon Inferior to the Aneto Glacier, avoid doing so as time will be wasted. Instead, bear right with the path as it climbs just below the crest, rises over Pico del Portillon Superior and comes to the gap of Portillon Superior. Descend the eastern side, scrambling down a short gully which is often rimed with ice early in the season. From the foot of the gully a trail heads roughly south-east towards Collado de Coronas, a deep col seen below the final cone of Aneto. Soon come to a low, natural pile of rocks, beyond which the glacier stretches at a regular angle. Early in the season the glacier will be snow covered, and safety precautions should be adopted (rope and ice axe essential) as you head across it towards Collado de Coronas.

Note: Later in the season (or if there is minimal snow cover and crevasses are open), the route does not cross at this point, but instead skirts round the base of the Portillon, then runs below the main ridge – but away from bergschrunds – to join the standard route at Collado de Coronas.

Packe tells of a lake that used to lie below the Collado until 'its waters...burst through the ice and found an outlet in August 1857.' Rising steeply above it a snow dome leads to the summit. Climb it, and at the top bear left to a portion of ridge that rejoices in the name of Puente de Mahoma (Pont de Mahommet). This is about 50 metres long, consists of great blocks of granite and presents no real difficulty unless coated with verglas. It provides an airy crossing and a satisfactory finale to the ascent. The summit, complete with large cross and statue of the Virgin, is just beyond it.

Allow about 3½ hours to descend by the same route.

Route 129: Refugio Forestal del Puente de Coronas (1990m) – Pico de Aneto (3404m)

Grade:	**F (via Valle and Collado de Coronas)**
Distance:	**6 kilometres**
Height gain:	**1414 metres**
Time:	**5–6 hours**
Equipment:	**Rope, ice axe, crampons**

Probably the easiest, and certainly the most direct, route from the Vallhiverna on the southern side of the massif. There's a small but steep glacier to tackle just below Collado de Coronas, but the majority of the ascent is over a rough terrain of rocks, boulders and scree.

From the unguarded forest hut walk downvalley until you reach the Rio Coronas where it flows from the north-east. The route now climbs through forest on the true right bank of the Coronas stream, gaining height in steep zig-zags until eventually emerging from the woods to arrive at a little tarn, Ibon de Coronas (2220m). Cross the stream just before the tarn and climb a very rough section of boulders. Cairns lead the way north-eastward until a sloping gully demands a more northerly course. Above this another tarn is reached. Pass round its northern bank and bear left (north-west) to reach the larger of the Coronas tarns at 2725 metres. From here head off to the right and climb to the small Glacier de Coronas which plasters the upper slopes of the corrie. Keeping more to its eastern side, climb steeply to gain Collado de Coronas, seen as a dip between the rocky features of Aneto to the right, and Cresta del Medio to the left. Once through the col join Route 128 to the summit.

Major Routes on Aneto:

There are many variations of routes, but two of the longest and finest are those that concentrate on the extensive ridge systems that continue either side of the summit. One involves a combination of **CRESTA DE SALENQUES** and **CRESTA DE TEMPESTADES**. Beginning at Coll de Salenques (2810m) the ridge is followed to Pico Margalida where the Tempestades crest is then joined. This is traced north-westwards to the summit of Aneto. The full route was first completed in 1934 (by Ollivier and Wild), and is graded AD sup. with rock pitches up to IV inf. About seven hours from Coll de Salenques to Aneto.

The other long route combines an ascent of **PICO DE LA MALADETA** with the complete **CRESTA DEL MEDIO** as far as Collado de Coronas, and continues above that on the ridge to Puente de Mahoma and Aneto's crown. This is a PD sup. route requiring 12–13 hours from the Renclusa and back.

PICO DE LA MALADETA (3308m)

Rising above the Renclusa hut, the Maladeta provides shorter routes than on Aneto but with more spectacular summit views. The Posets massif dominates the south-west; below lies the Cregüeña lake while above it, and to the west, the Cresta de la Maladeta looks superb. Aneto is seen clearly across its glacier and the Mulleres group given character by the Forcanada.

Route 130: Refugio de la Renclusa (2140m) – Pico de la Maladeta (3308m)

Grade:	**F** (*voie normale*)
Distance:	**3.5 kilometres**
Height gain:	**1168 metres**
Time:	**4 hours**
Equipment:	**Rope. Ice axe and crampons may be useful.**

From the Renclusa follow Route 128 to the base of the gully below Portillon Superior. Turn right and head south-west towards Collado Maldito, seen at the angle formed by the ridge of Cresta del Medio and the jutting southern ridge of Maladeta. About halfway along the Maladeta's southern ridge there are several gullies, short in length and of obvious qualities, which lead onto the ridge itself. Choose a gully to suit, climb it and cross to the western side. The granite is rough and delightfully firm. Turn right and wander along the ridge to the summit.

Pic de Paderna and its tarn, Maladeta massif

Route 131: Refugio de la Renclusa (2140m) – Pico de la Maladeta (3308m)

Grade:	**PD sup. (via Cresta de los Portillones)**
Distance:	**3 kilometres**
Height gain:	**1168 metres**
Time:	**4½ hours**
Equipment:	**Rope**

First climbed by Frederic Lung and the guides Castagne and Courrège on 9th August 1911, this is a more interesting route than the *voie normale* described above. Some rock scrambling involved (to grade II).

Follow Route 128 as far as Portillon Superior, cross beyond the gully and continue up the ridge which becomes broader above a 3-metre vertical slab (climbed with good holds), and reverts to an easy scramble. As the ridge dips to the level of the Maladeta Glacier note a tight chimney that has to be climbed (II) to regain the ridge above another steep pitch. At the top of the chimney turn right and continue along the ridge on firm granite blocks to gain the summit.

Other Routes in the Maladeta Massif:

Pico de la Maladeta and summits along the Cresta de la Maladeta to the north-west, have a variety of routes to them. From **LAGO DE CREGÜEÑA** a steep little PD route of 2–2½ hours heads up to the Maladeta via its western flank; another from the lake climbs **PICO LE BONDIDIER** (3185m) in about 1½ hours and is graded *Facile*. An extension of that climb takes in the summit of the Second Western Maladeta (**OCCIDENTAL 2**; 3220m) in just 30 minutes.

Using the Renclusa as a base both **DIENTE DE ALBA** (3136m) and the Third Western Maladeta (**OCCIDENTAL 3**; 3185m), linked by Collado de Alba, are easily gained by way of Lago de Paderna and the tiny Alba Glacier. Allow 3½–4 hours for the first, and an additional half-hour for the second.

PICO DE ALBA (3118m)

Pico de Alba is the most westerly of the massif's 3000 metre summits and makes a good acclimatisation scramble for newcomers to the Maladeta.

Route 132: Refugio de la Renclusa (2140m) –
Pico de Alba (3118m)

Grade:	**F** (*voie normale*)
Distance:	**3.5 kilometres**
Height gain:	**978 metres**
Time:	**3½ hours**

This ascent, first made in July 1868 by Henry Russell and Jean Haurillon, offers no serious difficulties, but ventures over some interesting terrain. Take the path leading from the hut in a south-westerly direction on the true right bank of the Renclusa stream. Cross to the opposite bank where a side stream (Torrente de Alba) joins the main one and follow a trail westwards to reach the little Lago de Paderna (2240m). Just beyond this is an even smaller tarn which is passed on the way up to a wide shelf of rock. On reaching the end of this descend to a chaotic region of boulders and cross with the guidance of cairns to mount rough slopes heading south-west to the broad ridge of Cresta de Tuca Blanca. Bear left and follow cairns heading due south towards Pico de Alba. From here Alba appears as a steep-walled peak, but as the edge of the little Alba Glacier is reached, a cairn marks the base of a gully offering an easy ascent.

Climb the gully on firm granite to gain the ridge north of the summit. Cross over and scramble along the rough western slopes below the ridge crest, led by more cairns, until the final slopes are mounted by a series of ledges and large granite blocks.

PICO FORCANADA (2881m)

The Forcanada is a fine double-pronged peak standing above the Valleta de la Escaleta in the extreme south-eastern corner of the upper Esera. First climbed by the young poet Alfred Tonnelle on 1st August 1858, the mountain offers an interesting scramble, although its rock is notoriously loose.

Route 133: Refugio de la Renclusa (2140m) –
Pico Forcanada (2881m)

Grade:	**PD** (via Collado Alfred)
Distance:	**8 kilometres**

Height gain:	981 metres
Height loss:	240 metres
Time:	5–5½ hours
Equipment:	Rope

Descend to the valley, bear right and walk up to the Forau de Aiguallut and Plan de Aiguallut beyond, then climb to the Escaleta glen. A path, then a line of cairns, leads deep into the glen, passes a string of tarns below Pico Forcanada, then climbs south-westward to find another tarn. Beyond this cut off to the south-east over a rough terrain of boulders to gain Collado Alfred (2844m; 4 hours), a dip in the ridge between Turo de 3 Puntes and Cap de Toro. Splendid views of the Maladeta massif to the west, and of the Besiberri and Montardo peaks further east.

Cross through the col and descend left over a boulder tip, often with snow patches, then climb to a *brèche* seen south of the Forcanada's south summit. From the cleft climb the ridge to this first summit (2875m), drop down into the gap between it and the main, north summit, which is then reached by way of an obvious gully.

Selected Climbs from the Upper Esera:

Various minor peaks walling the Upper Esera give interesting, if modest, ascents, and because of their geographical position in relation to the higher mountains, reward with summit panoramas of some splendour. The following outline routes are merely a sample.

CAP DE TORO (2978m) and **TUC DE MULLERES** (3010m) to the south of Pico Forcanada are reached by little more than a long walk, yet both offer fabulous views over the south-eastern flanks of the Maladeta massif and, across the Noguera Ribagorzana, to the Besiberri massif and a vast sea of peaks and hinted valleys. Approach to both summits is initially the same as that to Collado Alfred (Route 133). Good visibility is necessary because of an almost featureless region of glacial pavement. Allow about 4½ hours for Cap de Toro, 5 hours for Tuc de Mulleres from the Renclusa.

Nearby **PICO DE SOLENCA** (Pic de Salenques; 2990m), west of Tuc de Mulleres, is also worth ascending. Approached through the Valle de Barrancs by way of a col between Pico de Barrancs and Solenca itself, the summit can be gained in about 5 hours from the Renclusa, or 5½ hours via Valleta de la Escaleta.

On the frontier crest **PICO DE SALVAGUARDA** (Pic de Sauvegarde; 2738m) rising west of the Port de Venasque, has long made a popular tourist's excursion from the Hospice de France. Following the death of Archdeacon Hardwicke from a fall on the mountain in August 1859, a path was cut up the grassy flanks from the Port de Venasque and a toll of one franc levied on all who used it. The path is still there, the tax man is not. The normal route rises easily from just below the pass (Spanish side) and gains the summit in about 45 minutes. Views are even more extensive than from the Port de Venasque. An interesting scramble ascent may also be made direct from the pass along the ridge itself. (Not for the inexperienced.)

East of the Port de Venasque stands **PICO DE LA MINA** (Pic de la Mine; 2707m). Climbed much less frequently than its neighbour, it enjoys views every bit as interesting as those from Salvaguarda. The normal route climbs to the ridge just west of the summit and is more strenuous than the Salvaguarda path. There are also broken gullies to explore by scramblers (beware falling stones). The summit is broad, flat and featureless.

Situated in the north-west corner of the upper Esera **PICO DE SACROUX** (2676m) enjoys one of the finest views in all the Pyrenees. The south-east ridge offers a PD inf. route of about 4½ hours from the Renclusa. The ridge is gained at Port de la Glera (2367m), which is reached from the Hospital de Benasque (see Route 123). From the pass climb the ridge direct, turning one or two rock gendarmes on the right above the steep North Face. The summit is reached at the top of a broken, but broad final ridge. An alternative and easier route heads straight up snow slopes of the hanging valley above Lago de Gorgutes to reach a point just south of the summit. Grade F.

Selected Climbs from the Vallhiverna:

Less frequented than the Esera, the Vallhiverna which drains the southern flanks of the Maladeta massif, is nonetheless a charming glen and a favourite of both Packe and Russell in the 19th century. At its head several tarns lie in deep corries. Above rise attractive peaks, while the valley is lush with pines and extravagant alpine flowers.

Forming the south-eastern cornerstone of the valley **PICOS DE VALLHIVERNA** (3067m) offers a pleasant route via Coll de Vallibierna (2720m). Charles Packe and Captain Barnes, with Firmin Barrau as guide, made the first ascent by this route in 1865. From the Coronas refugio allow about 4–4½ hours to the summit (Grade F). The route leads into the cirque at the valley-head in which the Lagos de Vallibierna are cupped, then strikes up to the col overlooking Valle de Anglos to the east. From the col an easy ridge is then followed south-westward to the summit. Views of the southern slopes of the Maladeta massif are particularly fine.

West of Picos de Vallhiverna **TUCA ARNAU** (2820m) and **TUQUETA BLANCA DE VALLHIVERNA** (2790m) both offer easy ascents, while **PIC DE LLAUSET** (2910m) to the south, and separated from it by Collado de Llauset, is another summit that could be 'bagged' in the same outing. Allow 30 minutes from Collado de Llauset.

Route 134: Plan de Campamento (1460m) – Lago de Cregüeña (2657m)

Distance:	**4 kilometres**
Height gain:	**1197 metres**
Time:	**4 hours**

Like a huge teardrop cupped in the cirque formed by the Maladeta's extensive ridge systems, Lago de Cregüeña is the third largest (in terms of volume) of all lakes in the Pyrenees. From a camp or bivouac on its wild shore a number of climbing routes are made possible, and as a destination for walkers it provides a rewarding, if demanding, steep approach.

In the Valle del Estos, about 8.5 kilometres upstream of Benasque, the level pastureland of Plan de Campamento is popular with campers. An unguarded shelter nearby, Refugio de Pescadores, offers basic accommodation for those without tents. The walk begins at Puente de Cregüeña below the San Ferrer waterfall where a sign indicates the start of the trail heading east into forest.

The path is clear and well-trodden from the start. It climbs steeply in places through forest, then out to more open countryside, remaining on the northern side of the Cregüeña stream (true right bank) to its source at the lake itself. A number of 3000 metre summits project from the high ridges that contain it.

Selected Walking Tours from the Upper Esera:

The upper Valle del Esera and its tributary glens offer innumerable outings for walkers of all degrees of commitment. The following are just a few ideas.

A 6-hour tour of the **VALLES DE REMUNE** and **LITEROLA**, two glens that drain into the Esera just west of the sharp eastward bend of the upper valley, makes a long walk through quiet but attractive countryside. Highlights are the tarns that nestle in the wild inner heart of the valleys, and the crossing of Portal de Remune (2831m) which links the two. (Editorial Alpina map 'Posets' at 1:25,000 will be needed for the Literola section of this walk.)

Another 6-hour tour that takes in several mountain tarns is that which links both the **VALLE DE BARRANCS** and **VALLETA DE LA ESCALETA** at the extreme south-eastern end of the Esera's valley. First head up the Valle de Barrancs from Plan de Aiguallut, aiming towards Coll de Salenques, then bear left (east) to cross the rough granite ridge which leads to the Mulleres group, where you descend a broad glacier pavement to the lovely tarns that lie beneath Pico Forcanada.

By a combination of **COLL DELS ARANESOS** (2455m) below Pico Forcanada, and **PUERTO DE LA PICADA** (2470m) under the frontier ridge north of the Renclusa, a long and strenuous day's tour can be made by linking the Upper Esera, Valleta de la Escaleta, Vall de l'Artiga de Lin and Vall de Pomero in one grand circuit. By use of the unguarded Refugio Forestal del Pla de l'Artiga this circuit could be turned into an easy two-day tour.

Finally, a four-pass circuit via the Hospice de France, which of course involves twice crossing the frontier ridge, makes another very strenuous day out for energetic mountain walkers. From Plan d'Estan climb over the **PORT DE VENASQUE** by a good path and descend steeply to the Hospice de France. From the Hospice bear right and then follow directions given for Route 127 back to the Esera by way of **PAS DE LA MONTJOIE, PORT DE LA ESCALETA** and **PUERTO DE LA PICADA**. Splendid views are to be enjoyed from many points on this walk.

AIGÜESTORTES WEST –
BESIBERRI MASSIF

Position:	**In Spain. East of the Noguera Ribagorzana and south of Vall d'Aran.**
Access:	**From the west, on foot from the Viella Tunnel; from the north via Arties or Salardu, and from the south by way of Caldas de Bohi. Buses go as far as Bohi in the Noguera de Tor's valley from Pont de Suert.**
Maps:	**Editorial Alpina 'Val d'Aran' 1:40,000 and 'Vall de Boi' 1:25,000. IGN Carte de Randonnées No 6 'Couserans-Cap d'Aran' covers most of the region in one sheet at 1:50,000**
Valley Bases:	**Arties (1144m), Salardu (1268m), Bohi (1282m)**

The *Parque Nacional d'Aigüestortes i Estany de Sant Maurici* extends eastward from the valley of the Noguera Ribagorzana to enclose a series of landscapes of raw beauty. In a battleground of boulders, countless attractive tarns smile a benediction. High granite plateaux create a bewildering geography, giving birth to valley systems whose waters pour from one level to another in cascade after cascade. Cliffs rise smooth-faced from hidden tarns like misplaced fjords, while the big peaks seem to hold back as if reluctant to welcome the climber.

Packe had a taste of the area's possibilities in 1867 when he made a brief exploration, during which he climbed one of the Besiberri peaks and found scope 'for that spirit of discovery; which we can scarcely hope to evoke, among the higher, more difficult, but more trodden peaks of the Alps and the Pyrenees.' Russell too scrambled here, but his heart lay further to the west and it was left to men like Schrader and Gourdon to unravel its deeper mysteries.

It's a marvellous region for the hardened mountain walker, climber and scrambler. Any number of meandering tours could be dreamed by those inspired by a sense of exploration, while those who enjoy a day's scrambling on little-touched peaks will not go away disappointed. There are several wardened huts, but since the district is now designated National Park, wild camping is officially prohibited except in the peripheral zone, and even there you should first obtain a permit from the nearest village – although in practice if you choose your site with care and leave no trace behind, it's unlikely that you will be bothered by officialdom.

The highest peaks form a bold containing wall of around 3000 metres along the western rim: Besiberri Nord, Como lo Forno, Pic d'Avellaners and Pic dels Soldats (Pic de la Torreta). Besiberri Nord sends out ridges to the north-west and north-east, effectively creating a barrier to a wonderland of tarns that drain northward to the Vall d'Aran. The longer of these two ridges, the north-easterly (known as the Serra de Tumeneja), includes such summits as Pa de Sucre, Tumeneja Nord, Pic de Monges and Montardo; this last-named being a major cornerstone and superb viewpoint.

East of the Besiberri wall rise the jagged summits of the Agulles de Travessani, a bristling crest on a ridge that divides the headwaters of the Noguera de Tor from the Circ de Colomers, whose tarns and innumerable pools soak away north to the Vall d'Aran and the Riu Garona (Garonne). Country east of the Circ de Colomers is described in the following section: Aigüestortes East, which contains the original core of the *Parque Nacional d'Aiguestortes i Estany de Sant Maurici.*

Valley Bases:

ARTIES (1144m) provides access by way of the Val d'Arties to country north and west of Montardo. Nestled below the main road through Vall d'Aran, it has a few hotels, restaurants, a shop and a campsite just below the village, but it is really too far from the Besiberri region to serve as a useful base, other than for motorised visitors concentrating on the northern slopes.

SALARDU (1268m) lies a little over two kilometres upvalley of Arties and, after Viella, is the most important village in Vall d'Aran. There is plenty of accommodation in hotels, a youth hostel, in the 300-year-old Refugi Rosta (open July–September; 50 places, Tel: 973 64 53 08)

The Néouvielle region is noted for its many tarns, Routes 101–110

Approaching Pont de Mahomet, Pico de Aneto, Routes 128, 129

Granite and tarn region, Estanys Tort de Rius, Route 138 and High Route 18

The Sotllo tarns below Estats, Punta N.O., Route 153

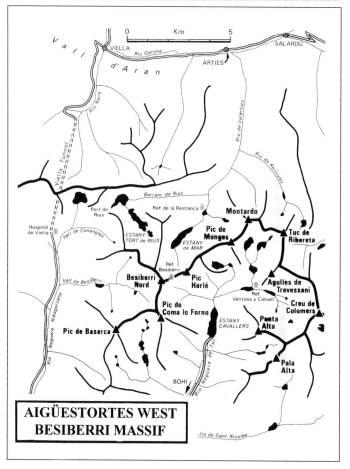

AIGÜESTORTES WEST
BESIBERRI MASSIF

and the CEC's Xalet Juli Soler i Santalo which has about 100 beds (open June–September, Tel: 973 64 50 16) Salardu has a few shops, restaurants and two banks. From the village narrow roads lead into the valleys of Aiguamotx and Riu de Ruda to give access to the Colomers and Saboredo regions respectively.

BOHI (1282m) or BOI, is situated about nine kilometres from the road-head in the valley of Noguera de Tor and stands at the entrance to the tributary glen of St Marti. A small but developing village noted for its 12th-century Romanesque shrine, it has several places offering overnight accommodation, plus restaurants, shops, bank and a National Park office (Casa del Parc Nacional) in the main square. Caldas de Bohi, further north on the way to the roadhead, is a spa with luxury hotel accommodation. Between Caldas and the Cavallers dam there's a free camping area just beyond the Park's information/control booth. Jeep taxis ferry visitors from Bohi to the control booth, although out of season it's possible to drive to the base of the dam and park there.

Mountain Huts:

REFUGI D'ESTANY LLONG (1985m) is managed by the National Park on the cross-country GR11 *variante* route between Bohi and Espot, and is situated at the western end of Estany Llong below Portarro d'Espot. Open with a guardian from mid-June to the end of September, when meals may be provided, it can sleep 53. Self-cooking is possible at this hut (Tel: 973 69 61 89). A metalled road, served by Jeep taxi, approaches through Valle de Sant Nicolau (begins about two kilometres south of Caldas de Bohi), followed by a walk of about an hour.

REFUGI VENTOSA I CALVELL (2220m) is reached by a walk of about two hours from the Cavallers dam at the roadhead above Caldas de Bohi, and is located just to the north of Estany Negre. Owned by the CEC, officially it has places for about 80, and there's a guardian in residence from 25th June to the end of September, when meals may be provided (Tel: 973 29 70 90).

REFUGI DE BESIBERRI (2826m) is a small, unguarded bivouac shelter with only basic facilities, perched in a dramatic setting just below the north-eastern ridge of Besiberri Nord. It could sleep about 10 in an emergency.

REFUGI DE LA RESTANCA (2010m) can accommodate 80 in its dormitories and has a guardian in occupation during the summer season. The hut is owned by the Federacio d'Entitats Excursionistes de Catalunya (FEEC) and is reached in about 45 minutes from Pont de Rius in Val d'Arties (Tel: 608 03 65 59).

REFUGI DE COLOMERS (2100m) stands beside the dammed Estany Major de Colomers, is owned by the FEEC, and has a guardian usually between mid-June and late September (Tel: 973 25 30 08). The hut can accommodate 30, but there's another refugi nearby that is permanently open with basic facilities only. Refugi de Colomers is reached from the north by way of a long, narrow road and dirt track through the valley of the Riu Aiguamotx, followed by a steep uphill walk of about half an hour.

REFUGI SANT NICOLAU (1630m), otherwise known as **BOCA SUD**, is located in the valley of the Noguera Ribagorzana just south of the Viella road tunnel, and is used by HRP trekkers travelling east from the Maladeta region. Open all year, 40 places, meals provided (Tel: 973 69 70 52).

Route 135: Estany de Cavallers (1782m) – Refugi Ventosa i Calvell (2220m)

Distance:	4 kilometres
Height gain:	438 metres
Time:	2 hours

The huge dam blocking the southern end of Estany de Cavallers above Caldas de Bohi effectively marks the Tor valley roadhead. Cars may be parked immediately below the dam wall. The walk to the hut begins on the eastern side of the dam.

A clear, well-trodden path leads along the eastern shore of the lake, and at its far end goes up boulder slopes into the pastures of the Riu Malo plain. Keeping to the true left bank of the stream for a short way, the path then crosses to the west bank on a simple footbridge, and heads in broad loops up a hillside of grey granite slabs to the north-east. Cairns and worn patches of path wind onward through a rocky terrain to reach the hut set high above Estany Negre on the edge of some wonderful wild country.

Route 136: Estany de Cavallers (1782m) – Refugi de Besiberri (2826m)

Distance:	4.5 kilometres
Height gain:	1044 metres
Time:	4–4½ hours

As mentioned above Refugi de Besiberri is a simple bivouac hut at the base of cliffs lining the north-eastern ridge of Besiberri Nord. All cooking equipment, fuel and water will need to be carried up to it should it be your intention to spend a night there.

From the Cavallers dam take the path along the eastern side of the lake as far as the Riu Malo pastures at the northern end. Cross the stream to the west bank by a simple footbridge and head west into the mouth of a narrow glen drained by the Riu Malo. Keep on the north bank of the stream following a trail which climbs into the gorge-like valley. Cairns lead the way. Beyond a junction with another stream draining from the south-west a second gorge is entered. Continue to climb through it, sometimes in the stream itself, but then taking the north bank path again to reach a small tarn, Estanyet de Riu-Malo (2450m). This is probably the last opportunity to collect water. The view west, above a wild and jumbled terrain, is to Besiberri Nord, but to the north-west in a gap in the ridge may be seen the Besiberri hut.

Move round the right-hand edge of the tarn and go up a grassy gully (cairns) which leads towards the hut. Above the gully you scramble up a slope of granite-dust, rocks and scree, so to gain Refugi de Besiberri.

Route 137: Pont de Rius/Val d'Arties (1700m) – Refugi de la Restanca (2010m)

Distance:	**1.5 kilometres**
Height gain:	**310 metres**
Time:	**45 minutes**

Visitors with their own transport will find the quickest approach to the Restanca hut is via Val d'Arties which projects south of Arties in Vall d'Aran. If you don't have your own vehicle it may be possible to hitch a ride. The first four kilometres are surfaced, but thereafter it's a dirt road as far as Pont de Rius. A cableway rises from a hut nearby, and behind the hut you will find the start of the path to the *refugi*. It is clearly marked and climbs forested slopes without difficulty.

Route 138: Refugi Sant Nicolau (1630m) – Port de Rius (2315m) – Collado de l'Estany de Mar (2468m) – Refugi de la Restanca (2010m)

Distance:	11 kilometres
Height gain:	838 metres
Height loss:	458 metres
Time:	8 hours

This western approach is one of the great hut walks of the Pyrenees; a superb day's journey across a wonderland of granite boulders and dazzling tarns. The route is only treated to a brief description here, however, as it forms part of the Pyrenean High Route and as such appears elsewhere in this book in more detail. See High Route 18 below.

From the refugi at the southern end of the Viella road tunnel in the valley of the Noguera Ribagorzana, a track heads east into Vall de Conangles. From this break away onto a path among beech trees and gain height steadily to reach Port de Rius in about two hours. Fine views west to the Maladeta massif.

Just below the pass on its eastern side lies the dammed Estany de Rius. A trail leads round the northern shore, then heads south over grass and boulder hummocks to gain the lovely Estany Tort de Rius. Cairns continue the way south-east up to the Collado de l'Estany de Mar (4½–5 hours). Descend steeply to Estany de Mar, go round its eastern shoreline, and then descend further to another dammed lake, Estany de la Restanca.

Route 139: Vall d'Aiguamotx (c1900m) – Refugi de Colomers (2100m)

Distance:	1 kilometre
Height gain:	200 metres
Time:	30 minutes

For motorised walkers coming from Vall d'Aran the following approach is the most practical. The valley of Riu d'Aiguamotx stretches south of Salardu; a gem of a valley that rises in steps and is extravagant with wild flowers in spring and early summer. The narrow road into the valley is surfaced until a little way south of the Baños de Tredos hotel. (Camping is forbidden in the valley below the Baños, but above it there are numerous idyllic wild sites.) A dirt track extends beyond the surfaced road and, rough in places and no doubt damaging to car springs, rises in tight bends before veering round the hillside that forms the upper valley's western wall. At the top of a series of bends a signpost on the left of the track marks the start of the path to the hut. Cars are often seen parked alongside the track just before this signpost, but for those who value their vehicles, it is probably better to park some way below, where the dirt road crosses a stream.

From the signpost simply follow the path that climbs quite steeply to the dammed lake of Colomers, beside which you will locate the hut.

Walks and Climbs from Refugi de Colomers:

Set beside Estany Major de Colomers this hut is in an ideal position to make the most of the mountains, lakes and wild plateaux of the Circ de Colomers spreading to the south. The Circ contains nearly 50 tarns and is certainly worth exploring, and given a day or two of fine, settled weather, one could wander for hours on end collecting some extraordinary views.

GRAN TUC DE COLOMERS (2932m) forms a cornerstone, and may be reached by a long walk and scramble by the following outline route: south-east to Estany Obago, then continue up to several more tarns beneath the retaining wall of mountains to reach Portell de Colomers (2731m) in the north-east ridge of the Gran Tuc. From the pass bear right and follow the ridge to the summit (about 4 hours from the hut).

A recommended six-hour **TARN CIRCUIT** links more than 20 tarns and pools, first by heading roughly south-west from Estany Major, rising towards Creu de Colomers, then breaking away at Estany del Port to cross the eastern dividing ridge just north of Tuc del Podu (not south of it as shown on the map), descending to the northern end of Estany Cap de Colomers and continuing downvalley, tarn to tarn, until you arrive back at the hut.

Walks and Climbs from Refugi Ventosa i Calvell:

Used as a base for several days this hut offers a variety of excursions for both walker and climber. A close study of the map immediately

In the Circ de Colomers

produces sufficient ideas to prove the point, for whichever direction you look there are tarns and ridges and beckoning peaks. From day trips to multi-day forays into the inner wilderness, prospects are exciting. The following suggestions immediately spring to mind.

The jagged **AGULLES DE TRAVESSANI** north-east of the hut offer assorted routes. **CREU DE COLOMERS** (2894m) to the south-east makes a pleasing ascent of little more than 2½ hours by its *voie normale*. There's the 3014 metre Punta Alta, the high peak of **PIC DE COMA LOS BIENES** off to the south, that could be linked in a circular outing or, perhaps the finest of the area, the high, lonely ridge of **BESIBERRI** which dominates country to the west.

BESIBERRI NORD (3014m)

The graniteland of Besiberri is immensely attractive. Below its long north–south wall the slopes are rough and uncompromising. There's little vegetation. Tiny streams weave among the huge boulders, and only the occasional lizard disturbs an aura of apparent lifelessness. For those of us who love the wilderness, it's a magical place.

Route 140: Refugi Ventosa i Calvell (2220m) –
Besiberri Nord (3014m)

Grade:	**PD** (*voie normale* from the Riu Malo pastures)
Distance:	**5 kilometres**
Height gain:	**1164 metres**
Height loss:	**370 metres**
Time:	**6 hours**
Equipment:	**Rope. Safety helmet advised.**

Go down from the hut to the Riu Malo pastures above the northern end of the Cavallers lake. From the western side of the stream (true right bank) head into the mouth of an obvious narrow valley to the west through which the Riu Malo stream emerges, and follow directions given under Route 136 as far as Refugi de Besiberri.

Go left below the hut to skirt the lower ridge wall. About 100 metres south-west of the hut a broad crack invites ascent. Climb it and come to a series of terraces and simple slabs leading to the ridge at Point 2832m. Bear left and climb along the exposed ridge directly to the summit.

Note: An alternative, easier, way onto the ridge, is to go beyond the crack referred to above, as far as the trace of a path below an obvious col. Climb up to this col and bear left to gain the summit.

The summit of Besiberri Nord gives magnificent views, and from it the vast expanse of empty countryside spread out below at last appears to reveal a semblance of order. Out to the west the Maladeta massif provides another wild prospect.

Other Routes on Besiberri Peaks:

This long ridge has several worthy summits on it. Other than Besiberri Nord there's **BESIBERRI DEL MIG** (Besiberri Central, 3003m), **BESIBERRI SUD** (3030m) and **COMO LO FORNO** (3032m). This last may be climbed in five hours from the thermal baths of Caldas de Bohi, by a PD ascent. There's also a classic traverse of the ridge, starting from the Besiberri hut and going south to link all the summits. First achieved by Jean Arlaud's party in 1926, it requires a long day's effort.

Route 141: Tour of the Agulles de Travessani

Start/Finish:	**Refugi Ventosa i Calvell (2220m)**
Distance:	**12 kilometres**
Height gain/loss:	**914 metres**
Time:	**7½–8 hours**

A wonderful long day's walk, this circuit of the Travessani peaks reveals a series of wild, untamed landscapes, among the finest to be found in all these mountains. It should only be attempted in settled weather, for there are remote sections where signs of a trail are few and far between, and where good visibility will be required for route finding.

Leaving the hut follow a footpath heading north. This leads to Estany Travessani, a large and attractive lake below the Agulles. The path leads up grass slopes above the south-eastern end of the lake, over rocky bluffs and on to another tarn which you skirt well to the left, heading north. Cairns trace routes in assorted directions, and it is necessary to remember that you are aiming for Port de Caldes, which lies to the north-east.

Heading north-east now above and beyond the tarn, cairns and occasional stretches of trail take you over a succession of granite terraces, each one giving better and more extensive views than the last. Eventually the way swings eastward (well above Estany del Port de Caldes) near the head of the valley system, and brings you easily onto the saddle of Port de Caldes (2550m) where views overlook a land falling away to yet more tarns caught in an idyll of confusing ridges and grassy banks.

The continuing path heads east down the left-hand side of a hanging valley, passes well to the left of a small tarn, then more steeply to reach a stream flowing from the right. Follow this down-valley, first on its left bank, then on its right, all the way to the dammed Estany Major de Colomers. (Two huts here; one with a guardian, the other unattended.)

Follow a vague path to the southern end of the lake, keeping above the shoreline, cross a stream coming from the south-west, then break away to climb southward (cairns, then path) so to reach a fine tarn in a grassy bowl. The path goes round its western end, climbs grass slopes, then among more rocky terrain to gain another tarn. Go

Estany Negre below the Besiberri massif, seen from Route 141

left round its northern edge to locate a clear mule path heading south. This leads to a number of other tarns and pools, sometimes near the linking stream, sometimes well to the left of it.

Keep alert for cairns, for eventually you cross to the right-hand side of the stream and continue to climb southward until, a little over a kilometre short of the headwall of the valley, a shallow granite 'gully' comes down from the western mountains. Cairns lead along its southern shoulder towards the hint of a pass, which becomes more obvious as you gain height. The route then zig-zags up a stony depression to gain Port de Colomers (2591m). Magnificent views west over a huge drop dominated by the Besiberri wall.

A clear path takes you down the western side to a lovely high pastureland whose stream leads to a tarn which you pass on the right, then continue down from one step to another. The way is now led by an occasional cairn, by which you come to a small tarn above the larger Estany Negre. Go round the right-hand side of this, then down to Estany Negre. At its eastern end a path leads up a slope to reach Refugi Ventosa i Calvell once more.

Route 142: Refugi Ventosa i Calvell (2220m) – Refugi de Colomers (2100m)

Distance:	5 kilometres
Height gain:	330 metres
Height loss:	450 metres
Time:	3 hours

This very pleasant hut-to-hut walk is easy, yet superb views almost every step of the way give it a classic status. Part of the route is used on the high Pyrenean traverse (HRP) as well as the Spanish GR11. The route is decribed above as the first part of Route 141.

Route 143: Refugi Ventosa i Calvell (2220m) – Refugi d'Estany Llong (1985m)

Distance:	7 kilometres
Height gain:	550 metres
Height loss:	785 metres
Time:	61/2–7 hours
Equipment:	Ice axe sometimes useful

A long and taxing cross-country route between these two huts, it should not be attempted by inexperienced mountain trekkers. The climb to Coll de Contraig (2770m) is often on snow or ice, particularly early in the season, when an ice axe would be very useful. No detailed route description is given here. Simply descend from the hut to Estany Negre and follow the cairned route towards Port de Colomers (Route 141 in reverse) until you reach the second lake above Estany Negre, at about 2185 metres. A cairned route heads away from the southern end of this and leads south-east to Coll de Contraig. From the col descend past Estany de Contraig and follow its stream towards Valle de Sant Nicolau. The hut is found at the western end of Estany Llong.

MONTARDO D'ARAN (2830m)

A magnificent viewpoint, the easy ascent of Montardo is often made by trekkers heading from hut-to-hut.

Route 144: Refugi Ventosa i Calvell (2220m) – Montardo d'Aran (2830m)

Grade:	**F**
Distance:	**3.5 kilometres**
Height gain:	**610 metres**
Time:	**2–2½ hours**

From the Ventosa hut head north to reach the Travessani lake, pass round the eastern end and continue north following a confusion of cairns. (The route marked on the Editorial Alpina map, however, is correct.) Make towards the north-eastern end of Estany Monges on the trail to Port de Güellicrestada, but break away from this some 400 metres or so before the pass. Montardo d'Aran rises to the north-north-west and the ascent route goes up a rocky gully, then to a false summit at 2781 metres before gaining the true summit. (If you plan to continue to the Restanca hut, it is possible to descend the south ridge to Port de Güellicrestada.)

Route 145: Refugi Ventosa i Calvell (2220m) – Refugi de la Restanca (2010m)

Distance:	**5.5 kilometres**
Height gain:	**255 metres**
Height loss:	**465 metres**
Time:	**3½ hours**

Another fine hut-to-hut route, this one takes you via Port de Güellicrestada to the north-western side of the region, from which there is more lovely tarn-jewelled country to explore.

There are various ways of reaching Port de Güellicrestada from the Ventosa hut, any one of which will reward with tarns, bluffs of grass-capped granite and beautiful views. The pass is located a little west of north from the Ventosa hut, just below Montardo d'Aran (which is worth a diversion – see Route 144 above), and the Editorial Alpina maps suggest various options to it. Take whichever assortment of tarn-trails suit. Port de Güellicrestada (2475m) is reached in a little under two hours.

Descend to Estany Cap de Port and take the right-hand path at its far end. This leads down to the dammed Estany de la Restanca and the Restanca hut.

Routes from Refugi de la Restanca:

With a glorious wild landscape of granite peaks and sparkling tarns accessible from it, the Restanca hut has much to commend it to walkers and climbers. The following outline routes offer just a few suggestions.

MONTARDO D'ARAN (2830m) has already been treated to an ascent route from the Ventosa i Calvell hut, but is just as easily climbed from the Restanca. The route goes by way of Port de Güellicrestada, then north along an easily-scrambled ridge to the summit. Allow about 2 hours from the hut.

A tough crossing of the **SERRA DE TUMENEJA** (the north-west ridge extending from Besiberri Nord) is possible for experienced mountain trekkers and scramblers, by either a pass west of Pic de Monges, or another between Pa de Sucre and Tumeneja Nord. This would lead down to Refugi Ventosa i Calvell and could be used as part of a two-day circuit.

A **WEST–EAST TRAVERSE** of the district, beginning at Restanca and ending at Refugi Colomers, is included as part of the High Route and is described elsewhere in this guidebook (High Route 19). But that route could be extended into a large circuit, by heading south from the Colomers hut into the Circ de Colomers and following Route 141 across Port de Colomers to the Ventosa hut, and continue from there via Port de Güellicrestada back to the Restanca for a long one-day, or easy **TWO-DAY**, **CIRCUIT**.

Perhaps the best of all circuits from Restanca, however, is that which goes south-west up to **ESTANY DE MAR**, climbs over Collado d'Estany de Mar and descends to the fabulous **ESTANY TORT DE RIUS**. From its northern end reach the outflow of **ESTANY RIUS**, bear right and follow an alternative trail back to the Restanca hut. A magnificent day's tour.

AIGÜESTORTES EAST – ENCANTADOS

Position:	**In Spain; east of the Besiberri massif and west of the Noguera Pallaresa. The northern boundary is Vall d'Aran.**
Access:	**From the west, on foot via Portarro d'Espot; from the east by road to Espot. There is no bus service to Espot, the nearest (Vall d'Aran–Pobla de Segur) passes about seven kilometres from the village. Southerly access is by a long walk from Capdella in Vall Fosca, reached by bus from Pobla de Segur.**
Maps:	**Editorial Alpina 'Sant Maurici' 1:25,000. The region is also covered by IGN Carte de Randonnées No 6 'Couserans–Cap d'Aran' 1:50,000**
Valley Bases:	**Espot (1321m) and Capdella**

Forming a major part of the *Parque Nacional d'Aiguestortes i Estany de Sant Maurici*, this region of wild jutting peaks, remote corries and rock-girt tarns has been aptly termed the Sierra de los Encantados (the Enchanted Mountains) after the showpiece of the area, the gaunt grey monolyth-with-two-heads, the Gran and Petit Encantat, that rise above the dammed lake of Sant Maurici.

Despite National Park status many of the lakes have been dammed for hydro-electric purposes. Bulldozed tracks have been scarred through the wilderness, and on the park's boundary at Espot there's a growing winter sports industry. However, an 'air of unquiet mystery' still prevails for those with a will to seek it out, and climbers and walkers have some magnificent country to explore where neither the hydro engineer nor holiday-making crowd has yet left a scar. Wander the more remote trails and you'll discover a harsh landscape, seemingly devoid of all life, where screes and rugged crags dominate, where hardly a scoop of snow remains in summer to soften the overall wash of grey. Then a corner is turned, a ridge gained and an explosion of lush vegetation greets the eye to woo the senses. A lake gleams in the sunlight; an alpine meadow dazzles with flowers, or a pine glade fills the air with its resinous perfume. And every horizon bears its fenceposts of stone.

The Encantat peaks are Siamese twins – erring shepherds turned to stone, in the mythology of the Pyrenees – that burst out of the deep green conifer woods overlooking Estany de Sant Maurici as though transported there from a luxurious Dolomite valley. The promise they offer to climbers is well-founded. The Gran Encantat has one or two modest lines, but the Petit Encantat has no easy route and should not be attempted unless a high standard of rock work can be sustained. Here, as in many other massifs of the Pyrenees, it was Henri Brulle whose pioneering instincts led to advanced routes being opened.

But neither climbers nor walkers should visit this region with only the Encantats in mind. The enchanted mountains have much to offer and the best advice that can be given is to pack a rucksack with supplies for several days, take a rope (if it's climbing you're after) and an open mind and wander into the chaotic glens and untouched cirques...and explore them for yourself.

Official campsites are found on the outskirts of the park. Wild camping is not allowed within the National Park itself, but there are a few mountain huts that provide accommodation and food. In reality, individual tents are seen in various idyllic spots, and it may be that the authorities turn a blind eye to discreet campers. If you should choose to camp wild, here as anywhere else, make sure you leave no rubbish, light no fires and be careful not to pollute streams and lakes.

Valley Bases:

ESPOT (1321m) has grown into a busy, if still small, tourist resort and ski station. It has several hotels, bars, restaurants, supermarkets and a National Park information office. There are three campsites on the approach to the village. Jeep taxis may be hired to ferry visitors the ten kilometres of metalled road that leads from Espot to the Sant Maurici lake. Taxis also continue as far as Refugi d'Amitges.

CAPDELLA, in the lovely, sparsely-populated Vall Fosca (30 kilometres north of La Pobla de Segur), provides a base for a southerly approach to the National Park, although it's still a half-day trek to the valley-head if you're without transport. (Capdella is served by a once-a-day bus from Pobla.) The village is on two levels with accommodation available in Hostal Leo (Tel: 973 66 31 57) and Hostal Monseny (Tel: 973 66 30 79). There are no shops, restaurants or banks, so go well prepared.

Mountain Huts:

REFUGI JOSE MARIA BLANC (2350m) is situated south-west of Espot on the east bank of Estany Tort de Peguera. Owned by the CEC it has room for 40, and a guardian is usually in occupation from mid-June to mid-September (Tel: 973 25 01 08). The hut is reached by a walk of about 3–3½ hours from Espot.

REFUGI DE COLOMINA (2395m) is the southernmost hut in the Encantados region and is found by Estany Colomina, south-west of Tuc de Peguera. Owned by the FEEC, this wooden chalet set in superb high mountain scenery can accommodate 40 and has a guardian from mid-June to the end of September when meals may be provided (Tel: 973 25 20 00). It is reached by a walk of about 2½ hours from the Sallente dam above Capdella, or from Refugi J.M. Blanc via Collado de Saburo.

REFUGI ERNEST MALLAFRÉ (1950m) stands snug among pines at the foot of the Encantats, just 15 minutes' walk from the roadhead at Sant Maurici. A small hut, owned by the FEEC, it is open with a guardian from mid-June to the end of September, and can sleep 36 (Tel: 973 25 01 18).

REFUGI D'AMITGES (2380m) enjoys fine views, not only of the Agulles d'Amitges that rise just to the north, but of the Encantats too, off to the south-east and looking rather insignificant from here. The hut is owned by the CEC and has 80 beds, with room for 12 in the winter annexe next door. There is usually a guardian from June to mid-September (Tel: 973 25 01 09). It is reached in 1½ hours from Sant Maurici by way of a rough dirt track.

REFUGI DE SABOREDO (2200m) is not strictly within the Encantados region, being located north of the watershed, but is included here as it forms an important link with the Amitges hut by way of Port de Ratera. Refugi Saboredo is reached in about 5 hours from Salardu in Vall d'Aran (see Aigüestortes West section), by way of the lovely valley of Riu de Ruda (Editorial Alpina map 'Val d'Aran'), or by

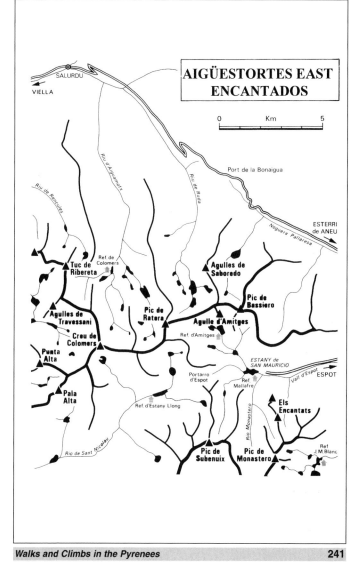

vehicle through the valley followed by 1½ hours walk. It belongs to the FEEC, is permanently open with a guardian in summer, and can accommodate about 20 (Tel: 973 25 30 15).

Route 146: Espot (1321m) – Refugi J.M. Blanc (2350m)

Distance:	**6 kilometres**
Height gain:	**1029 metres**
Time:	**3–3½ hours**

Walk upvalley on the road that winds above the village heading for the ski area of Super-Espot. When the road crosses the Riu Peguera immediately above Espot (at Pont de Fames) leave it and take a rough track (signpost GR11) heading to the right along the west bank of the stream. The track soon becomes a narrow path which climbs, steeply in places, among trees and shrubs. It remains almost all the way on the west bank and is soon high above the stream. There are several strands of path, all cairned. They lead through trees, over a couple of pastures, and sometimes climb very steeply to reach eventually the dammed Estany de Lladres (2026m) about two hours from Espot. Here you join a dirt road (also from Espot – possible to hire a jeep taxi from the village) and follow it upvalley heading south-west. In another hour or so you come to Estany Tort de Peguera and its small dam. The track passes within a few paces of the hut, which is found on the eastern shore.

Walks and climbs from Refugi J.M. Blanc:

With nearly three dozen tarns or pools accessible from this hut, it will be evident that there is a certain charm about the headwaters of the Riu Peguera. Add to that the curving, continuous line of peaks that form long grey walls to the valley, with tufts of pine, green hillocks and alpenroses clawing scarlet over boulders below, and explorations take on a special appeal. A number of summits can be reached from a base at the hut.

PALA SUDORN (2689m) is a modest peak south-east of the hut which shows the contradictory nature of the wild Vall de Peguera to the more gentle and rolling country on the eastern side of the ridge. It may be reached by way of a gully which seams the face of neighbouring Pala d'Ereixe, followed by a stroll along the ridge linking the two (about 2–2½ hours).

At the head of the valley **PIC MAINERA** (2905m) commands views not only of the Peguera glen, but also down to the attractive tarns and rocks of Colomina to the south-west. A climb of three hours or so will lead to the summit by way of Estany Cap del Port and the Cresta de Mainera.

Rising west of Refugi J.M. Blanc **PIC DE MONESTERO** (2878m) gazes onto the lower Encantats peaks which, from here, take on a different appearance from that normally seen from the north. A route goes to the pic by way of the tarns of Cabana, Escondits and Amagat (linked by a common stream), then up to a col on the mountain's short north ridge (two hours).

A magnificent tour of the lakes could be made, coupled with the crossing of **COLL DE MONESTERO** (2710m) – from which Pic de Monestero's summit may be gained by a 40 minute diversion – then descend to the lovely Monestero glen and wander down to Estany de Sant Maurici and Refugi Mallafré. This trek would take about six hours, plus extra time for Monestero's summit.

GRAN ENCANTAT (2747m)

The Gran Encantat is the south summit of the twin peaks known also as the *Sierra de los Encantados* or *Montagnes Enchantées* which look so appealing when viewed across the waters of Sant Maurici. It was first climbed in August 1901 by the team of de Negrin, Romeu, Ciffre and the guide Bernard Salles, who was noted for his enormous strength.

Route 147: Refugi E. Mallafré (1950m) – Gran Encantat (2747m)

Grade:	**PD (via the Central Gully)**
Distance:	**2 kilometres**
Height gain:	**797 metres**
Time:	**4 hours**
Equipment:	**Rope, safety helmet advised**

Refugi Mallafré is reached by a 15-minute walk from the dam at Estany de Sant Maurici. An alternative walking route from Espot leads along the GR11, which takes a high path on the south side of the metalled road.

Leaving the main path head south through the woods between the hut and the Encantats, then scramble up a steep slope to gain the base of the obvious Central Gully which clefts the North-West Face of the mountain. It is subject to stonefall, and caution is therefore advised on the ascent. The gully is not difficult, despite appearances, and is climbed by a series of rough slabs and broken rocky sections up its right-hand side. On gaining the Enforcadura, the cleft where the two summits strike out as individuals, scramble up the final 50 metres to reach the south summit. This final section offers no great problems and the scramble should be uncomplicated as there are traces of previous ascent routes as a guide.

Note: The easiest route of descent is by way of the Monestero Gully which cuts the south-west flank of the mountain and has less likelihood of stonefall.

Selected Routes from Refugi E. Mallafré:

A slightly easier route on the **GRAN ENCANTAT** than that of the Central Gully, is by way of the **MONESTERO GULLY**. Also graded PD it demands more 'scrambling' than rock climbing, although the final stretch from the head of the gully to the summit itself is the most demanding. The gully is located on the south-western flank of the mountain and is reached by way of the little Valleta Seca.

The **PETIT ENCANTAT** (north summit of the mountain; 2738m) has an AD route which extends from the Central Gully, described in Route 147. From the Enforcadura, where the two summits divide, the route descends for about 20 metres, then climbs by way of short gullies, ledges and a vertical pitch to the top.

PIC DE PEGUERA (2982m) is the highest peak in the Encantados section of the National Park and forms the south-eastern cornerstone of the delightful Vall de Monestero. The summit may be gained by a walk through the glen as far as Estanys de Monestero, from where you branch off to the south-east, so to gain Coll de Monestero, then head to the right along the ridge to the summit (about 3½ hours). Another route, graded PD, continues upvalley beyond Estanys de Monestero, then crosses boulder slopes to gain Coll O de Peguera (beyond which lie the Colomina lakes). From the col bear left and climb first the south summit, then the main summit of Pic de Peguera in about four hours.

A five-hour walk links the Mallafré hut with **REFUGI J.M. BLANC** by way of the **COLL DE MONESTERO**. Another, but shorter, hut-to-hut walk follows a section of the GR11 *variante* across **PORTARRO D'ESPOT** (2423m) west of Estany de Sant Maurici and descends easily to **REFUGI D'ESTANY LLONG** in the Valle de Sant Nicolau.

Route 148: Estany de Sant Maurici (1900m) – Refugi d'Amitges (2380m)

Distance:	**3.5 kilometres**
Height gain:	**480 metres**
Time:	**1½ hours**

This approach to the Amitges hut is straightforward for it takes a jeep track all the way from the roadhead at Sant Maurici. The track rises in bends above the Sant Maurici dam (a footpath short-cut can be taken at the start), then rises steadily in a north-westerly direction, giving occasional views back to the Encantats looking grand above the lake. Passing Estany de Ratera the track forks. Take the right-hand option, soon to gain height more steeply in a very wild and rocky landscape. In about 1½ hours from the roadhead you reach the hut, set above Estany

Agulles d'Amitges in the Encantados region (Route 149)

Gran. Above it to the north soar the dramatic Agulles d'Amitges, while from the bluff behind the hut superb views overlook jutting peaks of the south.

AGULLES D'AMITGES (2665m)

From the track approaching the Amitges hut one is suddenly struck by the formidable appearance of the twin Agulles *(aiguilles)* stabbing skywards from a rather desolate terrain. They rise a little north of the hut and are separated from the Saboredo watershed ridge by a low-slung col. The southern peak offers one or two exposed climbs on its South Face of varying qualities and grades of difficulty, while the northern, and higher, of the Agulles gives a modest ascent from the west, with some dramatic views from the summit.

Route 149: Refugi d'Amitges (2380m) – Agulle d'Amitges (2665m)

Grade:	**PD (northern aiguille, *voie normale*)**
Distance:	**1 kilometre**
Height gain:	**285 metres**
Time:	**1½ hours**
Equipment:	**Rope useful**

From the hut continue along the track a short distance until it ends. Cross the stream which links the two main tarns and work a way to the north on a vague path (some cairns) over a rough hillside leading into a corrie west of the Agulles, which from here assume a very different aspect. The path skirts the base of the *agulles*. Shortly after the obvious gap between the two peaks has been reached, a mini gully cuts the broken face of the northern peak. There are marks of previous ascents in grassy patches in the gully. Climb it without undue difficulty to reach a vegetated terrace leading right to a vague saddle giving fine views onto the exposed eastern side. From here one short pitch on firm granite up a broad crack leads directly to the summit block.

Other routes on the Northern Agulle:

The short north ridge of this peak has some exposed sections, but the West Face has several moderate gullies giving access to it, mostly of a maximum grade of PD, but the subsequent ridge scramble to the summit should not be underestimated. Another possibility is to go to the obvious saddle at the northern end of the ridge and climb south along its entire length.

Route 150: Estany de Sant Maurici (1900m) –
Refugi de Saboredo (2200m)

Distance:	7 kilometres
Height gain:	630 metres
Height loss:	330 metres
Time:	4½ hours

Useful for walkers departing the region who need to reach Salardu and Viella in Vall d'Aran for homeward journeys, or for those who wish to explore another side of the mountains, this route is convenient and full of interest.

Follow Route 148 as far as the fork in the track just beyond Estany de Ratera. Take the right-hand (Amitges hut) track and then break away from it to the left on a trail that works its way through the little Vall de Ratera heading north-west (some cairns and marker poles) alongside a stream to reach Estany d'Obago de Ratera. Beyond this the slope steepens, and eventually brings you to another tarn, Estany del Port de Ratera with the Port de Ratera (by which you gain access to the Circ de Saboredo) seen clearly to the north-north-east.

From the pass descend in a northerly direction to follow the course of a stream (left bank) which eventually flows into the first of a string of lakes. Skirt the left bank of two lakes, and when you reach the dam at the northern end of the second of these, descend north-westward to the hut, which is seen near yet more little tarns. (It's a 3½-hour walk from here down through the valley of Riu de Ruda to reach Salardu. See Aigüestortes West section for details of Salardu.)

From Refugi d'Amitges:
Descend the track towards Sant Maurici, but break away from it at the first sharp left-hand bend to cut across country heading south-west, soon reaching Estany d'Obago de Ratera. Now bear right and follow the path up through Vall de Ratera on the route described above.

Refugi d'Amitges with Els Encantat in the distance

Access to Refugi de Saboredo from Salardu:

A short distance upvalley from Salardu in Vall d'Aran, at a ski area on the main road above Tredos, a track breaks away and forges into the valley of Riu de Ruda. It follows the river on its west bank for much of the way; lush green pastures with craggy peaks of the Circ de Saboredo ahead. After about three hours or so of walking the track ends, and a trail climbs into the Circ, reaching Refugi de Saboredo in 4½–5 hours from Salardu. (See Editorial Alpina map 'Val d'Aran'.) From the Saboredo hut to Refugi de Amitges (Route 150 in reverse) allow about three hours.

Route 151: Capdella (Embalse de Sallente: 1790m) – Refugi Colomina (2395m)

Distance:	**5 kilometres**
Height gain:	**605 metres**
Time:	**2 hours 15 mins**

This is a varied and interesting hut approach on the southern rim of the National Park. Refugi Colomina stands in another tarn-sprinkled region, most of these tarns having been harnessed for hydro-electricity. In fact it was the electricity company that built the hut in the first place, and part of this route to it follows sections of narrow-gauge track left behind by the hydro-engineers. Several tunnels have to be wandered through, and a torch could be useful.

The road from Capdella continues upvalley for several kilometres before climbing to the large dam at the southern end of the Sallente reservoir. There are parking spaces at the eastern end of the dam wall, and a cableway at the northern end of the lake. The walk begins from the car park where a sign indicates the path to Colomina. At first stony, the way rises in long loops to the east and soon comes onto a grassy hillside where the path unravels into several braidings which reunite about 40 minutes from the start. Here you come onto a crossing track along which lies the old railway.

Bear left and immediately enter a tunnel, about 20 metres in length. A second tunnel, about the same length, is entered shortly after. The way then contours round the hillside and goes through a 100 metre tunnel. Emerge to a stonier landscape and curve round to a fourth (and final) tunnel, this one about 30 metres long. After this the track leads directly to the dammed Estany Gento (2142m), about one hour from the start.

Cross to the west side of the dam where there is a large new building and the cableway from the Sallente reservoir. Beyond the téléphérique the path slopes briefly downhill and forks. Take the upper trail, another rocky path which improves and is almost paved in places. It rises into increasingly wild country, and about 40 minutes from Estany Gento leads to another section of rail. (A diversion left will bring you in 5 mins to the long Estany Tort.) For Colomina turn right along the track for about 120 metres, then take a waymarked path slanting above the line. The path twists uphill to gain a broad rocky shoulder from which you can see the refugi ahead, just to the right of another dam wall. Skirt below the dam and then climb up to the hut. Ragged granite peaks gather round, with more lakes trapped below them.

Note: Just before reaching the hut another path cuts left to Collado de Saburo (for Refugi J.M. Blanc), and Coll de Paguera for Estany Sant Maurici above Espot.

ESTATS – MONTCALM

Position:	On the frontier between the valley of the Noguera Pallaresa and Andorra
Access:	From Llavorsi in the Spanish Noguera Pallaresa a road heads into Vall de Cardos towards Tavascan; another cuts away from that heading north-east through Vall Ferrera. It is possible to drive to within a short walk of Refugi de Vall Ferrera. From the north road access is via Vicdessos and Auzat to Mounicou. There is no public transport within 20 kilometres of Mounicou (in France), or Tavascan (in Spain).
Maps:	Editorial Alpina 'Pica d'Estats–Mont Roig' 1:40,000 IGN Carte de Randonnées No 6 'Couserans' and No 7 'Haute-Ariège–Andorre', both at 1:50,000 IGN TOP 25 series no: 2148OT 'Vicdessos, Pics d'Estats et de Montcalm' 1:25,000
Valley Base:	Àreu (1220m) in Spain, Vicdessos (708m) in France

Vall de Cardos and Vall Ferrera are two of the least-visited valleys in the Spanish Pyrenees, the mountain country of Haute-Ariège the most deserted on the French side of the watershed. But in that little-known lies much of the area's charm.

Deserted hamlets decay beneath the snows of winter and crumble in the summer heat. Land that once sustained a few remote farms has gone back to nature. Streams dance from tarn to tarn, and while the French slopes clutch damp forests, those on the Spanish side draw a balmy warmth and simmer with a wealth of aromatic plants. At the head of Vall de Cardos hydro engineers have been active, but as Robin Fedden noted of another corner of the Pyrenees in his classic book, *The Enchanted Mountains:* 'When the landscape has been scarred, the surgeons leave. Vegetation does its work. These valleys are not ruined.'

In the forests, it is claimed, wild boar, lynx and a few brown bear still roam unhindered, while on the heights self-contained walkers and climbers may spend days of activity in high summer and have the mountains virtually to themselves. Mont-Roig (2864m) lords it over the western part of the region, while Pica d'Estats and its neighbour Montcalm are the easternmost 3000-metre peaks in the Pyrenees. Standing astride the frontier they may be reached from either French or Spanish valleys; Vall Ferrera being the nearest. The nearest valley-based accommodation is still a long way from the main peaks, but a hut on either side of the frontier provides overnight shelter for climbers and walkers.

There is no intention here to reveal all the secrets of the region, but a handful of sample routes and suggestions will be made for those who are drawn by its quality of remoteness. The High Route makes a traverse of the south-facing slopes, and details of that route will be found elsewhere in this book (High Routes 21–24).

Valley Bases:

ÀREU (1220m) is the highest sttlement in the Vall Ferrera, an attractive medieval hamlet with one hotel, Hostal Vall Ferrera (Tel: 973 62 90 57), and two cheaper lodgings at Casa Gabatxò (Tel: 973 62 43 22) and Casa Xicot (Tel: 973 62 43 48). Àreu has a campsite and shop.

VICDESSOS (708m) on the French side of the mountains is about 11 kilometres from Montcalm as the crow flies. It has two hotels, a campsite and a tourist office (Tel: 05 61 64 82 59), but about 10 kilometres upvalley **MOUNICOU** has a *gîte d'étape* (Tel: 05 61 64 87 66).

Mountain Huts:

REFUGI DE CERTASCAN (2240m) overlooks the lake of the same name high above the right arm of the upper Vall de Cardos. Owned by the FEEC it can accommodate 40 people, and has a guardian from mid-June to mid-September when meals may be provided (Tel: 973 62 32 30). It is possible to drive to within a 40 minute walk of this hut.

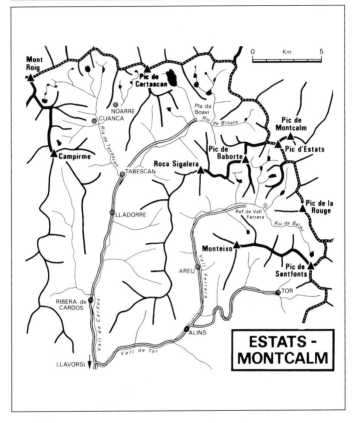

REFUGI DE BABORTE (2438m) is an unmanned metal hut provided by the UEC and with an official sleeping capacity of 16. Although basic, blankets are provided and there's an emergency first aid kit. The refuge stands on a bluff in the Circ de Baborte (south-west of Pico d'Estats) above Estany de Baborte. On the HRP, it may also be reached by a trail that climbs out of Vall Ferrera near Pla de Selva.

REFUGI DE VALL FERRERA (1940m) is the standard base for climbs on Estats, and is situated near the head of the valley on the lower slopes of Pic d'Areste. Owned by the FEEC it can sleep 35 and has a guardian from May to late September (Tel: 973 62 07 54). To reach it, follow the 4WD dirt road upvalley through Vall Ferrera. This ends shortly before Pla de Bouet where a signpost puts you on a path leading directly to the hut in about 20 minutes.

REFUGE DU PINET (2242m) has been built on the north-west slopes of Pic de Montcalm by the CAF. It can sleep 50, and there's a guardian from June to end of September (Tel: 05 61 64 80 81).

Route 152: Tavascan (1167m) – Refugi de Certascan (2240m)

Distance:	13 kilometres
Height gain:	1073 metres
Time:	5 hours

Since much of this route is along a dirt road, walkers with their own transport could make considerable time savings by driving to the end of the road and taking a short walk from there. The full walk, however, leaves Tavascan heading north-east up the right-hand branch of the valley on a dirt road that follows alongside the Noguera de Lladorre. After about six kilometres a track, signposted Certascan-Romedo, breaks away to the left and climbs in long sweeps up the hillside. Walk up this track for about three kilometres, then leave it for a trail on the left which rises to Estany de Naorte, from where you continue to Refugi de Certascan, found on the south side of its lake near the outlet stream.

Routes from Refugi de Certascan:

The uncomplicated two-hour ascent of **PIC DE CERTASCAN** (2853m) west of the lake makes an obvious goal. This is reached by way of **COLL DE CERTASCAN** followed by a 40 minute ascent of the mountain's southern ridge. Also using Coll de Certascan the attractive small hamlet of **NOARRE** is accessible in about four hours from the hut following part of a *variante* of the HRP. From Noarre a descent of just under two hours will take you back to **TAVASCAN**. Both the ascent of Pic de Certascan and cross-country walk to Noarre require good visibility.

Eastwards from the hut a tour of the **ROMEDO TARNS** will reward with a splendid five-hour day. There are about a dozen tarns and smaller pools gathered in a cluster below the frontier ridge that can be linked in a meandering circuit.

Various optional stages of the HRP can be used as onward routes from Refugi de Certascan. One goes by way of the Romedo lakes, crosses **PORT DE L'ARTIGA** on the frontier ridge, and descends to the *gîte d'étape* at **MOUNICOU** in about 7½ hours. Another descends to the Noguera de Lladorre roadhead at **PLA DE BOAVI**, enters the Sellente Valley, crosses **COLL DE SELLENTE** and from there reaches **REFUGI DE BABORTE**. An extra three hours from the Circ de Baborte takes walkers south-eastward below Pica d'Estats to **REFUGI DE VALL FERRERA**. Route descriptions for the stage Pla de Boavi to Refugi de Vall Ferrera are given under High Route 23.

PICA D'ESTATS (3143m)

Estats and its neighbour Montcalm came under the scrutiny of the military surveyors, Coroboef and Testu, during the 1820s and were climbed by them in 1827. The large cairn built on Montcalm's summit to aid their cartographic surveys is still there. The ascent of both peaks makes a fine day's outing from the south.

Route 153: Refugi de Vall Ferrera (1940m) – Pica d'Estats (3143m)

Grade:	**F (via Port de Sotllo)**
Distance:	**6 kilometres**
Height gain:	**1203 metres**
Time:	**5 hours**
Equipment:	**Ice axe, crampons useful**

From the hut take the path which rises steeply to the north, then forks at 2190 metres. Go left to skirt slopes of grass and shrubs and enter the Sotllo Valley, now heading north-west and sloping down into the glen. This is delightful with soft grassy levels split by meandering streams, with tarns, cascades and the huge face of Estats leering from the north. The path, which is clearly defined, wanders along the western side of the glen.

Note: At about 2150 metres on the west bank of the Sotllo stream, immediately before the first 'plan' is reached, a little cave, with straw and a rough wall at its entrance, would make a handy bivouac shelter.

Rise through the valley to reach the cirque at its head (Coma d'Estats) by way of a series of natural steps. From Estany d'Estats (2471m) go up scree and patches of snow to the obvious pass of Port de Sotllo in the ridge linking Pica d'Estats with Pic de Sotllo, about 400 metres above the tarn. Go through the pass and descend briefly on the northern side on snow, before making a traverse to the right, crossing a rib of rocks and more snow slopes until a point is reached between, and some way below, Montcalm and Punta N.O. Climb the steep slope of snow to reach Coll de Riufred (2978m). Bear right and climb easy slopes to gain the secondary summit of Punta N.O. (3126m), then the main summit of Pica d'Estats.

A fine panorama includes the tangled ridges of the Encantados region out to the west, Andorran peaks off to the south-east, and north where French valleys reveal their remoteness. Best of all are views down into the lovely Sotllo glen, all gentle pasturelands and a dazzle of tarns. As an alternative descent follow directions given below as Route 154 – but note that rope and safety helmets are advised (Grade PD sup.).

Route 154: A Traverse of the South-East Ridge

Grade:	**PD sup.**
Distance:	**13 kilometres (round-trip from Refugi de Vall Ferrera)**
Time:	**9–9½ hours**
Equipment:	**Ice axe, crampons, rope, safety helmet advised**

Estats's south-east ridge forms the frontier between France and Spain. Bearing two more 3000 metre summits and several over 2900 metres, it then descends to lesser altitudes and heads southward to Andorra. Linking some of these peaks on a traverse makes an interesting alternative route back to the valley. Beware, however, of loose rock.

Follow Route 153 to the summit of Pica d'Estats (five hours), then go down steeply along the narrow and broken south-east ridge. Three rock gendarmes are passed before reaching Sotllo (3115m) whose summit is marked with a concrete pillar. Continue without undue difficulty over Punta S.E. and Point 3004m. From this last summit descend on steep slopes of loose rock in a sweeping traverse to reach a little tarn (Estanyet, 2880m) cupped south of Point 3004m by great slopes of scree.

From Estanyet go down towards the southern end of Estany d'Estats, picking a route over broken rocks and scree, and at the lake join the path heading down-valley on the right bank of the stream.

PIC DE MONTCALM (3077m)

Montcalm is invariably included in any ascent of Pica d'Estats from which it is separated by the saddle of Coll de Riufred (2978m). It lies wholly in France; a broad, bald unattractive mountain when seen from Estats, it so dominates the valleys of Ariège to the north, that for centuries it was locally believed to be the highest in the range. The only ascent route given here is from the south, although Refuge du Pinet on the north-west slopes would be the obvious starting point for climbs from the French side.

Route 155: Refugi de Vall Ferrera (1940m) – Pic de Montcalm (3077m)

Grade:	**F (via Port de Sotllo and Coll de Riufred)**
Distance:	**5.5 kilometres**
Height gain:	**137 metres**
Time:	**5 hours**
Equipment:	**Ice axe, crampons useful**

Take Route 153 through Port de Sotllo and up to Coll de Riufred. From here bear left and wander up the wide southern shoulder of the mountain to reach the summit with its huge cairn. To gain Estats from Montcalm takes about 30 minutes.

Other Routes from Refugi de Vall Ferrera:

Rising to the west of Port de Sotllo is **PIC DE SOTLLO** (3075m), known to the French as Pic du Port de Sullo. This summit may be gained direct from the pass by a scramble demanding no more than about 30 minutes (4½ hours from the hut). To link Pic de Sotllo with Pica d'Estats by the joining ridge will involve moderate scrambling in and out of the Port; a total of about one hour, summit to summit.

A walking circuit combining the tarns below Estats and those of

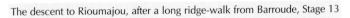
The descent to Rioumajou, after a long ridge-walk from Barroude, Stage 13

The Besiberri massif is seen from the route to Salardu, Stage 19

the **CIRC DE BABORTE** may be achieved by crossing two easy mountain spurs. First go up to Estany de Sotllo, then head east on a traverse of the southern slopes of Pic de l'Estany Fons to locate another tarn (Estany Fons). Now cross the northern spur walling the tarn to gain Estany d'Estats, climb west into the **CIRC DE SOTLLO** and cross Coll de Baborte (2618m) to the Circ de Baborte, making the descent to Vall Ferrera from there. This fine cross-country walk is likely to require about 6½–7 hours.

South-east of Refugi de Vall Ferrera the valley is blocked at the **CIRC DE BAIAU**, a charming pastureland set in a horseshoe of attractive peaklets that form the Andorran border. All this countryside is worth exploring; either from the hut itself, or from a wilderness camp.

ANDORRA

Position:	South of the watershed, and east of the Estats/Montcalm massif
Access:	By road from France through the valley of l'Ariège to Pas de la Casa and Port d'Envalira, or by rail to l'Hospitalet-pres-l'Andorre and bus from there. From Spain a road (with bus service) heads north through the Valira's valley from La Seu d'Urgell.
Maps:	IGN Carte de Randonnées No 7 'Haute-Ariège– Andorre' 1:50,000, Editorial Alpina 'Andorra' 1:40,000 or M.I.Consell General 'Valls d'Andorra' 1:50,000
Valley Bases:	Most of Andorra's towns and villages offer accommodation and because of its compact size all valleys are accessible in varying degrees to motorised walkers and climbers (see below for details).

The little mountain-locked State of Andorra comprises an area of only 487 square kilometres (48,692 hectares) and consists of one long main valley, the Valira, which runs from the French port of entry in the north-east at over 2400 metres, to the Spanish frontier in the south-west corner at an altitude of about 850 metres. All commerce is centred on this valley with cheek-by-jowl hypermarkets in Les Escaldes and Andorra-la-Vella offering duty-free goods as the main attraction; all transit traffic must use the single thoroughfare and since the Valira is a narrow, steep-walled valley, congestion is inevitable. But from this main valley a number of ridges radiate like the spokes of a wheel, and between these ridges lesser valleys give access to hills and corries in which some of the country's former charm may still be experienced. While the Valira, with its main town of Andorra-la-Vella, has been sacrificed to the very worst aspects of Western greed and tasteless development, it is still possible to find corners of seclusion and great beauty in flower-decked pastures, and in those high nestling corries that have not yet been adapted for skiing.

Beginning in the north and travelling anti-clockwise the main valleys are as follows: Vall d'Incles, Vall de Ransol, Vall del Riu, Valira d'Ordino (Valira del Nord), Vall d'Arinsol and Vall d'Aos. South of the main Valira are the Madriu and Cortals glens, with minor river valleys, or deep gorges, scarring the steep-walled mountains on either side.

Many upper valleys have been developed for skiing, with all that the downhill school demands: mechanical tows, bulldozed pistes and large car parks. Tourism has replaced pastoral economies, although tobacco is still grown and shepherds are seen grazing their flocks on pastures trod by their ancestors when hiding from Saracen invaders. The modern smuggler, replacing the romantic Andorran of old, now drives expensive French cars, leaving mountain paths to walkers of other nations.

Andorra's mountains are not really climbers' mountains. Invariably they offer ascents demanding little more than a steep walk, though in several areas rock will be found on which to climb or scramble if desired. Climbers in Andorra will find routes on Puig de Roca Entrevessada at the head of Vall d'Arinsal, on Pic d'Escobes (2778m) on the frontier above the little Vall de Juclar, and also on the Pessons to the south-east.

These mountains are not high by Pyrenean standards. Not one reaches 3000 metres; the highest being Pic Alt de la Coma Pedrosa at 2964 metres which stands above Vall d'Arinsal. Most offer grassy ridgewalks of some charm, and an opportunity to traverse from valley to valley in long outings. In spring and early summer botanists are drawn by a profusion of alpine plants that swamp the valleys and clothe hillsides in a kaleidascope of colour.

Mountain Huts:
REFUGI DE COMA PEDROSA (2260m) is the only hut in Andorra with a guardian in summer (meals provided). It can accommodate about 70 people, and is located by the little Estany de les Truites to the south of Andorra's highest mountain (Tel: 376 32 79 55). Reached in about 1½ hours from Arinsal.

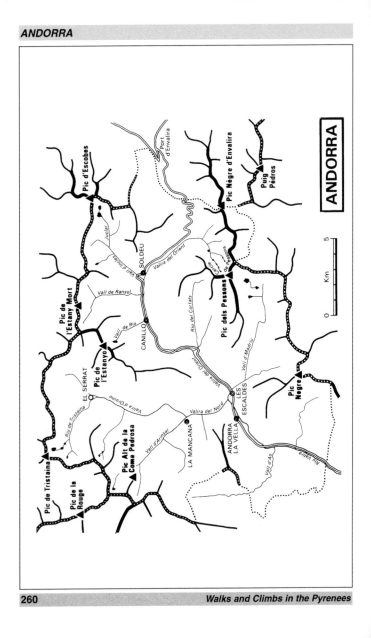

VALL D'INCLES

The glen which drains out of the hills above Soldeu, north-west of the Envalira, is a fine stretch of pastureland scooped between unpretentious mountain walls. One or two farms are situated in Vall d'Incles, and there's a campsite near the roadhead (Camping d'Incles 1875m; bar/restaurant and provisions) at the junction of two streams. That which flows from the east comes from Vall de Juclar, at whose head lie the two tarns known as Estanys de Juclar, below Pic d'Escobes (2798m). A *variante* of the HRP crosses Collada de Juclar above the tarns and, when used in conjunction with Col d'Albe, provides a useful, if strenuous, route of entry for walkers having arrived by train at l'Hospitalet or Mérens-les-Vals. The northern stream converging at Camping d'Incles is the Manegor, whose little glen has the Port d'Incles at its head. Beyond this pass, in France, lie the gleaming Etangs de Fontargente. Other tarns are caught in the hills that form the western wall of the valley, and beside the largest of these, Estany de Cabana Sorda, stands a small hut (Cabana Sorda 2295m) with room for about half a dozen.

Route 156: Camping d'Incles (1875m) – Collada de Juclar (2442m)

Distance:	5 kilometres
Height gain:	567 metres
Time:	2½ hours

Walk along a broad track heading east into Vall de Juclar on the south bank of the stream, then cross to the true right bank by a footbridge at about 1927 metres. The track becomes a climbing path that crosses and recrosses the stream on the way to the lower of the two Juclar tarns. This is reached at a dam at its south-western end. Bear right round the southern shore, then head between this and the next tarn and climb north-east along a trail that leads directly to the col, from which you look down into France onto more tarns, with Pic de Fontargente and Pic de Ruille projecting along a ridge ahead.

Other Routes from Vall d'Incles:

An extension of Route 156 can be turned into a grand six-hour circuit which visits **ETANG DE JOCLAR** on the northern, French, side of

Collada de Juclar, descends past more small tarns and reaches the rather basic Refuge de Garsan (1900m) in the Jasse de Pinet. From the hut turn south and rise to the **ETANGS DE FONTARGENTE**, then cross Port d'Incles in the frontier ridge, returning to Andorra with a descent to Camping d'Incles.

The ascent of **PIC D'ESCOBES** (2798m) via Collada de Juclar, Col d'Albe and the mountain's north ridge is made in 3–4 hours. Also using Collada de Juclar and Col d'Albe, 6–7 hours of cross-country trekking will lead to **l'HOSPITALET** by way of several tarns, a descent through the Jasse de Brougnie and the Siscar Valley on the HRP.

A crossing of **PORT D'INCLES** (2262m) to visit the **ETANGS DE FONTARGENTE** in France makes good use of a day too, but it would be possible to extend this into a long east-west trek (another HRP *variante* recommended only to experienced trekkers and in good weather) on the French side of the border, returning to Andorra at Port de Banyells above **EL SERRAT**.

VALL DE RANSOL

More narrow than that of Incles, Vall de Ransol is entered from the Valira at the village of Ransol, which has a few apartments and stands above the main road some two kilometres west of Soldeu. It is a valley to suit the flower specialist, as well as the walker planning a traverse of the valleys. A road projects into the glen for about four kilometres. Beyond and above it in the north-west, tucked beneath the frontier ridge, lie several small tarns, while Refuge de Pala de Jan (2218m) provides basic accommodation for about a dozen walkers. By crossing Coll de la Mina above the tarns access to Valira d'Ordino is gained. On the eastern side of the valley there are two ways of crossing into Vall d'Incles, both of which are options on the Pyrenean High Route.

Suggested Route from Vall de Ransol:

A **RIDGE-WALK** along the mountains that contain the valley in a horseshoe curve will reward mountaineers and trekkers experienced in scrambling with some fine views and interesting challenges. This can be a serious outing, for which clear settled weather is essential. Allow 7–8 hours for the route outlined as: Estanys de Ransol – Coll de la Mina – Pic de la Serrera – Pics del Mener – Pic de l'Estany Mort – Portella de Jan – Portelles and Pic de Queralb – Pic de la Passada – Punta de Querol – Pic del Cap d'en Tor – Vall de Ransol.

VALL DEL RIU

This short, narrow and steep-walled glen lies immediately to the west of Vall de Ransol and is entered by a trail that extends from Plan (els Plans), a huddle of buildings at the west side of Vall de Ransol's opening. One and a half hours of walking from Plan lead to Refugi de la Vall del Riu (2160m), another simple hut that could sleep about a dozen people. The glen does not reach as far north as the frontier with France, but is enclosed by ridges that splay out from Pic del Estanys de la Vall de Riu (Pic de la Cabaneta). A few tarns and pools are cradled by the undulations of the valley's western flanks, and may be reached by a pleasant walk of about three hours from Plan.

VALIRA D'ORDINO (VALIRA DEL NORD)

Disgorging into the main Valira at the fume-choked conurbation of Andorra-la-Vella and Les Escaldes, Valira del Nord is the longest of the northern valleys and, after the Valira itself, the one that has seen most development. Sections of the valley retain some of their former beauty; tobacco grows in the fields, and cattle graze pastures that in early summer are a mass of wild flowers. But at its head hillsides have been sacrificed to the ski industry. The Valira del Nord forks at La Massana (La Macana), with Vall d'Arinsal slanting off to the north-west while the main road continues roughly northward (north-east at first) as the Valira d'Ordino. At El Serrat streams converge from tributary glens. The road heads off to the north-west and climbs to the purpose-built ski resort of Arcalis (Ordino-Arcalis), but from this road too the popular Tristaina lakes are made accessible by a short walk (see Route 157). North-east and east of El Serrat trails head up into the high hills where there are two or three mountain huts, the busiest being Borda de Sorteny (1969m; 30 places) to the east, which is accessible in only ten minutes from a road that climbs from El Serrat. More up-market accommodation in Valira d'Ordino is available at La Massana, Ordino and El Serrat.

Route 157: Arcalis (1940m) – Estanys de Tristaina (2249m)

Distance:	**2 kilometres**
Height gain:	**309 metres**
Time:	**1–1½ hours**

The three Tristaina lakes lie one above another in a cirque crowned by Pic de Tristaina in Andorra's north-western corner. To the south the ski-slopes of Ordino-Arcalis have been cluttered with tows, but the Tristaina cirque remains delightfully untouched.

An extensive parking lot by the ticket booths of the Ordino-Arcalis chairlift (served by local bus) marks the start of this walk. Wander along the road a short distance beyond the ticket booths and at the first hairpin bend break off to the right on a minor road/track. In a few paces this crosses a stream, and 150 metres later you cut left on a narrow path. This climbs steeply up the hillside and leads to the same stream crossed below on the road. Stepping stones may be needed to cross here, then continue uphill to top a rise overlooking a rough grassy basin with two cascades pouring into it. This is a very flowery area in the spring and early summer.

The path is now rather faint, but a few cairns and occasional red spots serve as waymarks as the route makes for the 'saddle' ahead from which one of the waterfalls appears. There are several streams to cross, sometimes by stepping stones. After the first of these streams note the small shelter on the right – a domed hovel of stone roofed with turf.

As you progress towards the waterfall the path becomes more clearly defined, and you gain the saddle after 40 minutes. A signpost stands at a junction of paths. Bear right (the way ahead is to Port de Rat) and climb the steep hillside in a series of loops waymarked with yellow. About 15 minutes from the junction come onto the rocky ridge to discover the first of the Estanys (lakes) of Tristaina below – a lovely scene of lake, rocks, grass slopes and a curving wall of mountains which carries the Franco/Andorran border. Go down to the outflow stream and take the path on the right-hand side of the lake. This leads up to the second tarn in 15 minutes, and the upper lake about 15 minutes after that.

Return by the same path, and not by the alternative seen tracing the north side of the outflow stream, for this is thin and exposed and potentially dangerous where it crosses a series of narrow rock shelves.

Other Suggested Routes from Valira d'Ordino:

Using El Serrat as a base a day-long circuit is possible by heading north-east up the **RIALB VALLEY**, following the Riu de Rialb to its head beneath **PORTELLA DE RIALB** (Portella de Varilles; c2500m),

The second of the Tristaina lakes in early summer (Route 157)

then descending the far side of the pass through the glen drained by the **RIU DE VARILLES**. This brings you back to the road at El Castellar, three kilometres upvalley of El Serrat.

The ascent of Andorra's third highest mountain, **PIC DE L'ESTANYO** (2912m) is made from either El Serrat or Borda de Sorteny in about 4–5 hours. The route heads up alongside the stream flowing from Estany de Sorteny which lies below and to the west of the peak. The summit is reached by a steep haul from the lake to a point on the Cresta de l'Estanyo a little south of the peak itself.

A popular stage of the HRP traverses below the northern headwall of Andorra in an eight-hour day from El Serrat to Camping d'Incles, and may be followed as far as **COLL DE LA MINA** (3½ hours) on the ridge above Vall de Ransol.

VALL D'ARINSAL

Breaking away from Valira del Nord at La Massana, Vall d'Arinsal leads peak-seekers to Andorra's highest, Pic Alt de la Coma Pedrosa, and for long-distance trekkers a variety of passes leading over the mountains to both Spain and France. Arinsal has been transformed by high-rise apartment blocks and hotels, and comes alive in winter with its 12 ski lifts lacing crowds to the western slopes, but in summer it is still possible to find peace in the mountains that, though they may not be as attractive nor as dramatic as many found elsewhere in the Pyrenees, are not short of charm. Two huts serve the Coma Pedrosa massif: the unmanned Refugi du Pla de l'Estany (2060m), with places for about six, and Refugi de Coma Pedrosa (2260m), with 70 beds and a guardian in charge.

PIC ALT DE LA COMA PEDROSA (2946m)

Rising to the north-west of Arinsal, Coma Pedrosa is Andorra's highest peak; a large bald mountain cluttered with rocks and screes in its upper reaches, but lush with pastures, shrubs and trees lower down. The ascent makes for an enjoyable day's outing, and summit views include a wild and tangled landscape out towards the Estats-Montcalm massif and the forested Ariège. Eastwards and to the south-east, Andorra's heights and depths are spread in patterns of harvested meadow, shadowed hamlets and barren mountains. Spain's sierras disappear in a haze of blue.

Route 158: Arinsal (1467m) –
Pic Alt de la Coma Pedrosa (2946m)

Grade:	F
Distance:	5 kilometres
Height gain:	1479 metres
Time:	4 hours

During update research in the early summer of 2000 the route out of Arinsal was seriously disrupted by construction work. Suffice to say that you head upvalley from the centre of the village and go through a short road tunnel. On emerging from this remain on the road twisting uphill and follow GR11 waymarks, eventually turning west into the valley of the Riu de Coma Pedrosa a little over two kilometres from Arinsal.

The way cuts round to reach the stream, then comes to a delightful platform stepped naturally into the hillside, surrounded by trees and rocky bluffs and watered by meandering streams. Cross this area and climb steeply to a minor pass (2240m) opening into a lovely upper valley out of which rises the South Face of Coma Pedrosa (about 1½ hours from Arinsal). The Coma Pedrosa refugi is above to the left.

Go down to the marshy area beyond the pass and bear right to find a sloping grassy gully. There were neither cairns nor marked trails when I was last there, but the route is not difficult; merely arduous. Climb the gully, and at the top continue to reach the grassy shoulder of the mountain, at which point bear left to gain the south-east ridge. Then turn right and go up the ridge to the summit, which is marked by an enormous cairn.

For an alternative descent, thus making a traverse of the mountain, go down the ridge to the south for a short distance to reach a bare, wind-swept col, then bear right and make a long scree run to the tarn seen far below, all green and trapping echoes among its surrounding rocks. Go round the left-hand (south) shore and work down to the head of Pla de les Truites, led by cairns – Refugi de Coma Pedrosa can be seen beside the lake. Then eastwards down-valley to pick up the route of ascent from Arinsal.

Route 159: Via the South-West Ridge

Grade:	**F**
Distance:	**5.5 kilometres**
Time:	**5½ hours**

Take Route 158 above to reach the marshy section of valley beyond the minor pass at 2240 metres (1½ hours from Arinsal). The Coma Pedrosa hut is off to the left, while ahead stands a shepherd's *cabana*. Go upvalley beyond the *cabana*, beside streams and over soft turf levels with the mountains ahead forming the attractive Cercle de Coma Pedrosa. Waymarks guide you, at last climbing to the right (north) to reach a tarn fed by streams falling from a second, upper, lake. Estany Negre is found through a rocky defile formed by the lower crags of the south-west ridge of Coma Pedrosa. (Up to this point the route has been that suggested as the descent following Route 158.)

Immediately before the second tarn is reached, waymarks lead right to climb the long, rocky ridge all the way to the summit.

The Cercle de Coma Pedrosa (Route 159)

VALL D'MADRIU

On the south side of the main Valira, the valley of the Madriu river is a narrow, steep-walled and wooded shaft which slices the mountains to the east of Les Escaldes, and provides a convenient entrance for those wishing to make a traverse of these Eastern Pyrenees, avoiding ski areas and traffic-congested roads. The Val d'Perafita is a tributary of the Madriu, joining the latter near the stone-built hamlet of Entremesaigues, an hour or so upvalley from Les Escaldes. At its upper levels the Madriu broadens into a high cirque with a number of tarns to mirror the Cresta de Pessons which forms its northern wall. Beside the largest of these Gargantilla tarns stands the recently restored Refugi de l'Estany de l'Illa (2485m), a hut with a sleeping capacity of about 20. This is reached by a walk of about 4½ hours from Les Escaldes. There are several other huts and *cabanes* accessible from the Madriu, but apart from l'Illa, they are all small and very basic.

Suggested Routes from Vall d'Madriu:

A two-day cross-country loop from **VALL D'MADRIU to VALL DE CORTALS** via **REFUGI DE L'ESTANY DE L'ILLA** will provide a challenge for mountain trekkers. Apart from Vall d'Madriu itself, the upper tarns will be a real highlight, but then a crossing of the Cresta de Gargantilla is made in order to gain the drainage system that feeds the Cortals Valley. Another small hut, Refugi de les Agols (2280m) will be passed on the descent. It would be possible to achieve this in one long day, but in order to make the most of the fine lake scenery, it is advisable to take two short days.

Another loop, shorter than the above, links Val d'Madriu with Vall d'Perafita by way of Coll de la Maiana (2421m). This pass lies south of Pic Maiana and the route to it begins a short way upvalley of the Collet de l'Infern. The round-trip requires about 4–5 hours.

CERCLE DE PESSONS

The ski station of Grau Roig, south-west of the Port d'Envalira, is linked with the architectural monstrosity of Pas de la Casa to provide nearly 60 kilometres of ski pistes. In summer the tows and carved hillsides proclaim an environmental horror story. But above and to the south-west of Grau Roig the Cercle de Pessons is a splendid amphitheatre of shrubs, rocks and more than a dozen little tarns and pools. The cirque wall begins in the north with Pic de Cubil, works south-west to Pic d'Ensagents and Pic de Pessons, then south-east along the Cresta de Pessons (beyond which lie the Gargantilla tarns at the head of Vall d'Madriu), to rise again at Pic de Ribus. Pic d'en Gait forms the south-eastern cornerstone, before the eastern wall projects northward as the final curve of the horseshoe. A short walk of a little over two hours is required to explore the most distant of the tarns within the Cercle de Pessons, but a delightful day could easily be spent wandering from one to another, with the ascent of a peak or two to add interest. It is also possible to cross the Cresta de Pessons and descend to the Gargantilla tarns on the route of the GR7, continuing down through Vall d'Madriu to Les Escaldes; or also on GR7 head south-east to escape Andorra at Portella Blanca d'Andorra (2517m) and descend through Vallée du Campcardos to Porte-Puymorens, thereby being in a good position to explore the Carlit massif, described in the next section.

ANDORRAN RIDGE-WALK

A classic challenge is the circumnavigation of Andorra's mountain rim. It should not be undertaken lightly, but treated as an expedition of some seriousness. Although there are no major climbing obstacles, the overall circuit demands expertise on rock and long spells of settled weather. Andorra's peaks and ridges are not friendly places when storms are raging.

Route 160: A Circuit of Andorra's Frontier Peaks

Distance:	**About 160 kilometres**
Height gain:	**The circuit involves about 15,000 metres of ascent in all**
Time:	**12 days**
Equipment:	**Rope, camping or bivouac gear necessary**

In all this expedition is comparable to the Cuillin ridge, but is about six times as long. The amount of time to be taken depends, of course, on weather conditions and expertise of the party. Food caches should be arranged in advance to avoid long descents to villages for restocking. Water flasks are essential. The route is best undertaken in an anti-clockwise direction on account of difficult sections which are mainly: Pic d'Escorbes, Cresta de Varilles, west of Port d'Incles, and the Cresta del Forat on the frontier west of Coma Pedrosa.

CARLIT MASSIF

Position:	Situated to the north-east of Andorra and lying entirely in France. Bordered to the south by the Cerdagne and to the east by Capcir.
Access:	By road from the north via Ax-les-Thermes and the Vallée d'Orlu; from the south-west by the Col de Puymorens and Vallée de Lanous, and from the south-east via Mont-Louis and Lac des Bouillouses. There are railway stations at Ax-les-Thermes, Mérens-les-Vals, l'Hospitalet, Porta and Latour de Carol. Mont-Louis is reached by la Petit Train Jaune from Latour de Carol or from Villefranche-de-Conflent.
Maps:	IGN Carte de Randonnées No 8 'Cerdagne–Capcir' 1:50,000 IGN TOP 25 series nos: 2249OT 'Bourg Madame, Col de Puymorens, Pic Carlit' and 2249ET 'Font-Romeu, Capcir' both at 1:25,000
Valley Bases:	Ax-les-Thermes (810m), Porté-Puymorens (1623m), plus various villages in the Cerdagne

The Carlit (or Carlitte) massif marks the eastern extremity of the High Pyrenees. Between it and the Mediterranean sprawl rolling sierras and the singularly attractive Pic du Canigou (2784m), lording it over the eastern hills as the symbol of independence-seeking Catalonia. To the south of the Carlit lies the broad sun-trap of the Cerdagne, which holds the sunshine record of all France, but to the east is the chill, north-facing high valley of Capcir. Waters from Carlit lakes flow into both these valleys, as well as to others in the north and west, making this rocky upland a surprisingly generous fountain despite the efforts of Electricité de France to tame the largest of its lakes.

The Carlit is predominantly granite; a rough-grained land scoured by long-departed glaciers, with jagged spires and rounded domes mirrored in countless lakes; 'a sterile waste...sprinkled with mountain tarns' is how one mountaineer described it a hundred years and more ago. On the outer edges a thin mattress of boggy, flower-starred turf oozes with moisture. Birch trees line low-valley streams, while massed pines darken the lower slopes of the mountain rim. In the heartland raw granite plateaux dominate with tarns of all shapes and sizes. Mouflon were introduced to the outer area in 1957, and by 1996 the population had grown to 1000. Chamois are also plentiful.

It's a very popular region for walking. Both the GR10 and Pyrenean High Route cross the massif, while the Tour du Carlit makes an interesting multi-day circuit. But there are numerous possibilities for creating your own tours and traverses, as well as enjoying day walks to the interior from valleys on the outer rim. In addition several summits are accessible to walkers with only a modicum of experience, although no-one should ever dismiss these mountains lightly. They have their serious side too.

Pic Carlit (2921m) is the highest. Rising to the south-east of Étang (or Lac) de Lanoux it has some attractive features, provides an easy ascent by its *voie normale*, and rewards with a huge panorama from the summit. Tarns lie wherever you look; jewels flashing from a desert of stone.

Visitors with their own transport could explore the outer Carlit on day excursions from centres such as Ax-les-Thermes, or from villages in the Cerdagne. However, there are a few spartan refuges and one or two more substantial huts within the massif to form an overnight base, but camping will be the only real answer to those wishing to experience its true nature, or who plan to conduct more intensive explorations of the heartland. Supplies may be obtained from Ax, Mérens-les-Vals, Porté or villages in the Cerdagne.

Valley Bases:

AX-LES-THERMES (810m) is a spa town cursed by through-traffic, but a good place from which motorists can set out on tours of the surrounding countryside. It scores with walkers and climbers from Britain by having rail access with Paris via Toulouse. There are several hotels, restaurants, shops and banks, a tourist information office and campsite. Access to the Carlit region is best via Vallée d'Orlu, which strikes off to the south-east. **Note**: Orlu village has a campsite and accommodation for 34 in the *gîte d'étape* Relais Montagnard (Tel: 05 61 64 61 88).

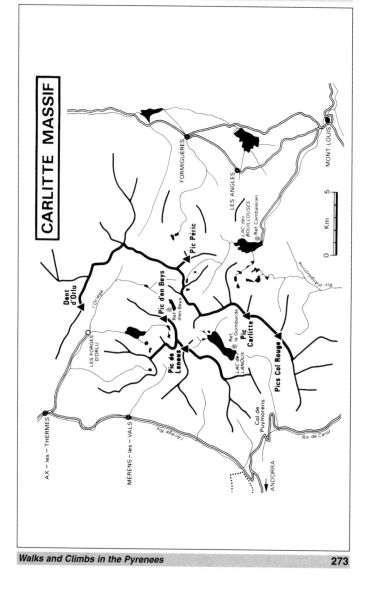

CARLITTE MASSIF

MONT LOUIS

FORMIGUÈRES

LES ANGLES

LAC des BOUILLOUSES

Ref. Cambaleran

Pic Péric

Dent d'Orlu

L'Oriège

Pic d'en Beys

Ref. d'en Beys

Riv d'Angoustrine

Ref. la Guimbarde

Pic Carlitte

LES FORGES D'ORLU

Pic de Laneus

LAC de LANOUX

Pics Col Rouge

AX – les – THERMES

MÉRENS – les – VALS

L'Ariège Riu

Col de Puymorens

Riv de Carol

ANDORRA

0   5
Km

PORTÉ-PUYMORENS (1623m) as its name suggests, is situated just below Col de Puymorens midway between Andorra and the Carlit massif. Only a village, with ambitions for expansion, it nonetheless has a campsite, hotels, the popular Auberge Cajole (Tel: 04 68 04 85 47), a restaurant and shop. The charming Vallée de Lanous stretches to the east, with Pic Carlit accessible from it.

Elsewhere, **MERENS-LES-VALS** upvalley from Ax and on the route of the GR10, has a *gîte d'étape* (Tel: 05 61 64 32 50), as do **L'HOSPI-TALET** (Tel: 05 61 05 23 14) – also a campsite – and **PORTA** (Tel: 04 68 04 95 44) below Porté-Puymorens. On the southern side of the massif, overlooking the Cerdagne, the tiny hamlet of **BÉNA** also has a *gîte d'étape* on the Tour du Carlit (Tel: 04 68 04 81 64). Beyond these places, there are several villages enjoying a certain tranquillity on the outlying slopes, in which hotel accommodation may be found.

Mountain Huts:

REFUGE D'EN BEYS (1970m) is situated on the shores of Étang d'En Beys, one of the sources of l'Oriège, on the northern side of the region. Accessible by a walk of about 2½ hours from the roadhead in Vallée d'Orlu, the hut can sleep 50 in its dormitories. There is a guardian from the end of May to the end of September, when meals may be available (Tel: 05 61 64 24 24).

CHALET-REFUGE DES BOUILLOUSES (2005m) is owned by the CAF, officially has places for 45, a guardian from June to the end of September, and for the ski season January to April (Tel: 04 68 04 20 76). This hut is on the route of the GR10, HRP and Tour du Carlit, and is accessible by car from Mont-Louis (the D60). It stands to the south of the dammed Lac des Bouillouses to the east of Pic Carlit.

There are several other huts scattered about the region, but they are invariably small and offer only basic facilities.

Route 161: Walking Tour of the Vallée de Lanous

Distance:	12 kilometres
Height gain/loss:	327 metres
Time:	4–5 hours
Base:	Porté-Puymorens (1623m)

The actual circuit starts and finishes at the roadhead in Vallée de Lanous. Walkers with their own transport can save eight kilometres of exercise by driving into the valley and parking at the roadhead near the base of an electricity works cableway. It is an attractive walk, especially in spring or early summer when wild flowers are at their best, but it should be pointed out that paths are not always clearly defined.

From Porté-Puymorens wander eastwards into the Vallée de Lanous on a narrow road which ends after four kilometres. It's a gentle walk with rough pastures to one side, mountain slopes on the other and the Carlit massif directly ahead. The road ends beyond a lake and the circuit begins 50 metres north of an electricity works building.

A narrow trail climbs among pines and alongside a small stream. There are various alternative paths after a while, but you should keep just to the left of overhead cables until emerging in an open meadow. Wander up its right-hand edge and climb to a second meadowland where you bear right on a clear waymarked path which leads to Étang de Font Vive. Go along its northern shore to the far end. Leave the lake and continue heading east across a pasture and descend among trees into the head of the valley where you find a wooden bridge over a stream below some cascades. Across this bear right at a path junction. The trail meanders above the stream, then veers left near a ravine. Climb to a grassy saddle. The way (cairns) now gradually loses height and grants views to Andorra's mountain border. Pass through walled meadows and pinewoods and come to a broad track. Bear right, cross a bridge to reach the Lanous valley roadhead, and wander down the road back to Porté.

Route 162: Porté-Puymorens (1623m) –
Refuge de la Guimbarde (2250m)

Distance:	**7.5 kilometres**
Height gain:	**627 metres**
Time:	**2½–3 hours**

Refuge de la Guimbarde is a small, basic hut (marked as Abri on the map) with room for about half a dozen on two sleeping platforms. Its situation is idyllic, standing on a bluff above Étang de Lanoux and with views up to Pic Carlit.

There are three ways of reaching the hut from Porté: a) take the clear path (GR7) that leaves the eastern-most hairpin bend of the Puymorens road just above the village, and follow it rising gradually along the northern slopes of the Lanous Valley as far as the dam at Étang de Lanoux. Cross the dam to its eastern side and go along a narrow path vaguely heading north-east with Pic Carlit ahead. After a few hundred metres a small dam is seen off to the left with Refuge de la Guimbarde perched upon a grassy bluff above it.

Alternative route b) leaves Porté by the narrow road running east into the Lanous Valley. Shortly before you reach a point almost level with the dam at the end of the lake seen below, a path climbs away from the road to the left. This path rises steeply for about ten minutes before joining the main path referred to in option a). Turn right and follow round to the hut as described above.

The third option c) begins at the roadhead in Vallée de Lanous, and follows Route 161 as far as Étang de Font Vive. A path then climbs steeply from the western end of the lake to join the main GR7 path described in the above two options.

PIC CARLIT (2921m)

First climbed by Henry Russell in 1864, Pic Carlit (or Carlitte) makes an obvious goal for all who are drawn to the massif. Though not at all difficult by either of its standard routes, the mountain is nonetheless an enjoyable one, and a traverse from one side to the other, as experienced by trekkers on the Pyrenean High Route, provides a rewarding exercise. Most visitors tackle the peak from Lac des Bouillouses, so the following routes from the west will be slightly less busy in the height of the season.

Route 163: Refuge de la Guimbarde (2250m) – Pic Carlit (2921m)

Grade:	**F (North-West Face)**
Distance:	**3 kilometres**
Height gain:	**671 metres**
Time:	**1½–2 hours**

Head into the Fourats glen on a winding path with Pic Carlit ahead. Follow a line of cairns over boulders as far as the little tarn (Étang des

Fourats; 2457m) under the north-western face of the mountain. A choice of routes presents itself, the first of which is easier to follow.

From the tarn head east towards the face of Carlit, crossing a long slope of shale to reach the foot of an obvious Y-shaped gully up which a steep zig-zag path is clearly seen. There is nothing difficult about the ascent of this gully, which works up the right arm of the Y to gain a small pass (2910m), with the summit above to the right. To reach the summit bear right at the pass and walk up the ridge, reaching the top in a little under two hours from the hut.

If your plan is to return to la Guimbarde or Porté-Puymorens, an alternative descent is suggested; by reversing the following route (164 below), an interesting traverse may be accomplished.

Route 164: Refuge de la Guimbarde (2250) – Pic Carlit (2921m)

Grade:	F (via the South Ridge)
Distance:	4 kilometres
Time:	3 hours

This route is the original one taken by the pioneers, and is more interesting and varied than that previously described, but is more tiring too. It is also much less used, which in itself is a benefit on a summer's day when all the world has come to visit.

Follow Route 163 as far as Étang des Fourats, then continue through the glen, keeping to the left of centre, until you reach the foot of scree slopes coming from Carlit's south ridge. An obvious saddle is seen above to the left, on the southern ridge. Climb the screes to reach this saddle, which is more arduous than difficult, and at the saddle bear left to scramble up the steep (and loose) ridge towards the summit. Keep to the eastern (right) side where holds are plentiful.

Route 165: Chalet-Refuge des Bouillouses (2005m) – Pic Carlit (2921m)

Grade:	F (*voie normale*)
Distance:	7 kilometres
Height gain:	916 metres
Time:	3–3½ hours

From the western side of the Bouillouses dam follow a clear path branching left among trees, then turn north-west to pass along the edge of Étang du Vive. Continue through an attractive landscape of streams and pools (the so-called Desert du Carlit), still heading north-west to a string of tarns, which you pass to your right. The first of these is Étang des Dougnes, with the smaller Étang de Balleil on your left. All around are tiny pools, many of which are not shown on the map; alpenroses, juniper and mattresses of heather create a wonderful natural garden through which the clear trail leads, now making a more westerly course towards Pic Carlit. Beyond the last of the tarns, Étang de Soubirans, you lose a little height on grass and come to the start of the stony ascent of Carlit itself. The path continues to be clearly defined with cairns and waymarks, and leads interestingly, and with a little scrambling, to the small pass (2910m) just below and to the right of the actual summit. Bear left and walk to the top.

Route 166: The Carlit Lakes Tour

Distance:	**39 kilometres**
Height gain/loss:	**1719 metres**
Time:	**2 days**
Start/finish:	**Porté-Puymorens (1623m)**
Accommodation:	**Chalet-Refuge des Bouillouses (2005m)**

A moderate-grade walk but a fine circuit that includes the summit of Pic Carlit, displays some remarkable scenery and enables the walker to explore some of the best that the area has to offer.

The first section of this tour, from Porté to Étang de Lanoux, has already been described as Route 162 (Refuge de la Guimbarde). Follow the standard route from there to the summit of Pic Carlit (Route 163), and from the summit to Lac des Bouillouses reverse Route 165. This is straightforward and clearly defined and it leads through the wonderland of dwarf pine, tarns and pools and extravagant vegetation curiously known as the Désert du Carlit.

Lac des Bouillouses, at the head of a road from Mont-Louis, is extremely popular with anglers, walkers and picnic parties. Spend the night at the Chalet-Refuge, and next day walk north along the western shore of the lake following the clear path of the GR10 among

The Désert du Carlit

pines and over rough boulders. At the far end of the lake the trail bears left to enter the valley of the Grave de la Tet. Now the way becomes faint in places, but nowhere is it difficult to find. Soon rise towards the head of the valley by a series of short grass steps. Near the valley-head the path veers left where you enter an upper level of pastureland and find a small tarn (Étang du Pradet). Cross its outlet stream (cairns) and make the ascent to Porteille de la Grave (2426m), a broad grassy saddle. Down to the west lies the huge Étang de Lanoux; to the south rough slopes rise to Pic Carlit.

Continue on the GR10 path down towards the lake, but when it forks, break away on the left branch which skirts above the south bank. This is the route taken by the GR7. It's an interesting traverse route leading over various knolls before reaching the dam at the lake's southern end. Here you rejoin the path which brought you up from Porté-Puymorens.

Route 167: A Traverse of the Carlit Massif on GR10

Distance:	25 kilometres
Height gain:	2088 metres
Height loss:	1128 metres
Time:	10–11 hours (2 days)
Start:	Mérens-les-Vals (1052m)
Finish:	Chalet-Refuge des Bouillouses (2005m)
Accommodation:	Refuge du Barrage des Bésines (1975m)

This diagonal crossing of the Carlit massif from north-west to south-east is worth tackling whether or not you undertake the full GR10 Ocean to Sea traverse. Food and cooking equipment will have to be carried from Mérens-les-Vals because the Bésines hut is only very basic (six spaces) and there is no possibility of buying anything between Mérens and Lac des Bouillouses. Mérens has *gîte d'étape* (Tel: 05 61 64 32 50), food stores and a railway station. The Chalet-Refuge at Bouillouses has a guardian in summer residence when meals should be available (Tel: 04 68 04 20 76). Mont-Louis in the Cerdagne is reached by another three hours of walking, or you may be able to hitch down the road from Lac des Bouillouses.

The route is decribed in detail in Alan Castle's guidebook, *The Pyrenean Trail GR10* (Cicerone Press), but is briefly outlined below. It is clearly waymarked almost throughout this particular traverse.

Mérens-les-Vals – Vallée du Nabre – Porteille des Bésines – Refuge du Barrage des Bésines (5 hours) – Col de Coume d'Agnel – Étang de Lanoux – Porteille de la Grave – Lac des Bouillouses – Chalet-Refuge des Bouillouses (5½–6 hours)

Route 168: A North–South Traverse
(Vallée d'Orlu to Vallée de Lanous)

Distance:	28 kilometres
Height gain:	1642 metres
Height loss:	852 metres
Time:	2 days
Start:	Orlu (833m)
Finish:	Porté-Puymorens (1623m)
Accommodation:	Refuge d'En Beys (1970m)

Another fine two-day traverse, this has the benefit of a guardianed hut with the possibility of meals, so trekkers could travel lightly laden. The village of Orlu is easily reached from Ax-les-Thermes. Accommodation is available in the Relais Montagnard d'Orlu. The village also has a campsite on the south side of the main valley stream.

The first stage is easy. It heads south-east upvalley through the Vallée d'Orlu (take the side road left just after passing a power station) and passes beneath the unseen granite tooth of Dent d'Orlu. When the road ends at 1180 metres follow the GR7 path rising steadily, still to the south-east. Coming to the Jasse Justiniac the valley veers south and the trail climbs along the west bank of the Oriège stream all the way to its source at Étang d'En Beys. The refuge is found on the northern shore (Refuge d'En Beys; 50 places, guardian end of May to end-September, meals provision. Tel: 05 61 64 22 24).

Leaving the hut walk to the far end of the lake (still on GR7), and from the south-western corner climb over boulders and up into a delightful valley. The waymarked path leads into the upper part of the horseshoe that dominates d'En Beys. Where the path divides near the top, take the left fork over boulders until a damp, flat area is reached. On the map this is shown as a small tarn. Above, the saddle of Porteille d'Orlu is seen. Go up to this and follow through to descend to Étang de Lanoux where you join another path, the GR10. Bear left, and when the path forks, head to the right to make a traverse of the slopes that form the lake's left bank.

On reaching the dam at the southern end of Étang de Lanoux, cross to the western side and follow a clear path down to Porté-Puymorens.

PIC PERIC (2810m)

Seen from Lac des Bouillouses Pic Peric appears as a conical mountain rising at the far northern end of the lake. From a distance it gives an impression of being quite separate from its neighbouring peaks, although the Petit Pic (2690m) is below to the east, and to the north-west, but hidden from the south, are Pic de la Grande Porteille and Pic de Morties. Pic Peric reveals a splendid panorama from its summit, a contrast of rugged peaks to the west, and the green luxury of pasture and forest to the east. Off to the south-east Canigou may be seen on a clear day, while rising above valleys to the north-west, the amazing profile of Dent d'Orlu.

Route 169: Chalet-Refuge des Bouillouses (2005m) – Pic Peric (2810m)

Grade:	**F**
Distance:	**7 kilometres**
Height gain:	**805 metres**
Time:	**3½–4 hours**

From the western side of the Bouillouses dam follow a clear path (GR10) that heads north along the west bank of the lake among trees and, later, boulders. On reaching the grassy plain of the Tet Valley at the far end of the lake bear right and cross the stream on a waymarked path. Soon after bear left up the hillside, veering away from the route that leads into the Llose glen below and to the left of Pic Peric, and instead heading a little east of north to reach the tarn, Étang de l'Esparbe. From here choose one of two alternatives.

a) Leave the tarn at its western end and follow the path until it bears right at the foot of a ridge. Climb the ridge, following it to the summit by a broken and indistinct path.

b) Head north from the eastern end of the tarn making for a second tarn, Étang de la Llose (2238m), then go upvalley under the south-eastern face of the mountain, following a stream. Climb to the ridge, which is gained just before the summit.

Other Routes in the Carlit Region:

Possibilities for walks and tours within the Carlit region are almost inexhaustible. The map is criss-crossed with suggestions, though it must be stated that not all routes marked on the map have obvious trails on the ground. West of Pic Peric **GRANDE PORTEILLE D'ES-PAGNE** at the head of the Llose glen offers a way over to the Vallée d'Orlu for trekkers planning a south to north traverse. Walkers should be warned, however, that the descent on the northern side of the pass is far more serious than the ascent to it from the south.

North-east of Pic Peric lie the **ÉTANGS DE CAMPORELLS**. Though they may be reached by a cross-country walk from Bouillouses (on the Tour du Capcir), they are more easily gained from a narrow road climbing from Formiguères down in the Capcir, to the Fontane de la Calmazeilles. Beside one of the tarns is Refuge de Camporells (2240m) with spaces for 25. **A TOUR OF THE CAMPORELLS TARNS**, using the refuge as a base, links almost a dozen tarns and smaller pools, with Pic Peric rising to the south-west. An ascent of Pic Peric is also possible from the hut, by a route which climbs first over the Petit Pic.

North of Refuge de Camporells is **PIC DE LA MONTAGNETTE** (2436m) which may be climbed from the west – a recommended long (7–8 hour) circuit from Formiguères via the Vallée du Galbe includes this summit, plus that of the Serre de Maury to the east.

Route 170: Tour du Carlit

Distance:	**45 kilometres**
Time:	**3 days**
Start/Finish:	**Chalet-Refuge des Bouillouses (2005m)**
Accommodation:	**Auberge at Porté-Puymorens, *gîtes d'étape* at Porta and Béna**

The Carlit massif wears two faces. In the north and central regions it is a harsh, bold land of granite and water; but its other face smiles at the sun. Soft and green the southern slopes overlook the warm expanse of the Cerdagne, and the waymarked Tour du Carlit provides an opportunity to explore both sides of its character.

The first stage of the walk heads north along the shores of Lac des Bouillouses, then north-west to cross Porteille de la Grave (2426m), traverses above Étang de Lanoux and descends to Porté-Puymorens (Auberge Cajole, Tel: 04 68 04 85 47). This is described in more detail as the second part of the Carlit Lakes Tour (Route 166). A combination of path and track then heads easily downvalley to the stone-built village of Porta for an overnight in a *gîte d'étape* (La Pastorale, Tel: 04 68 04 83 92).

The shortest of the three stages of the tour goes from Porta to Béna. Immediately upon leaving Porta a climb of some 800 metres leads to a spur projecting west from Pic de Comaou. From the high pastures leading to Col de l'Homme Mort (2300m) a fresh appreciation of the mountains is revealed, for a vast rolling country spreads out to the east and drains down into the Cerdagne. From here to the hamlet of Béna (with its very pleasant *gîte d'étape* – d'Enveitg, Tel: 04 68 04 81 64) the walk is almost entirely downhill, with glorious views that seem to grow broader with every step.

Leaving Béna the tour continues eastward and passes through yet more tiny, time-forgotten hamlets like Fànes and Brangoly, then crosses Col de Jouell to slope down to Dorres, a handsome place and one of the jewels of the Cerdagne. Shortly after this the tour breaks off to the north, working a way through the peaceful Vallée d'Angoustrine. Modest hills guarded by granite tors form the walls to this valley that is headed by Puig del Cap de l'Homme. Skirting below the Puig you enter a new landscape for the final stretch leading to Lac des Bouillouses.

THE PYRENEAN HIGH ROUTE

Introduction:

The High Route across the Pyrenees, officially known as the Haute Randonnée Pyrénéenne (HRP), is a challenging traverse of the range which begins on the shores of the Atlantic and takes 45 days or so to reach the Mediterranean at Banyuls-sur-Mer.

It's the mountain trekker's dream of a route; always demanding, ever-varied, passing through some of the most deserted and spectacularly scenic regions in all of Europe. At no time is it dull. Neither should it ever be treated lightly, for although in many areas the route has been adequately waymarked, there are sections, especially on the Spanish side of the frontier, where route-finding calls for experience and cool reasoning and where the ability to use map and compass is essential. Sometimes a very long day's journey has no accommodation at the end of it, so camping or beneath-the-stars bivouac are the only options. Rarely does the route pass near a village for the restocking of supplies. Food, therefore, has to be carried in those regions where manned refuges are uncommon.

Since there are at least 45 day-stages between Ocean and Sea, the complete traverse must involve more than six weeks of walking, without taking into consideration off-days and bad-weather days when high level trekking is out of the question. Few are fortunate enough to have this amount of time to devote to one long walk, so the following High Route sections, leading from Lescun to Andorra through the very best of the High Pyrenees, have been designed to afford two or three separate holidays broken by rail links with Paris. The length of this section of the HRP is no more than 24 days, and as some stages are of fairly short duration, it would be possible to reduce this time even more. Two holidays of a fortnight each would be sufficient to complete the trek through the High Pyrenees. Better still, take three holidays over it, and spend the occasional day exploring specific areas that entice you with their mystery and magic, or make the ascent of one or two peaks along the way. There should be enough suggestions and route details contained in this book to help you create some truly memorable days and weeks in the mountains.

The route through the High Pyrenees may conveniently be broken into three separate expeditions governed by rail access as follows: 1) Lescun to Gavarnie, 2) Gavarnie to Maladeta, 3) Maladeta to Andorra. It should be borne in mind, however, that the 'official' HRP is in a state of constant revision, with numerous *variantes* being devised and subsequently waymarked. The route described below is just one of several possible traverses from Lescun to Andorra.

Trekkers with sufficient time at their disposal to attempt the complete Ocean to Sea traverse are recommended to obtain a copy of Georges Véron's admirable guide, *Pyrenees High Level Route* published by Gastons-West Col.

HIGH ROUTE SECTION ONE:
LESCUN TO GAVARNIE

Maps:	**IGN Carte de Randonnées No 3 'Béarn' and No 4 'Bigorre' 1:50,000**
	IGN TOP 25 series nos: 1547OT, 1647OT and 1748OT at 1:25,000
Accommodation:	**Mountain huts or gîtes d'étape on all stages except one**
Access:	**Train from Paris to Oloron-Ste-Marie via Pau, then SNCF bus to Bedous and taxi to Lescun**
	At the end of the walk: bus from
Gavarnie	**to Lourdes, and train Lourdes–Paris**
Time required:	**10 days**

The High Route proper reaches the Cirque de Lescun after ten days of journeying from the Atlantic. For the purposes of this guide the route begins at Lescun village, with a short first stage leading to the Cabanes d'Ansabere. Those who have travelled on the overnight express from Paris will find that three hours of walking from the village will be sufficient for a first day's activity. Although trekkers have in the past sometimes been offered basic overnight accommodation at the shepherd's cabanes beneath the Aiguilles d'Ansabère, there is little chance today and one should not expect it, but instead be prepared either to camp, or to bivouac. One day, it is hoped, a proper hut will be provided here to service the needs of trekkers and climbers.

Overnight accommodation is possible on every subsequent stage of the walk to Gavarnie.

Lescun is beautifully set amid sloping pastures high above, and to the west of, the Aspe Valley. Rising at the head of a tributary glen to the west of the village is Pic d'Anie, first of the High Pyrenees over whose shoulder the High Route comes from La Pierre-St-Martin. To the south stands a veritable barrier of rocky fence-posts; the so-called Cirque de Lescun.

All but a very small part of the route from Lescun to Gavarnie passes through the *Parc National des Pyrénées*. Having entered the Cirque de Lescun, the way then heads south-eastward keeping close to the border, briefly crosses into Spain, and comes to the Aspe Valley at the end of day three. Pic du Midi d'Ossau is next. The HRP climbs over Col d'Ayous, traverses the southern side of Pic du Midi and descends into the Ossau Valley before working eastwards to the stony desert of the Balaitous. There are two ways round this, the first of the 3000-metre peaks met on the route; one makes a strenuous loop round its northern slopes, the other passes below the south face on a rough trek that emerges to meet the main route in the pastures of the Marcadau Valley, back in France.

From the Marcadau to the foot of the Vignemale is a classic stage that involves the crossing of three high passes, but this may be broken by a night spent in the Refuge des Oulettes de Gaube between the second and third of these. All that remains thereafter is a walk into Gavarnie to complete Section One.

Opportunities abound for interrupting the route with an exploration of country through which you pass, or for the ascent of an occasional peak. Of particular interest will be the Pic du Midi region, Balaitous, the Marcadau Valley and Vignemale. The Cirque de Gavarnie also has obvious appeal and, time permitting, there will be plenty to do there. Consult the relevant sections of this guidebook for ideas and route details.

High Route 1: Lescun (900m) – Cabanes d'Ansabère (1560m)

Distance:	9 kilometres
Height gain:	660 metres
Time:	3 hours
Accommodation:	Lescun: hotel, *gîte d'étape*, campsite. Ansabère: none

As far as Pont Lamary, a little over six kilometres from Lescun, the

On Stage 23 the High Route edges Estany de Baborte above the Vall Ferrera

Knot of peaks forming the borders of Spain, France and Andorra, Stage 24

way follows a surfaced road then forest track, and is accessible by vehicle. Unless you have reason to visit Lescun, there is no need to go up into the village when approaching from the Aspe Valley, but instead branch off on a minor road heading left (south-west) just below the village itself.

For walkers starting from Lescun, find a GR10 signpost near the general stores which directs you through the alleyways heading south-west until a narrow road is reached. A sign here shows the way to 'Cirque d'Ansabère'.

Keep on this road as it threads initially among pastures, then after several kilometres becomes a forest track gaining height through woods well above the right bank of the Gave d'Ansabère. The track reaches a clearing beyond a gateway, and comes to Pont Lamary (1171m) where vehicles are often parked (about 1½ hours from Lescun).

Cross the bridge and follow a clear path heading south-west in and out of woods as it gains height with the Ansabère needles soon luring you on. At the top of a rise a large pastureland clearing is reached; a lovely bowl of mountains with streams meandering through, dark woods on the far side and the Aiguilles d'Ansabère rising dramatically above.

Descend into the bowl, cross the stream and climb steeply among the woods beyond, and continue on the true left bank of the meagre Gave d'Ansabère until the Cabanes d'Ansabère are located below screes fanning from the base of the needles.

Note: An easy 2½ hour ascent of Pic d'Ansabère is described as Route 5 (Aspe Valley and Cirque de Lescun section).

High Route 2: Cabanes d'Ansabère (1560m) – Refuge d'Arlet (2000m)

Distance:	14 kilometres
Height gain:	915 metres
Height loss:	475 metres
Time:	7½ hours

This is quite a demanding stage, especially on a hot summer's day, for there's practically no shade for the greater part of the walk. Water supplies are few and far between and paths are not always evident.

Find a path which strikes off to the south from the shepherds' huts to cross pastureland, rising steadily then to the south-east and growing clearer until shortly before the little Lac d'Ansabère (1859m) is reached. Leaving the tarn behind to your left, climb the steep hillside aiming towards the frontier ridge, which you gain south-west of the tarn, at an obvious saddle east of Point 2028m on the map. Views into Spain are of gentle rolling hills that fold into the haze of southern sierras. Below lies a charming, empty valley.

Go left along the crest of the ridge for a short distance, then make a descending traverse southward over steep grass slopes (care required, especially if wet), aiming towards a jutting spur beyond which lies Ibon de Acherito, a delightful tarn. A steep descent is guided by red–white paint flashes to the lake's southern outflow (about two hours from the Cabanes d'Ansabère). The tarn is set in an attractive amphitheatre of cliffs, while to the south a series of smooth folding hillsides breathe an atmosphere of peace and tranquillity.

Before leaving it is important to fill water bottles. Cross the stream flowing from the tarn and follow a waymarked path heading south-east. It soon begins to lose height, whilst remaining still some considerable way above the valley. At about 1620 metres, half an hour from Acherito, a well-vegetated area adorned with clumps of box is reached. It is now essential not to lose more height, but instead take a narrow path going vaguely north-east, and then climb through a shallow hillside coomb to gain broad open pastures with the frontier ridge above enlivened by rocky crests. The path disappears, but by crossing these pastures heading east, Col de Pau (1942m) will be located to the left of Pic de Burcq (4½ hours from the cabanes).

Note: Should you roam too far east (an easy mistake) climb to Col de Burcq (2063m) instead, the saddle to the right of Pic de Burcq, where the correct path is met on the northern side.

Although a further three hours will be needed to reach Refuge d'Arlet, the path gained at either Col de Pau or Col de Burcq signals the end of any route-finding difficulties for the day. Both cols mark the Franco-Spanish border and entry to the PNP. Bear right on a clear path round the head of the Labadie Valley among first rocks, then grass, along the ridge. Leave the ridge at Col de la Cuarde (1970m) to cut eastwards across to the lower Col de Saoubathou (1949m). Over this the path then rises and falls in varying degrees until at last a sharp series of twists brings you onto a grassy plateau with Refuge d'Arlet set above its lake on the right.

Refuge d'Arlet: PNP owned, 43 places, guardian from mid-June to mid-September (Tel: 05 59 36 00 99) when meals may be provided. Winter quarters can sleep about ten.

High Route 3: Refuge d'Arlet (2000m) –
Col du Somport (1632m)

Distance:	**13 kilometres**
Height gain:	**312 metres**
Height loss:	**680 metres**
Time:	**5–5½ hours**

After the exertions of the previous stage, this comes as a welcome relief. It's predominantly a downhill – or at least a level-section – day, offering no real difficulties. The only major uphill effort comes at the end of the day with 2.5 kilometres and over 300 metres of height gain to reach a *gîte d'étape* near Col du Somport.

From the hut go down to the lake and take a path which skirts its left (north) shore and leads round to the so-called Cirque de Banasse; a gentle pastoral amphitheatre. Passing several rough *cabanes* (those of Caillaous on the right and Gourgue Sec beside a little pool on the left) the path then rises slightly to pass through Col de Lapachouaou, then bears south-east to traverse the mountainside towards an obvious spur which has to be crossed. On the south side of this spur the descent leads into a minor valley and over a stream on a footbridge below Cabane Grosse. The way then climbs suddenly to cross Col Plâtrière before plunging into the shade of the Espelunguere forest (2½ hours from Arlet).

The forest path brings you onto a road at the grassy Pla d'Espélunguère, with a stream coming down from frontier peaks in the south-west. Cross the stream by a footbridge and follow the continuing path for about 400 metres until a sign directs you left-wards to Sansanet. Here the trail rises to a grassy saddle bordered by trees. In a south-easterly direction the route comes to a broad forest clearing and shortly after this a track is reached. (A number of tracks are being bulldozed throughout the forest and this one may have been extended. Waymarks should keep you on route.)

Waymarks lead to a more attractive path which in turn goes to a rough pasturage with Cabane d'Escouret commanding some rather picturesque country. A little beyond the hut a signpost marks the way down, once more in forest shade, to Sansanet. The Gave d'Aspe is crossed by a bridge, and beyond this you come to a picnic site and the Somport road (1320m).

Bear right and walk up the road, noting as you do a path breaking away to the left at a hairpin bend – this is the path to refuges Larry and d'Ayous adopted on High Route 4. Continue up the road to find the Gîte du Somport, just below Col du Somport, for overnight accommodation.

Gîte du Somport: owned by the Aspe Valley Communes, 12 places, restaurant nearby (Tel: 06 08 22 23 31).

High Route 4: Col du Somport (1632m) –
Refuge d'Ayous (1982m)

Distance:	**16 kilometres**
Height gain:	**755 metres**
Height loss:	**405 metres**
Time:	**5½ hours**

Note: An alternative, shorter (3½–4 hours) route to Refuge d'Ayous via Col des Moines (2168m) is described as Route 17 (Aspe Valley and Cirque de Lescun section).

From the Somport retrace the last of yesterday's route downvalley for about two kilometres to a left-hand hairpin bend where a footpath signposted Refuge de Larry breaks away to the north. Follow this among clumps of heather and juniper, steadily gaining height above the valley with fine views back to the Cirque d'Aspe. About 1½ hours from the road brings you to Col de Lazaque where the continuing path is seen some way off to the east. Now a descent is made in woodlands, turning south-east into a short glen. Over the Arnousse stream the way veers to the north and passes a small *cabane*. Another stream is crossed, then the path goes up, once more among trees, gaining height quickly.

Eventually woodland shade is traded for open hillside just beyond the Gouetsoule stream and, heading north-west, makes a few wide loops before coming to Cabane de Gouetsoule (a rough shelter for 4–5 people). Col de Gouetsoule (1845m) marks another change of direction. Now the trail heads north-east descending among rocks

Refuge de Larry (High Route 4)

with Refuge de Larry (1724m) soon coming into view. This is reached 3½ hours from the road.

Refuge de Larry: a small, basic PNP hut with sleeping space for about ten people. A water pipe outside is worth noting.

At the refuge a sign gives 1½ hours to Col de Larry. The route to it heads in a rough easterly direction, easily defined, and gains height steadily with a steep zig-zag for the final pull onto the pass itself. Beyond Col de Larry (2130m) the way continues round to the right, still with more height to gain before reaching Col d'Ayous (2185m) about 15 minutes later. A dramatic view of Pic du Midi d'Ossau is gained from this pass. Descend by way of the GR10 path that leads directly to Refuge d'Ayous seen below on the shores of a peak-reflecting lake.

Refuge d'Ayous: another PNP hut in the same style as Refuge d'Arlet, with 30 beds and a guardian from mid-June to mid-September when meals may be available (Tel: 05 59 05 37 00). Superb views of Pic du Midi across Lac d'Ayous.

High Route 5: Refuge d'Ayous (1982m) – Refuge de Pombie (2032m)

Distance:	8 kilometres
Height gain:	754 metres
Height loss:	704 metres
Time:	4 hours

A magnificent stage with ever-changing views of Pic du Midi almost every step of the way. Although not a long walk, it is quite strenuous, but with sufficient time in hand to enjoy the splendours of the area.

From the hut take the path heading south-west and rising to Lac Bersau. Continue along the left-hand shore of the tarn to cross a minor col (2100m) below Pic Casterau, and descend eastwards to a smaller tarn, Lac Casterau. After this the path descends more steeply in zig-zags to reach the Bious stream draining from a small glen on your right. Cross the stream, below which another knuckle glen cuts back to the south near Cabane de Cap de Pount (1½ hours from Refuge d'Ayous). Climb a grassy gully which rises above the cabane to the north-east, and when it levels out bear right to gain a pastureland overseen by Cabane de Peyreget.

The trail continues on a mostly level stretch to gain a major path where you bear right. Follow this to Lac de Peyreget, then head north-east led by cairns across a region of huge rocks, and climb to Col de Peyreget (2300m). Descend on the eastern side of the pass without difficulty and reach Refuge de Pombie with its direct view of the South Face of Pic du Midi.

Refuge de Pombie: CAF owned, 55 places, guardian from end of June to end of September when meals may be provided (Tel: 05 59 05 31 78). Room for 20 in the winter quarters. Wild camping is restricted to 48 hours in the vicinity of this hut.

Note: An ascent of Pic du Midi by the *voie normale* will take about 3–3½ hours from Pombie (see Route 23). The Tour of Pic du Midi, a classic of its kind, is also worth considering on a day-off from the High Route, and is described as Route 25. Consult the section above headed Pic du Midi d'Ossau for further details and suggestions.

High Route 6: Refuge de Pombie (2032m) – Refuge d'Arrémoulit (2305m)

Distance:	7.5 kilometres
Height gain:	960 metres
Height loss:	687 metres
Time:	5–5½ hours

Note: Early in the season snow may severely hamper the crossing of one or two high passes between the Pombie hut and Refuge Wallon in the Marcadau Valley, so assess conditions before committing yourself to this and the following two High Route stages.

Take the path that goes almost directly from the hut door down into the scoop of hillside to the east, winding at first until the stream is reached. This is followed on the left bank, then on the right until shortly after passing Cabane de Pucheoux when the left bank is regained. On coming to woods cross the stream once more on a footbridge and follow the continuing trail losing height through the woods.

Eventually the path makes a left-hand slant and cuts steeply down to the floor of the main valley. Cross the Gave de Brousset by a footbridge and go up to the road above and to the left of two buildings known as Caillou de Soques (about 1hr 45 mins from Pombie). On occasion snacks and some provisions may be obtained here.

Cross the road and enter more woodland near a large boulder on a path that rises north-eastward to enter the Arrious Valley. Emerging from the woods a bridge takes the path over the Arrious stream, then you wander up the north side of the stream heading east for some distance. Behind, Pic du Midi shows itself with a fresh profile. After a while the path climbs in zig-zags and levels to a narrow false col; an idyllic spot with flat turf, a clear stream and fine views. Col d'Arrious (2259m) is reached soon after, and the path forks.

Note: The right-hand trail crosses the Passage d'Orteig. Although exposed, this artificial ledge cut in the rock face has been safeguarded, but trekkers unhappy about it should take the alternative path which descends on the eastern side of Col d'Arrious towards Lac d'Artouste, then climb again south-eastward on a steep waymarked path which leads to Arrémoulit.

The right-hand path at Col d'Arrious brings you to the narrow Lac d'Arrious. Keep to the left-hand side of the tarn where the trail rises over a low ridge, curves to the right and then narrows as the Passage d'Orteig which traverses the North Face of Pic du Lac d'Arrious. Climbing out of it cairns lead over a very rough landscape of boulders, more or less eastward, then down to Refuge d'Arrémoulit which is found squat upon the northern shore of its lake.

Refuge d'Arrémoulit: CAF owned, 45 places, guardian from mid-June to mid-September, meals available (Tel: 05 59 05 31 79). Pic Palas (Route 37) and Balaitous (Route 38) are just two of the peaks accessible from this hut.

High Route 7: Refuge d'Arrémoulit (2305m) – Refuge de Larribet (2070m)

Distance:	**5 kilometres**
Height gain:	**310 metres**
Height loss:	**545 metres**
Time:	**3½ hours**

For experienced mountain trekkers and in good conditions only. An alternative stage, which traverses south of Balaitous and goes as far as Refuge Wallon in the Marcadau Valley, is described below, but that is also a demanding trek.

Leave the Arrémoulit hut, bear left and cross some granite boulders above the lake to gain the hanging valley which rises a little south of east, and has Col du Palas at its head. Cairns lead beyond a small tarn and up to the col, about an hour from the hut. The west ridge of Balaitous is clearly seen from it.

Descend a short way to the upper screes plunging to the Lacs d'Arriel, then traverse left (eastwards), keeping as high as possible. A few cairns indicate the way to the steep wall linking Pic Palas with Batcrabère, which you climb to gain the narrow Port du Lavedan (2615m), often in snow. In places the descent on the north-eastern side is precarious and caution is necessary. Trekkers with some mountaineering experience could descend by a series of gullies direct from the col. Otherwise paint flashes direct you towards the east, now steadily descending over snow, scree blocks and boulders, before reaching the tiny Lacs de Micoulaou. From the lower of these the path goes north-east to the larger of the Lacs de Batcrabère, which is passed along its right-hand side, then up and down until the Brèche de la Garènere brings you into view of Refuge de Larribet.

Refuge de Larribet: Owned by the CAF, 62 places, guardian from May to end-September, meals possible (Tel: 05 62 97 25 39).

High Route 7 Alternative: Refuge d'Arrémoulit (2305m) – Refuge Wallon (1864m)

Distance:	**15 kilometres**
Height gain:	**778 metres**
Height loss:	**1219 metres**
Time:	**8 hours**

Although this is an easier alternative to the crossing of Port du Lavedan described above, it is still a serious undertaking, with some rough ground to cover and a long day's trekking hut to hut. It passes to the south of Balaitous and is mostly on Spanish territory. The route could be broken by a night spent in the very fine Refugio Respomuso, four hours or so from Arrémoulit.

Follow directions to Col du Palas as given in High Route 7. From the col descend steeply to the northern end of the Lacs d'Arriel and go along their eastern (left-hand) side. Between the two tarns a high point is passed on your right, beyond which a path descends a little west of south. Go between two further lakes and follow the outflow stream. Keep above a much smaller tarn and trend left (south-east) towards the Respomuso dam. A good path now remains high above the stream flowing from the Respomuso lake, and brings you to some ruins and a chapel. The path now climbs in zig-zags, then contours to the right above the lake before slanting down to Refugio Respomuso (2200m).

Refugio Respomuso: FAM owned, 120 places, permanently manned, meals provided (Tel: 974 49 02 03).

Continue heading south-east to reach the dam and lake of Campo Plano. East of the lake Col de la Fache dips between Pene d'Aragon and Grande Fache. A stream flows from just below the col and a cairned route leads alongside it and brings you to the Lacs de la Fache, half an hour below the col which forms the border.

Col de la Fache (2664m) is reached about six hours after leaving Arrémoulit. Back in France a PNP path takes you easily down past one or two small tarns to the Marcadau's lovely pastures, and across its stream to reach the Wallon hut.

Refuge Wallon: Managed by the CAF, 120 places, guardian from June to end of September, meals provision (Tel: 05 62 92 64 28). (See the Marcadau section above for details of this enchanted area.)

High Route 8: Refuge de Larribet (2070m) – Refuge Wallon (1864m)

Distance:	**14 kilometres**
Height gain:	**1143 metres**
Height loss:	**1349 metres**
Time:	**7 hours**

In good conditions this stage makes a very pleasant trek, but snow can turn the crossing of Col de Cambales into a difficult and potentially hazardous epic. Likewise mist can also make this an awkward place to find. Early in the season an ice-axe can be very useful; at all times a compass should be kept handy.

A good path descends from the Larribet hut into the little valley to the north-east, and crosses to the left bank of a stream flowing through it. It becomes a delightful, flowery walk. In and out of trees the path comes to the more open Arrens Valley about an hour from the hut, where it is advisable to leave the path in favour of cutting across to the right to find a clear trail on the east bank of the Gave d'Arrens. Bear right along this and wander upvalley, now heading roughly south.

After crossing a level section of valley the trail climbs in numerous zig-zags to enter a long, rocky glen, narrow and steep-walled, with the Lacs de Remoulis spread in its floor. The path leads through and heads for the frontier at Port de la Peyre-St-Martin, which is reached about four hours from Larribet.

Shortly before the pass, about 100 metres to the north, an alternative path breaks away to the left (north-east) near what appears to be a ruin. A sign indicates 1½ hours to Col de Cambales. Take this path, climbing into savage country that is often sheathed in snow throughout summer. Another trail is seen heading off to the left, but this should be ignored. Keep going in a vague easterly direction until a gap to the north of Pic de Cambales demands a southerly turn. So reach Col de Cambales (2706m; 5 hours).

Invariably littered with snow, the eastern side of the col demands continued care. First descend a little to the south, then make a northerly turn to cross a slope of scree, then along a rough rocky 'ridge' above some tarns. Boulders, scree and the occasional snow patch slowly give way to smiling lakes and lush vegetation. The path goes down into the Marcadau near a waterfall, and leads unerringly to the large Wallon refuge.

Refuge Wallon: Managed by CAF, 120 places, guardian from June to end of September, meals provision (Tel: 05 62 92 64 28).

Note: Given sufficient time it would be worth interrupting the High Route here to explore the Marcadau Valley. There are many fine walks and easy climbs to be made from a base at the Wallon hut. For suggestions and route descriptions see Marcadau section above.

High Route 9: Refuge Wallon (1864m) – Refuge de Bayssellance (2651m)

Distance:	**11 kilometres**
Height gain:	**1438 metres**
Height loss:	**651 metres**
Time:	**7½ hours**

This walk is a true classic, either as one section of the High Route proper or as an outing in its own right. With three high passes to cross it makes a strenuous day out but, time permitting, it could be broken into two separate stages by a night spent at the Refuge des Oulettes de Gaube beneath the Vignemale's North Face, thereby saving the third pass (Hourquette d'Ossau) for the second day.

On leaving the hut take the down-valley path and cross the Gave de Marcadau by footbridge at the mouth of the Arratille glen. A path leads south into the glen, soon on the true right bank of the Arratille stream. Gain height, exchanging grass for glacier-polished rocks, then back to grass again. Streams and cascades brighten the way. Shortly before reaching Lac d'Arratille a footbridge takes the path across to the left bank of the stream, then heads round the lake's western shore (about 1¼ hours from Wallon).

Cross back to the stream's right bank, south of the lake and below a small tarn, and follow waymarks that lead in a circuitous route among broken rocks. In case of obliteration by snow, the general direction to be followed is south, keeping to the left of the path of a stream until a desolate upper corrie is gained where you find Lac du Col d'Arratille. Traverse the screes well to the left of this lake to reach Col d'Arratille (2528m; 2 hours). The Clot de la Hount face of the Vignemale shows clearly across the intervening Ara Valley.

What follows is a brief Spanish interlude, as the upper reaches of the lovely Ara Valley are crossed. Red and white waymarks direct the way down, first south-eastward, then in an easterly trend, traversing on difficult broken rocks and scree before climbing (cairns) to the rather pleasant pass of Col des Mulets (2591m; 4 hours from Wallon).

A narrow, steep little glen takes you down eastwards, often crossing long snow patches, and brings you without difficulty to a flat marshy plain out of which rises the huge North Face of the Vignemale. Keep left to pick up a clear path coming from down-valley. This takes you to the right over the stream on a footbridge and up to Refuge des Oulettes de Gaube (2151m).

Refuge des Oulettes de Gaube: CAF owned, 75 places, guardian from Easter to mid-October, meals provision (Tel: 05 62 92 62 97). (See Vignemale section above for further details about this particular region.)

The continuing path rises south-eastward with fine views to the Couloir de Gaube, but soon heads north, climbs in zig-zags and comes to a trail junction. Ignore the left-hand path (which leads to Col d'Arraille and the Vallée de Lutour) and continue, now curving south through a region of boulders with the Petit Vignemale seen directly ahead. Sometimes snow patches litter the path, but the trail should be clear all the way to Hourquette d'Ossau (2734m). Refuge de Bayssellance is seen below to the east. But if you have time and energy to spare, it is worth heading up to the right where an easy ridge leads from the pass to the summit of Petit Vignemale (3032m). Allow a little over an hour for this diversion, then descend directly from the pass to the Bayssellance hut.

Refuge de Bayssellance: CAF owned, 70 places, guardian from May to late September, meals provision, 45 places in winter (Tel: 05 62 92 40 25). This hut is invariably very busy in summer.

High Route 10: Refuge de Bayssellance (2651m) – Gavarnie (1365m)

Distance:	**17 kilometres**
Height gain:	**140 metres**
Height loss:	**1426 metres**
Time:	**6–6½ hours**

This particular stage adopts a *variante* of the GR10 as the most interesting route down to Gavarnie, without making the long detour to the Port de Gavarnie and Refuge de la Brèche, as does the official HRP.

The route down-valley from the Bayssellance hut is an old and well-established one, the trail soon coming in view of the Ossoue Glacier (largest in the Pyrenees) which flows down the eastern flanks of the Vignemale. Ignore the path which branches off towards the glacier and instead continue to lose height, passing three of Henry Russell's caves. Shortly after these go below an old glacial moraine and curve round a projection to enter a small bowl through which streams spray. Here, and elsewhere on the path, snow often lies in great cones throughout summer and care should be exercised when crossing.

Now the trail climbs against a cliff, then descends into a long, flat area containing a small lake blocked by the Ossoue dam. Cross a footbridge over the stream and walk along the north shore of the lake, reaching the dam about two hours from the Bayssellance hut. (Cabane d'Ossoue here provides basic emergency shelter.) Beyond the dam a track leads to Gavarnie (8kms) and offers the shortest route down.

Cross a footbridge over the outflow stream and head south following waymarks over grass, then on a clear path up to a level area criss-crossed with streams draining the Vallée de la Canau. Here the Cabane de Lourdes offers more emergency shelter. Cross the main Canau stream by footbridge. The GR10 path then breaks from the 'official' HRP route and cuts off to the north (left), then eases round towards the south-east to pass yet another basic hut, Cabane de Sausse-Dessus in the indented glen of the same name. North again, then eastward on a fairly level course high above the Ossoue Valley, you wander over several streams and leave the PNP. A steady descent, and an interesting trail, takes you down to the Gavarnie-Port de Gavarnie road. Bear left and follow this into Gavarnie, passing on the way **Grange de Holle**, a CAF refuge with 48 beds and meals provision (Tel: 05 62 92 48 77).

See section headed Gavarnie above for details of accommodation, facilities, route suggestions etc for this, the most visited and best-known of all Pyrenean villages. There is an infrequent bus service from here to Lourdes.

HIGH ROUTE SECTION TWO:
GAVARNIE TO MALADETA

Maps:	IGN Carte de Randonnées No 4 'Bigorre' and No 5 'Luchon' 1:50,000; Editorial Alpina 'Posets' and 'Maladeta–Aneto' 1:25,000 IGN TOP 25 series nos: 1748OT, 1748ET and 1848OT at 1:25,000
Accommodation:	Mountain huts or inns on all stages except one
Access:	Train from Paris to Lourdes, or by air from London to Tarbes-Lourdes. Then bus from Lourdes to Gavarnie. At the end of the walk, train from Luchon to Paris via Toulouse. Or by air from Toulouse to London.
Time required:	7–8 days

Between Gavarnie and the Maladeta massif there is some very fine trekking country; mountain cirques, unfrequented valleys, empty ridges, high passes, and always with big mountains in view. There are no villages on the route once you leave Gavarnie, and only one hamlet, Héas. All refuges and inns along this section, however, provide meals during the main summer season. But the Hospice de Rioumajou, at the end of the third day's walk from Gavarnie (High Route 13), has only light snacks and drinks for sale, and closes at 6pm. No accommodation is available, so camping is the only option here. If you plan to backpack throughout you will need to carry food and cooking fuel for at least five days before there is an opportunity to make a short diversion (to Benasque) to restock.

The route climbs out of Gavarnie to cross the high ridge walling its valley to the east, then descends steeply towards the Cirque d'Estaubé before heading north through the Estaubé glen to reach Héas, an unpretentious hamlet that gazes into the larger Cirque de Troumouse. On the next stage two passes separate Héas from the Cirque de Barroude, the eastern side of Cirque de Troumouse, where accommodation is in a PNP refuge. Early in the summer snow can make this crossing difficult and ice-axes could be helpful.

From Barroude to Rioumajou is a long, hard day along the frontier ridge, left foot in France, right foot in Spain for some of the way. Then at the end of it comes a tiring descent to the valley. Next day necessitates climbing all the way out again in order to cross the frontier ridge and descend to Viados, a collection of barns idyllically set beneath Pico de Posets, second highest mountain in all the Pyrenees.

From Viados to the Estos Valley is a very pleasant stage, crossing the easy Puerto de Gistain on a northern projecting spur of Posets, with views towards the big Maladeta massif. The stage from Refugio de Estos to the Maladeta unfortunately involves a certain amount of road walking, although strong and experienced mountain trekkers could make a high crossing over the Lliterola and Remune ridges to avoid the worst of it (study the map for possibilities).

Leaving the Maladeta for the home-bound train involves crossing back into France by way of the Port de Venasque, thereby deserting the High Route, and descending through the Vallée de la Pique to Luchon.

Walkers with plenty of time at their disposal will find lots of opportunities to divert from the High Route along the way in order to explore neighbourhood valleys, peaks and hillsides. Relevant sections of this guidebook to study for ideas are: Gavarnie; Estaubé, Troumouse and Barroude; Posets and Maladeta.

High Route 11: Gavarnie (1365m) – Héas (1500m)

Distance:	**16 kilometres**
Height gain:	**1115 metres**
Height loss:	**1080 metres**
Time:	**7 hours**

After a long train journey through France, followed by the bus ride from Lourdes, this seven-hour walk (plus rests) will no doubt be found somewhat taxing. Walkers not carrying a tent will find there is only one possibility to interrupt this stage, and that is by spending a night at the Refuge des Espuguettes, just two hours above Gavarnie.

Wander south out of Gavarnie towards the cirque on a broad mule track. About one kilometre beyond the village the track crosses a stone bridge to the left-hand (east) side of the Gave de Pau, and soon a path breaks away to the left. Follow this as it climbs grass-covered hillsides heading roughly south-east and with good views to the cirque. The path rises without difficulty and brings you to the Plateau de Pailla. The trail veers left in a northerly sweep, gains more height and, heading back to the south-east, comes to Refuge des Espuguettes (2027m).

Refuge des Espuguettes: Owned by PNP, 60 places, guardian from July to mid-September, meals provision (Tel: 05 62 92 40 63).

The path continues beyond the hut, rising towards the ridge linking Piméné and Pic Rouge de Pailla, and divides at about 2260 metres. The left-hand option climbs to Piméné, but the main trail sweeps to the south-east and continues to gain height to the Hourquette d'Alans (2430m; 3hrs 15 mins) which separates the valleys of Gavarnie and Estaubé. Descend into the Estaubé glen by way of numerous zig-zags, soon heading north-east. Once in the valley proper the path wanders along the left bank of the stream.

At the far end of rough boulder-strewn pastures you come to the Gloriettes lake, blocked by a huge dam. Cross the dam to its eastern side and walk down to a car park, where a service road winds down to join the Gedre–Héas road. There you turn right and walk up to the hamlet of Héas.

Héas: accommodation at the *gîte d'étape* Auberge Le Refuge (Tel: 05 62 92 47 74), at Auberge de la Munia (Tel: 05 62 92 48 39) and La Chaumière – also camping – (Tel: 05 62 92 48 66).

High Route 12: Héas (1500m) – Refuge de Barroude (2373m)

Distance:	**10 kilometres**
Height gain:	**1227 metres**
Height loss:	**354 metres**
Time:	**6 hours**

A pleasant day's journey with a wide variety of scenery; in early summer snow may create difficulties when crossing Hourquette de Héas and Hourquette de Chermentas.

Just beyond the chapel in Héas, on the road that leads to the Cirque de Troumouse, there is a rough car park. On the left of the road the path to Hourquette de Héas begins, signposted as 3½ hours away. It climbs steeply up the hillside to the right of the Aguila stream. When the incline slackens Cabane de l'Aguila (1910m) is passed on the opposite bank. After this the path cuts away from the stream, returning near some cascades before heading off to the south-east.

The route is clearly defined, mostly on a well-trodden path, but sometimes aided by cairns. It climbs the grassy Montagne des Aiguillous, then goes through a shallow gully to emerge near Cabane d'Aiguillous which stands above the stream. Go over the stream to the right of the hut and cross a broad undulating depression. Above, mountains walling the valley appear incapable of offering a route through, but a path toils up the eastern slopes on long winding sweeps, offering fine views back to the west where the Vignemale commands the horizon. Near the head of the pass the trail has been cut as a ledge, and Hourquette de Héas (2608m) is gained with a mixture of surprise and relief, about 3–3½ hours from Héas.

From this rocky pass descend in zig-zags, first to the north until another path is met, then bear right, still losing height but more gradually now. Make a traverse of mountainside going south-east, before climbing once more to reach the next pass, Hourquette de Chermentas (2439m), where a fresh vista opens out.

Go down in tight zig-zags on scree, and bear right to pass close below cliffs that form the eastern wall of Pic des Aiguillous. The path then climbs once more on scree towards a minor pass. Leading round below the long Barroude wall the path is met by another coming from Plan d'Aragnouet on the left. Continue on, now heading south-east on boulder-strewn grass and sometimes snow, with several pools lying around. Lac de Barroude is seen to the right. The little Refuge de Barroude is located above the path on the left, standing on a grassy bluff.

Refuge de Barroude: PNP owned, 20 places inside, plus 10 in tent annexe, guardian from July to mid-September, meals provision (Tel: 05 62 39 61 10).

Note: For further information regarding this region of lakes,

Lac de Barroude (High Route 12)

mountain walls and rolling pasture, please consult the relevant section above, headed Estaubé, Troumouse and Barroude.

High Route 13: Refuge de Barroude (2373m) – Hospice de Rioumajou (1560m)

Distance:	17 kilometres
Height gain:	472 metres
Height loss:	1285 metres
Time:	9–10 hours

Do not set out for Rioumajou unless you can be sure of fine settled weather. For several hours the way traces a high exposed ridge with few opportunities to escape should a storm appear. Mountain walkers of limited experience are advised against tackling it. Begin as early as possible, and fill water bottles before starting as it's a very long way before water is found again. A less-demanding two-day Spanish alternative, leading to Viados, is briefly outlined at the end of the Estaubé, Troumouse and Barroude section above.

Go down to the stream flowing from the eastern end of Lac de Barroude, cross it and take the left of two marked paths. Waymarks lead round to the north, gaining height steadily and traversing a steep hillside on narrow terraces to come onto a grassy spur projecting north from Pic de Port Vieux. Descend its eastern side along a vague line of cairns to reach a mule path ascending from the left at about 2280 metres. Turn right on this and climb to the pass of Port Vieux (2378m; 1½–2 hours).

It is not necessary to follow waymarks climbing steeply left; instead head east across steep grass slopes, but taking care especially when the ground is damp from past rain or heavy dew. Steadily gain height to reach the frontier ridge a little north of Port de Bielsa, a narrow pass guarded by rocks, whose historic use has been overtaken by the road tunnel far beneath. Descend across the pass, keeping on the Spanish side, then traverse the steep mountainside below Pic de Marioules – grass and lines of rocks – heading east-south-east. Do not lose too much height, but aim for a metal marker pole painted red–yellow–green (there are several of them) on a plunging spur. On reaching this spur climb north on a marked route towards the ridge once more. Now head east towards Pic de Bataillance (2604m), which is gained 3½–4 hours after setting out.

Now follows a pleasant stretch of ridge work involving a little scrambling. The route remains mostly along the crest itself, heading south-east with very fine distant views. On reaching Port de Hechempy (2450m) the pyramid of Pic de Marty Caberrou rises ahead. Fortunately our route skirts it.

Continue to rise towards the peak, going round two rocky lumps on the ridge, keeping to the south of them, and at about 2500 metres leave the ridge to go left (north-east) on the French side. Follow a line of animal tracks across grass, then scree, rising to cross a rocky rib beyond which descend on more scree to a small, low plateau south of Pic de la Hount (about 5 hours from Barroude).

Note: A little below and to the east of this plateau a stream offers the first opportunity to restock with water since leaving the hut. Bear in mind too, that another 4–5 hours will be required to reach the Rioumajou. If the weather remains settled, trekkers with a tent could find space to camp near the stream, on a grassy spur which projects over the Vallée de Moudang, thereby turning this into a two-day crossing.

The continuing route descends slightly east of the plateau, then, passing below rock bands, rises once more with tracks to lead you back onto the ridge at Port de Moudang (2495m). Go up screes on the south side to reach a vague pass at a junction of ridges below Pic de Lia. This little notch of a pass (2752m; 6½ hours) offers a sobering view of the way down into the depths of Rioumajou. Ahead the great mass of the Posets massif is clearly seen, while behind Monte Perdido dazzles its snow and ice.

Descend towards Rioumajou with great care, going north-east on extremely crumbly schist, followed by broken 'crests' which lead down to scree proper. The first 50 metres are the worst. Near the foot of the steep descent waymarks are found which lead right to climb and cross a rocky spur bordering a depression littered with boulders and scree. Grass slopes take the place of ankle-twisting rocks, the route being led by infrequent waymarks.

Although high ridges have been left behind, and it is all vegetation down into the valley, the route is not an easy one. At all costs avoid being drawn into a direct descent to the valley as large outcrops form major obstacles. Instead, veer south-eastwards, keeping alert to the few markings that exist. Losing height diagonally on grass and among juniper and alpenroses the route leads to the occasional flat area, sometimes boggy with cotton grass, and at about 2100 metres a cluster of pine trees on a ridge. Go down to the south into the valley moulded by Pic de l'Espade, making for the large flat area from which a stream flows out to the left. Leave this valley heading south-east, and then make directly for the Hospice de Rioumajou seen on the left bank of the stream to the north-east.

Hospice de Rioumajou: Former ancient hospice; no accommodation, but open until 6pm for snacks and drinks in summer. Wild camping tolerated in pastures nearby.

High Route 14: Hospice de Rioumajou (1560m) – Refugio de Viados (1810m)

Distance:	**11 kilometres**
Height gain:	**1126 metres**
Height loss:	**876 metres**
Time:	**6½ hours**

This stage is a real joy. After a remorseless haul out of the valley, Port de Caouerère provides a magnificent introduction to the western face of the huge Posets massif. A descent into the valley of the Cinqueta de la Pez on a bright summer's afternoon is to walk in the land of dreams, while the hamlet of Viados at the end of the day comes as no anti-climax. A night spent in the shadow of Posets can well be a night to remember.

Several passes into Spain are accessible from Rioumajou, but the route to follow from the courtyard of the Hospice is that marked red. It goes south on the true left bank of the Rioumajou, crosses a side-stream flowing from the west and continues up-valley. Cross the Rioumajou stream by a bridge and head east, gaining height steeply among trees above the left bank of the Millarioux stream in its narrow glen.

The path divides after about 1¼ hours from the Hospice. Ignore that which heads off to the right, and instead go down to the stream, cross it, and climb south-eastward towards a grassy bluff with a stream on either side. Waymarks, and an occasional direction post, lead the way, although it is easy to lose sight of the markings. Keep the ravine through which the Caouerère stream flows on your left, and clamber among shrubs and trees until a long, seemingly endless slope of scree is reached. A path is seen climbing this, which leads directly to the Port de Caouerère (3 hours).

The pass itself is not particularly attractive, but the views are sufficient reward for gaining it. Spain lies spread below to the south-east, with the hint of sun-trapped valleys and dipping ridges leading the eye irresistibly towards the Posets.

At first the descent, east-south-east on slopes avoiding deep beds of springtime's streams, threatens to be a little tedious. But soon grass-covered hillsides and acres of alpenroses offer a fair substitute, and a vague path leads through woods (**Note:** I am informed it is best to 'keep towards the path by a ruined cabane'), losing height towards the Cinqueta de la Pez. Again, it is easy to lose the way. Work a route down to the main valley and reach a flat area with a rain gauge near a bend in the stream. The path here resumes along the right bank (4½ hours).

Rising above the stream, pass a shepherd's cabane, and then continue across a slope to a side-stream which you cross before returning to trees. Continue along the Cinqueta's right bank to reach a broad forest track. Keep walking downhill on this until you come to a bridge with a cascade on your left. Cross the bridge and bear left on the dirt road that leads to Viados. The refugio stands on a grassy bluff above the summer farming hamlet.

Refugio de Viados: privately owned, 40 beds inside, 6 in the annexe, guardian from July to late-September, meals provision (Tel: 974 50 60 82). See Posets section above for details and alternative routes.

High Route 15: Refugio de Viados (1810m) – Refugio de Estos (1835m)

Distance:	**11 kilometres**
Height gain:	**793 metres**
Height loss:	**768 metres**
Time:	**5 hours**

The standard High Route returns to France above Viados by way of Col d'Aygues-Tortes, but a two-day *variante* remains south of the watershed and skirts the Posets massif in order to approach the Maladeta via the Esera Valley. This is the route chosen here; a very fine walk and a good opportunity to explore the delightful valley of the Rio Estos. Between Viados and the Estos hut the route crosses Puerto de Gistain (2603m), an easy pass that gives long views to the distant Maladeta.

Leaving the Viados hut descend a little towards a collection of barns. A clear path heads north-east across the hillside just above the barns and is followed for about three kilometres, mostly well above the true right bank (west side) of the Cinqueta de Añes Cruces. (Various editions of the Editorial Alpina map wrongly show this path as being on the east side; it is important to follow the path on the west bank.)

The valley narrows and about 1½ hours after setting out a stream is seen appearing from the east to discharge into the main stream. Before reaching this emergent stream, leave the main path which continues upvalley towards the frontier ridge, cross the Cinqueta and find a path which climbs up the eastern side towards the Puerto de Gistain. As you gain height so the path becomes less evident, but a line of cairns leads to the pass itself; a broad saddle divided by a

Puerto de Gistain between Viados and Refugio de Estos (High Route 15)

rocky bluff (3 hours). From it the Estos Valley looks inviting below, while far off the Maladeta makes an obvious goal.

Pass the bluff on its right-hand side and descend, steeply at first, crossing snow patches and boulders, until at last the infant Estos stream is seen. From the start keep to its left bank and, crossing assorted tributaries, come to a path that leads all the way to the Estos hut.

Refugio de Estos: Owned by the FEM, it is the largest in the Pyrenees with room for 180, guardian in permanent occupation, full meals service (Tel: 974 55 14 83). (The Estos Valley is a tempting place to stay for a day or two in order to explore further. See Posets section above for route ideas.)

High Route 16: Refugio de Estos (1835m) – Hospital de Benasque (1750m)

Distance:	**18 kilometres**
Height gain:	**530 metres**
Height loss:	**615 metres**
Time:	**4–5 hours**

There is a similarity between the valleys of the Estos and the upper Esera on the north side of the Maladeta, and the massifs they moat are the two highest in the Pyrenees, now protected within the *Parque Natural Posets-Maladeta*. Unfortunately, this link route necessitates walking along a road for some distance – the first since leaving Héas several days ago. Purists will want to walk all the way; others less committed may be tempted to try hitching. If you need to restock with food, or have a longing for the 'fleshpots', Benasque lies 3.5 kilometres off route down the road.

A path heads down-valley directly from the Estos hut, and keeps on the left bank, in and out of trees, until losing height where the valley opens and a bridge crosses the stream opposite Cabane de Turmo. Cross the bridge and bear left on the continuing path which becomes a major track. It moves away from the stream for some way, then returns to it near a small gorge at the mouth of the valley. Cross back to the left bank and descend beyond a small dam to the confluence with the Esera. Benasque is a short distance down-valley to the right. (Hotels, restaurants, shops, post office, banks etc. See Maladeta section for full details.)

Bear left in the valley and walk up the wide metalled road. A short distance beyond a dammed lake a choice of routes is offered: a) the continuing west bank road, or b) a dirt road which follows the east bank. If taking option a) walk to the end of the road, then descend to the Rio Esera, crossing a few streams on the way, then over a bridge to the Hospital de Benasque. Option b) leads directly to the Hospital de Benasque building via the Baños de Benasque spa (shown on the map as Bañs de Benás). The renovated Hospital (a former *hospice*) is located beside the Esera where it curves south-westward out of the upper pastures.

Hospital de Benasque: Hotel-refuge accommodation in three grades, meals provision, open all year, 18 places (Tel: 974 55 10 52).

Note i: With a wide variety of walks and climbs to be had in and around the Esera/Maladeta, the Hospital de Benasque makes an obvious base. Consult the Maladeta section above for ideas.

Note ii: For the continuing HRP see High Route 17. If, however, your High Route trek ends with this stage, see High Route Departure Link below.

High Route Departure Link: Hospital
de Benasque (1750m) – Luchon (625m)

Distance:	**19 kilometres**
Height gain:	**694 metres**
Height loss:	**2049 metres**
Time:	**5–6 hours**

A return to France for the journey home is made over the classic Port de Venasque, a very fine rocky pass in the frontier ridge. From the Port there follows a steep descent to the ancient Hospice de France, and a long road walk through the Vallée de la Pique to Luchon.

From the Hospital go down to the Esera and follow it upstream for about three minutes, then cross by a log footbridge. Continue upvalley to a second log bridge and recross to the right-hand side of the stream. The path now rises up a grass slope between streams to a fork. Take the left branch to climb the valley's walling hillside with views growing in extent as you gain height. About two hours from the Hospital you should arrive at the Port de Venasque (2444m; Portillon de Benas on the Editorial Alpina map). Looking back the Maladeta forms a great block, the moulding of its fast-receding glaciers clearly evident.

Descend into France on a trail that cuts down over screes towards several tarns, the Boums de Port, beside the largest of which is a small hut.

Refuge du Port de Venasque (2249m): CAF owned, 16 spaces, guardian from June to September, meals provision (Tel: 05 61 79 26 46).

Continue down to the right of the tarns. The path is steep in places and crosses and recrosses the stream flowing through the narrow glen. Having returned to the left bank the way zig-zags down to the Vallée de la Pique and the Hospice de France. Bear left and walk down the road to Luchon, about 11 kilometres away.

Bagnères de Luchon: Hotels, campsites, restaurants, shops, banks, post office, railway station (north of town) with trains to Paris via Toulouse.

HIGH ROUTE SECTION THREE: MALADETA TO ANDORRA

<table>
<tr><td>Maps:</td><td>IGN Carte de Randonnées No 5 'Luchon', No 6 'Couserans' and No 7 'Haute-Ariège–Andorre' 1:50,000. Or Editorial Alpina 'Maladeta–Aneto' 1:25,000, 'Val d'Aran' 1:40,000, 'Montgarri' 1:25,000 and 'Pica d'Estats–Mont Roig' 1:40,000</td></tr>
<tr><td>Accommodation:</td><td>Mountain huts or inns, and wild camping</td></tr>
<tr><td>Access:</td><td>Train from Paris to Luchon via Toulouse; or by air from London to Toulouse. At the end of the walk, bus or taxi from Andorra to l'Hospitalet-près-l'Andorre, and train from there to Paris via Toulouse; or by air from Toulouse to London.</td></tr>
<tr><td>Time required:</td><td>8–10 days</td></tr>
</table>

This final third section of the High Route across the High Pyrenees is almost entirely in Spain and is the most demanding of all, with several remote areas and high passes to negotiate. Since accommodation is not possible at the end of each stage, camping equipment and some food should be carried. It is not recommended for inexperienced mountain trekkers, but for strong walkers with an ability to read both a map and the country itself. Given favourable conditions the wild landscapes of the Spanish Pyrenees will provide plenty of rewards. An ice-axe could be useful at any time of year.

Leaving the Maladeta behind the highest pass of the whole route is crossed in order to gain access to the valley of the Noguera Ribagorzana. This in turn allows a climb eastwards to the lovely lake-gleaming wilderness of the Aigüestortes-Besiberri region. The trek continues across its northern limits before sloping down into the pastures of the Vall d'Aran and the village of Salardu, from whose alleyways the Maladeta can be seen far off over intervening ridges.

A long but easy day's walking out of Salardu follows a curving valley for several hours to put you in line for a hard ten-hour stage that crosses three high passes on ridges splaying out from Mont Roig. Two more, but less arduous, stages bring you down into the Vall Ferrera in readiness for a final trek out of Spain and into France, and straight out again by crossing Port de Rat into Andorra.

High Route Access Link: Luchon (Hospice de France, 1385m) – Esera Valley (1990m)

Distance:	**8 kilometres**
Height gain:	**1059 metres**
Height loss:	**454 metres**
Time:	**4–4½ hours**

From the railhead at Luchon to the Forau dels Aigualluts where this link route joins the main HRP requires a long walk. The route begins with 11 kilometres of road journey to the Hospice de France (hitch or taxi), then a steep climb over the Port de Venasque – but note that there is some avalanche danger until the mountains have shed their winter/spring snow. It might be worth spending the first night at the Refuge du Port de Venasque, about half-hour below the frontier crossing, and tackle Stage 17 of the High Route fresh next day.

From the Hospice de France a clear signed path leads south-west across a stream (the Pique) and climbs, easily at first, then more steeply with zig-zags through a narrow valley towards the frontier ridge. The historic mule path mounts to a high stony corrie to find the Boums de Port tarns and Refuge du Port de Venasque (2249m) about 2–2½ hours from the roadhead at Hospice de France.

Refuge du Port de Venasque: CAF-owned, 16 places, guardian from June to September, meals provision (Tel: 05 61 79 26 46).

Remaining left of the hut the path skirts the base of Pic de la Mine, then rises in more zig-zags over scree to find the narrow cleft of the Port de Venasque (2444m) about 30 minutes from the refuge. Descend on the Spanish side to the lip of a grassy terrace and continue down the hillside towards the Maladeta massif, until you come to a major path in the valley bed near the head of a dirt road.

When the path forks take the left branch (the main trail climbs to the Renclusa refuge for ascents of Aneto, Maladeta, etc), rising gently, then in zig-zags to mount a minor ridge. This leads into an upper level of the valley. Slope down to a pastureland which leads directly to the pit of the Forau dels Aigualluts into which streams draining the next valley level pour in a waterfall, about two hours from Refuge du Port de Venasque. Here you join High Route 17.

High Route 17: Hospital de Benasque (1750m) – Refugi Sant Nicolau (1630m)

Distance:	**15 kilometres**
Height gain:	**1178 metres**
Height loss:	**1538 metres**
Time:	**7½–8 hours**

This stage of the High Route to Refugi Sant Nicolau in the valley of the Noguera Ribagorzana crosses Coll de Mulleres, at 2928 metres the highest point on the full Ocean to Sea traverse. It should not be attempted if there is any chance of a storm, nor in poor visibility.

Leaving Hospital de Benasque go down to the Esera and bear right upstream for about three minutes to find a log footbridge. Cross the stream here and continue upvalley to a second long bridge by which you recross to the right-hand side. The path rises up a grass slope between streams and in 10 minutes comes to a signed junction of paths. Ignore the left fork (to Port de Venasque), cross a pine-topped bluff and go along the edge of two or three shallow marshy troughs to gain the Plan d'Estan. Skirt the left-hand edge of the Plan – a lake is sometimes found here, although this has usually disappeared by mid-summer – and at the far end veer right to join the unmetalled road from the Hospital de Benasque. Bear left and follow the road to its end at a rough parking area known as Besurta (1915m).

Cross the stream and at the end of the track take the continuing footpath which is partially paved. When it forks take the left-hand option (the alternative climbs to the Renclusa refugio) and about 30 minutes later come to the Forau dels Aigualluts (Trou de Toro), a large hollow with a waterfall plunging into it. This is reached about two hours from the Hospital de Benasque. Go beyond this and head across the left-hand edge of the Plan de Aiguallut towards a stream

The Valleta de la Escaleta – the head of the Esera Valley (High Route 17)

flowing from the hinted Escaleta glen to the south-east. Cross this stream and climb into the Escaleta on a good path rising above its true left bank. Ahead the double-pronged Forcanada dominates the view.

The path goes towards a cascade, then rises above it. Shortly after cairns lead you scrambling to mount a rocky bluff, then left on a broad shelf above a minor gorge. Continue deeper into the valley to reach the first of several tarns. Pass this on the right, cross the stream which feeds it and follow the path up to another tarn. Go round this to the left and gain height on the true right bank of a stream washing down rocks to the south-east, draining from a third tarn.

On reaching the upper tarn (2459m) cross its outlet and mount south-westwards up a rough landscape of boulders. Above to the south smooth glacial slabs form a low skyline with cairns leading up it. Follow these to reach a granite plateau with a few clear streams and pools trapped in shallow dips. Now bear left and rise eastwards toward Tuc de Mulleres, keeping left of an easy ridge running north-east between Tuc de Mulleres and Cap de Toro (about 4½ hours from the Renclusa).

Follow the ridge a little north of its lowest point (Coll de Mulleres) to find a small cairn. Cross the ridge here, taking great care down the steep eastern side. At the foot of the initial rocks bear left in a diagonal descent over rocky terrain, cairns leading away from a line of cliffs that plunge to the Estanys de Mulleres. Continue to follow cairns that lead down, sometimes steeply through minor gullies, now and then on poor grass, sometimes looping to the left to avoid more rock bands. Keep well away from the upper Mulleres tarn, but come down to meet the outflow of the second, larger, lake, keeping left to reach two more tarns.

Note: On a bluff above the left shore of the lower lakes there stands an orange-painted metal shelter, Refugio Mulleres (Molières; 2360m), permanently open, unguarded and with space for about 12.

Now skirt in a wide left-hand loop, with cairns becoming a little scarce, to avoid yet more rock bands, then go down where practicable to the valley floor. Bear left along the valley and descend a narrow path beside the stream which cascades to a lower level. Take the path along the left bank of the stream, crossing after a while to the right, and back again a few minutes later by stepping-stones. The trail loses height, goes through trees and comes to a broad meadowland with the end of the Viella road tunnel projecting ahead. Near its southern end is the site of the ancient Hospital de Viella.

Refugi Sant Nicolau (Refugi de Boca Sud): Open all year, 40 places, meals service (Tel: 973 69 70 52).

High Route 18: Refugi Sant Nicolau (1630m) – Refugi de la Restanca (2010m)

Distance:	11 kilometres
Height gain:	838 metres
Height loss:	458 metres
Time:	8 hours

A lovely trek through a landscape of lakes and granite wilderness, it is however, another fairly long and taxing stage, but the scenery never wanes and in good weather few difficulties should arise. The main problems come from a constant desire to throw off the rucksack and soak in the views!

From the south end of the tunnel go up a dirt road leading into Vall de Conangles to the east. Follow the track as far as a bridge which takes it over to the left bank of a broad stream. Immediately before the bridge turn off the track to the left and cross the stream flowing from Estany Redo, hidden above to the north. Across this take a narrow path leading among beech trees, maintaining an easterly course. Beeches are traded for conifers after a small clearing has been crossed, and soon after the path opens to rock-pitted meadows with a pleasant grassy cirque ahead.

Halfway through the valley the path becomes faint, but a few ill-spaced cairns guide you north-westward, across a minor stream and then up its left bank, before heading up a little gorge. On reaching a path going off to the right (2100m), follow it heading east, and gain height to reach in half an hour or so, Port de Rius (2315m; 2 hours). The first of the day's lakes lies ahead, but spare a moment to gaze back the way you have come. A fine panorama includes the long Mulleres glen, its high ridge and the snows of the Maladeta beyond that.

Follow a clear and easy path along the northern shore of Estany de Rius. At its outflow bear right on a cairned trail, leaving an alternative path which heads into the valley spreading below to the east.

Note: This alternative path (GR11) goes along the right-hand side of the valley of Arties from the lake's outflow, and offers a useful short-cut to the Restanca hut. Should the weather be threatening this is the path to take, saving about three hours of walking. A water source about 200 metres along this path is worth noting.

Our path goes south, working a way over a rock and grass hummock, passes a couple of pools and shortly after reaches the northern end of the lovely Estany Tort de Rius. Cairns continue to lead the way along the left-hand (eastern) side clambering over white granite boulders and slabs that wall it. At the south-eastern end of the lake go up an easy scoop of valley coming from the south, and having attained the upper level on a slight depression, follow cairns that lead left (east) to gain Collado de l'Estany de Mar (2468m; 4½ hours). Views are stunning in all directions.

The descent to Estany de Mar below is rather dramatic and very tiring. It goes down eastwards on a tightly winding narrow path. Spongy turf at the foot of crags is very welcome, then you head to the right (south-east) to cross streams flowing to the lake, and go along the eastern shoreline following cairns and vague hints of path. The route rises over projecting cliffs and eventually reaches the northern end of the lake.

Veer left to descend steeply on a continuing but now clear path to reach a grassy bowl through which the lake's outflow stream drains, having first been diverted through a conduit. Across this stream go steeply down on a path heading north to reach the dammed Estany de la Restanca. The refugi has been relocated to its eastern shore.

Refugi de la Restanca: FEEC owned, places for 80, guardian in summer, meals provision (Tel: 608 03 65 59). (All the country to the south and east is described in the section headed Aigüestortes West – Besiberri Massif.)

High Route 19: Refugi de la Restanca (2010m) – Salardu (1268m)

Distance:	18 kilometres
Height gain:	708 metres
Height loss:	1450 metres
Time:	7½ hours

This day's journey noses along the northern uplands of the Besiberri region, a trek of simple pleasures and wide vistas where a compass, accurately read, will be welcome should mists come drifting. Tarns and streams promote day-dreams and inspire further visits.

Take the path which climbs to the south-east, steeply in places, to emerge at the western end of Estany de Cap de Port with the cliffs of Pic de Monges looming above. Follow round the north shore of the tarn, and from its end steadily gain height among boulders, the way always clearly defined with numerous cairns. Port de Güellicrestada (2475m) is topped in just under 1½ hours from the hut. Above to the left rises Montardo d'Aran (see Route 144).

On the eastern side of the pass go down to a low-slung grassy plateau with Estany de Monges below to the right, and head south-east towards a brief saddle in a rocky spur. Pass through this and descend to a tarn below, going along its eastern shore shortly before heading left to cross a bluff which leads down to the outflow of the large Estany de Mengades (2307m). Port de Caldes is seen to the north-east, Agulles de Travessani to the south-east, and off to the south-west the long ridge of Besiberri forming a magnificent skyline.

A path coming from the Ventosa hut leads up the granite boulder-land above which Port de Caldes is found. Port de Caldes (2550m; 2½

Estany de Monges (High Route 19)

hours) is a grassy saddle from which the onward route appears inviting. Go down the eastern side, by-passing a little tarn, then keep left of a stream, still heading east. In a lower level of valley join a second stream flowing from the right. Bear left and follow this down-valley all the way to the dammed Estany Major de Colomers (3½ hours).

Refugi de Colomers (2100m): FEEC owned, 30 places, guardian from mid-June to late September, meals provided (Tel: 973 25 30 08). Another hut nearby, basic facilities only, is permanently open.

From the dam descend steeply on a clear path towards Vall d'Aiguamotx, soon joining a dirt track. Follow this down-valley, taking short-cuts where possible. The track leads all the way to Salardu and is unsurfaced until it draws near the fancy hotel/spa at Baños de Tredos (8kms from Salardu). The valley through which it runs is a pure delight. In spring and early summer meadows are flush with wild flowers, later cattle and horses graze here, and in full summer Spanish families gather to picnic. In the upper part of the valley there are numerous idyllic wild campsites; below the Banos camping is forbidden.

About 6½ hours from Restanca reach a large dammed lake. Continue along the road and a little under an hour later arrive in Salardu. It would be prudent to stock up with provisions before departing the village as there's no other opportunity for shopping for at least 2½ days.

Salardu: accommodation in hotels, youth hostel (180 places, Tel: 973 64 52 71), in Refugi Rosta (open July–September, 50 places, Tel: 973 64 53 08) and the CEC's Xalet Juli Soler i Santalo (100 beds, June–September, Tel: 973 64 50 16). The village has shops, restaurants and a bank.

High Route 20: Salardu (1268m) – Palanca de Pine (Barranco de Comamala, 1339m)

Distance:	30 kilometres
Height gain:	612 metres
Height loss:	541 metres
Time:	8 hours

This long valley walk (accommodation in 4 hours but not at the end of this stage) turns a pleasant day's trek into one of some consequence. Campers will have the reassurance of a tent, but those relying on a bivouac will keep a jaundiced eye on the weather.

Leave Salardu to head north-east up a narrow lane which goes to Bagergue. Either follow the road all the way as it climbs in long sweeps up the eastern hillside, or take a footpath which branches off to the right about 400 metres beyond Salardu. The path (not always easy) eventually rejoins the road which you then follow round the southern shoulder of Serra de Comalada to reach the flat plain of Pla de Beret where a number of streams converge to form the Noguera Pallaresa. Looking back a panorama of jostling peaks confuses the southern skyline. Far off can be seen the snowy mass of the Maladeta.

Head along the valley track without diversion to reach the ruined hamlet of Montgarri (1640m; 4 hours). The Sanctuari de Montgarri, dating from 1117, is seen first on the far bank of the stream. Next to it is the Refugi Amics de Montgarri (1600m).

Refugi Amics de Montgarri: Open all year except November and early May, 30 places, meals provision (Tel: 973 64 50 64).

Continue along the track on the right bank of the Noguera Pallaresa as it makes a long sweep to the right, for some time through forest. About 1¾ hours from Montgarri cross a wide open area and curve right to lose height. On the left is a large building, and it is possible here to make a short-cut to rejoin the track where it crosses a bridge to the left bank (**Refugi El Fornet**, Bonabé, 40 places, meals provided; Tel: 973 62 65 22). Shortly after, pass a row of granaries; a side stream is crossed and later another stream gushes from the left to pass beneath the track in a concrete drain. The track then generally loses height and near a bend in the Noguera recrosses to the right bank over a bridge (about 7½ hours from Salardu).

Note: From this point on there are few sites for a tent until a sharp climb has been made into the valley of the Comamala, whose terrain only encourages the camper a further 1½ hours on. Farther along the Noguera, another 45 minutes or so away, is the picturesque hamlet of Alos de Isil, with restaurant, grocery and Refugi Casa Sastrés (45 places, meals provided; Tel: 973 62 65 22). But this is not on tomorrow's route and will therefore add extra time to an already heavy day's trekking.

Continue along the track going south. Soon a bridge is seen suspended over the Noguera on the left, the Palanca de Pine. Cross this for the route to Coll de la Cornella.

High Route 21: Palanca de Pine (1339m) – Bordes de Graus (1360m)

Distance:	17 kilometres
Height gain:	1414 metres
Height loss:	1305 metres
Time:	10 hours

Note: The 'official' HRP does not descend to Bordes de Graus, but cuts away from the route described here some way above the hamlet of Cuanca, to visit Noarre. But this has no facilities, and is still a long way from the next manned refugio. Our route makes a southward loop to Tabescan (Tavascan) for a chance to restock on High Route 22.

This epic stage crosses several high passes with few signs of a path. Although not especially difficult in fine weather, it is a serious trek which should not be undertaken lightly. Only experienced mountain walkers should tackle it, and then only in settled conditions. Campers may find a suitable site for a tent beside the Curios tarn (5½–6 hours after setting out), and so split this into a two-day stage. It should be borne in mind that Bordes de Graus has a 2-star campsite and nothing more. No provisions or conventional accommodation available until Tabescan, a further 1½ hours further on.

From the bridge over the Noguera follow a track on the north side of the Barranca de Comamala; this later deteriorates to an indistinct footpath which brings you up through a rough glen to a second valley level of pastureland, across which a cascade dashes down its south-eastern corner. Keeping to the left of the stream aim for the cascades, guided by cairns across little tributary streams, and then climb slopes of rock and shrubs keeping the cascades to your right. So arrive in a little enclosed pasture with a small tarn off to the right (about 3 hours).

From here the route heads up a sloping glen in the east to reach two false saddles (2190m and 2340m), between which a rough boulder region is crossed. Beyond the second false saddle lies a bowl of mountain debris; huge boulders forming a depressing, tortuous obstacle. Skirt this bowl to the right, and then clamber up to the east on scree and boulders to emerge, surprisingly, on Coll de la Cornella (2495m), a narrow V cut into the south-west ridge of Mont Roig (Mont Rouch) (about 4 hours from the start).

A steep gully leads down the eastern side; take care on the descent on tufted grass, loose rocks and scree, then veer left to aim for the stream linking two tarns below. Cross the stream and head south, avoiding the loss of too much height, before bearing left and mounting south-east to gain a broad pass in the Sierra de Mitjana, the ridge falling south from Mont Roig. This is Coll Curios (2428m), from which there are more fine views over a region of tarns and remote distant valley systems.

Bear left to find a stream which drains Estanyol Curios (the upper Calverante lake) and follow it up to the lake; a lovely tarn, trapped in a remote cup of mountainside with soft turf at its edges, it would make a tranquil site for a tent – weather permitting (2490m; 5½ hours).

Go round the tarn to the right and then head steeply east on a line of cairns to reach a high col (Col de Calverante?; 2610m) some 20 minutes above the tarn. A low stone wall marks the pass which is on yet another of Mont Roig's ridges. Views from this point are quite remarkable and call for a long rest to enjoy them. Steeply below to the east a descent is made to Estany Major, then bear left to skirt its north-west shore, reaching its natural embankment from whose lip yet more tarns are seen way below.

Cairns lead to the outflow of Estany Major then descend, crossing the stream to its right bank; a lovely stream washing over smoothed rocks and swirling in silver runnels – with the three Gallina tarns shining below. Taking care, go down to pass the first lake above it on the right, then to the second which must be passed some 30 metres above, and then to the larger lake, keeping well to the right, following cairns which lead through this landscape of glacier-smoothed boulders. At the far end of Estany de la Gallina is the small metal Refugi Enric Pujol (Refugi de Mont-Roig; 2280m).

Refugi Enric Pujol: FEEC owned, basic facilities, ten places.

Continue to descend, now eastwards, to reach the grassy bank of Estany Llavera (2200m). Go left round the western shore until you meet its outflow stream. A path climbs down its left bank into a deep grass-bottomed cirque overshadowed by the huge East Face of Mont Roig. Bear right to find the stream flowing out of the cirque and keep on its left bank. This has cut a deep channel in the rock, a micro gorge through which the stream flows, and the path stays fairly close to it before descending to a grassy region. Trees and shrubs become increasingly common. A side stream, the Ribereta, is crossed, and shortly after this you pass a rough hut.

Beyond the hut the path descends steadily across the hillside, but well above the valley which is cutting a deep ravine. Then the Riu dels Escobes is crossed; a few paces beyond this bear right, descending to a grassy shoulder of hillside bordered by luxurious shrubs. The way is unclear, but go left across this shoulder, once more among trees, to find the path again. It leads out of trees to a sloping meadowland formed by a valley out of which flows the Riu del Port from the left. A hut is seen some 200 metres off to the left. Cross the stream and follow the clear path south.

The trail becomes a forest track, but now and again reverts to path; after a while it descends in long and tedious zig-zags. Eventually the path-cum-track slips into the upper grasslands of the Tabescan Valley at the tiny hamlet of Cuanca. Pass alongside the buildings and walk down the track. At the far end of a small dammed lake you come to the campsite of Bordes de Graus.

Note: Hotel accommodation and supplies in Tabescan an hour or so down-valley. See High Route 22 following.

High Route 22: Bordes de Graus (1360m) – Pla de Boavi (1460m)

Distance:	**13 kilometres**
Height gain:	**293 metres**
Height loss:	**193 metres**
Time:	**3½–4 hours**

After the previous day's exertions this is an easy stage of valley walking, an opportunity to relax and at the same time reach a good position from which to set out on tomorrow's trek to the Vall Ferrera. There is no accommodation to be had at Pla de Boavi, but camping used to be one of the highlights of the trek. Regrettably this is now forbidden here, so campers will need to continue to find a suitable site (recommendations invited).

From the Bordes de Graus campsite follow the track down-valley on the bank of the Riu de Tavascan, crossing to the left-hand side where the track becomes a narrow metalled road. This winds down to the valley of Lladorre with Tabescan (complete with electricity 'nursery') seen lying a little way off to the right and reached an hour or so from the start.

Tabescan (Tavascan; 1167m): Hotels, restaurant, shops. Food shops here will apparently open upon request.

Head north-east from Tabescan along the road. It steadily gains height through the valley of the Noguera de Lladorre (the upper branch of Vall de Cardos) which becomes lovelier the deeper you go towards its head. There are meadows and woodlands, barns, streams and cascades emerging from side glens. The road, which becomes a track, remains on the west bank of the Lladorre, and after nine kilometres crosses the Planell dels Castellassos – a beautiful flat area landscaped with birches. Immediately beyond is Pla de Boavi; another level region beside the stream almost at the junction of two valleys. Birch, spruce and shrubs make it seem like a parkland. It is understandably very popular with Spanish picnic parties. To find a suitable (and not forbidden) campsite, follow directions for High Route 23.

High Route 23: Pla de Boavi (1460m) – Refugi de Vall Ferrera (1940m)

Distance:	**11 kilometres**
Height gain:	**1165 metres**
Height loss:	**615 metres**
Time:	**6–6½ hours**

Under misty conditions this section of the route could be a little problematic, but in the brilliance of a Spanish summer's day it is a real joy, with some fine scenery to pass through. Set out early in order to reach Coll de Sellente before the sun is too high.

From the eastern end of Pla de Boavi cross the stream by a footbridge and follow a well-constructed path – quite possibly the best of the whole trip – as it winds in long sweeps through forest heading south-east. Cross the Sellente stream at 1660 metres by another footbridge, and shortly after the path forks. Ignore that which heads east (left) for the Broate glen, and climb to the south. The path returns to the west bank and climbs in zig-zags, then heads clearly along the slopes of the Sellente Valley, crosses the stream once more and enters a rough, flat pastureland (2 hours from Pla de Boavi).

Follow the path which goes first along the eastern side of the pasture, then crosses three or four minor streams to gain the western side, there to climb in long sweeping zig-zags towards the south-west. On gaining a higher level of pasture at 2240 metres, pass a ruined building (Refugi de Sellente) and continue to gain height heading south-east to reach a false pass from which Coll de Sellente (2485m) is clearly seen as a grassy saddle above. This is gained about 3½ hours from Pla de Boavi.

Views from this saddle overlook a folding hillside dominated by the Baborte lake. To the left rises the Circ de Baborte, below and far-off hinted valleys draw your attention, while on a knoll above the northern end of Estany de Baborte is an unmanned metal hut, Refugi de Baborte (2438m).

Refugi de Baborte: UEC owned, 16 places, blankets and emergency first aid supplied.

Go down to the northern end of the lake, then wander along a cairned footpath to the left, past a metal sign pointing back to the refugi. A well-trodden path zig-zags downhill through pine trees and shrubs (light green waymarks) to arrive at the Cabane de Basello (5 hours), which sits on the lip of a flat shelf of hillside overlooking Vall Ferrera.

The Vall Ferrera hut is signposted from here, with the route being led by circular red waymarks. The path is an undulating one, gaining and losing some height, and eventually joins a forest track in the valley of the Noguera de Vall Ferrera. Bear left and soon come to the hairpins used as parking spaces by visitors to the refugi. Shortly after these you will see a signpost directing a path left to Refugi de Vall Ferrera. Cross the river on a footbridge and walk up the slope. An alternative path here cuts right to Pla de Bouet, but we go ahead along the right-hand side of the Barranco d'Areste, then across it by footbridge by a cascade to gain the hut at 1940 metres.

Refugi de Vall Ferrera: Owned by FEEC, 35 places, guardian from May to late-September, meals provided (Tel: 973 62 07 54). (See Estats–Montcalm section above.)

High Route 24: Refugi de Vall Ferrera (1940m) – El Serrat (1560m)

Distance:	**15 kilometres**
Height gain:	**1260 metres**
Height loss:	**1640 metres**
Time:	**7½–8 hours**

Descend from the hut to the Noguera de Vall Ferrera. Do not cross the bridge but bear left to enter the open pastures of Pla de Bouet where there's a campsite. The path goes behind a large farm building (Cabane de Bouet) and works its way up the hillside heading more or less in an easterly direction, then becomes confused among animal trails and disappears. There is no difficulty about finding a route. The way climbs on grass and through one or two marshy sections, now and then with a small cairn to give encouragement. A false saddle is reached, and beyond it a second from which Port de Bouet is clearly seen across a moorland-like hillside. Circ de Baiau off to the south-east appears most attractive.

Port de Bouet (2520m) is topped about two hours from the hut. Ahead lies France in the shape of a long valley beyond which rise the mountains enclosing Andorra. Go down through jumbled rocks north-east towards a little lake, Etang de la Soucarrane. After about 150 metres of descent the cairned route leads away from the lake to the south-east and drops into a pleasant grassy glen with some boggy areas.

Follow this glen to the head of a narrow ravine with a stream cutting through. A clear path goes down its left bank, and immediately below the ravine crosses to the right bank and winds among some crags. Beyond the crags cut across the hillside to reach the Franco-Andorran road (2000m).

Walk up the road until the ruins of a stone cabane (Orris de Rat) are seen to the left near a stream. Go down to join a waymarked path rising past the hut. Bear right on the path and follow its devious route up the mountainside towards Port de Rat. It's a delightful ascent on a fine old path; peaks jutting at the head of the valley look splendid. Port de Rat (2540m) is reached five hours after leaving Refugi de Vall Ferrera. France and Spain are now behind you, Andorra ahead.

The path goes down slanting left, north-eastwards, keeping above the road which it reaches all too soon. A large marshy bowl is gained and it is possible to exploit this to avoid walking on the road, although it is only a brief escape. At the earliest opportunity head left away from the road to join the much-used path heading for the Tristaina lakes hidden from view above to the north. Then bear right and follow down to the valley below, once more to rejoin the road. Continue down to reach El Serrat.

El Serrat: a collection of hotels and restaurants with a few original farm buildings incongruously tucked in the hillside. Andorra-la-Vella lies about 16 kilometres to the south, approached through the Valira del Nord. (See Andorra section for route suggestions and further details.)

Note: To return to the 'world beyond', either take a bus or hitch down to Andorra-la-Vella where buses head north to France and l'Hospitalet for the Paris train.

High Route Note:

The 'official' High Route continues beyond El Serrat and crosses Andorra by way of **COLL DE LA MINA** (2713m), the upper reaches of **VALL DE RANSOL** and **VALL D'INCLES** (8 hours), then departs for France across one of two different passes heading towards the **CARLIT MASSIF**. Eleven days after leaving El Serrat the HRP achieves its goal of reaching the Mediterranean at **BANYULS-SUR-MER**.

APPENDIX A

USEFUL ADDRESSES

1: Tourist Information:
French Government Tourist Office
178 Piccadilly
London W1V 0AL (Tel: 0891 244 123)
E-mail: piccadilly@mdlf.demon.co.uk

Spanish National Tourist Office
22–23 Manchester Square
London W1M 5AP (Tel: 020 7486 8077)

Andorra Tourist Delegation
63 Westover Road
London SW18 2RF (Tel: 020 8874 4806)

2: Specialist Organisations:
Rando Éditions
4 rue Maye Lane
BP24 – 65421 Ibos cedex
France (Tel: 05 62 90 09 90)
www.rando-editions.com

CIMES-Pyrénées
(Centre d'Informations Montagnes et Sentiers)
1 rue Maye Lane
BP2 – 65421 Ibos cedex
France (Tel: 05 62 90 67 60)
E-mail: cimes@randopyrenees.com

Association Randonnées Pyrénéennes
(address as for CIMES above)
E-mail: asso@randopyrenees.com
www.cimes-pyrenees.com

Club Alpin Français (Section de Tarbes)
46 Boulevard du Martinet
65000 Tarbes
France (Tel: 05 62 36 56 06)

3: National Parks Administration:
Parc National des Pyrénées
59 rue de Pau
65000 Tarbes
France (Tel: 05 62 44 36 60)
E-mail: pyrenees.parc.national@wanadoo.fr
Website: parc-pyrenees.com

Parque Nacional de Ordesa y Monte Perdido
Plaza de Cervantes 5
22071 Huesca
Spain (Tel: 974 24 33 61)

Parque Nacional d'Aiguestortes i Estany de Sant Maurici
C/ Camp de Mart 35
25004 Lleida
Spain (Tel: 973 24 66 50)
www.gencat.es/darp/medi/pein/cparcs05.htm

Parque Natural Posets-Maladeta
Avda. de La Paz
5 bajo
Huesca
Spain (Tel: 974 23 06 35)

4: Map Suppliers:
Cordee Ltd
3A De Montfort Street
Leicester LE1 7HD (Tel: 0116 2543579)
www.cordee.co.uk

Edward Stanford Ltd
12–14 Long Acre
London WC2E 9LP (Tel: 020 7 836 1321)
www.stanfords.co.uk

World Leisure Marketing/Map World
Unit 11
Newmarket Court
Derby DE24 8NW (Tel: 1332 573737)
www.map-world.co.uk

APPENDIX B

Maps and Continental Guides

The 1:50,000 series of maps published by **IGN** in conjunction with Rando Éditions provides excellent coverage, and will be adequate for most routes included in this guide. The series goes under the general title of *Carte de Randonnées* and covers the Pyrenees from coast to coast in 11 sheets (six for the region described in this book). Although primarily intended for the French side of the mountains, there is sufficient cross-border overlapping to enable walkers (if not climbers) to do without Spanish maps for all but a few isolated regions; but study requirements listed. Details of specific sheets needed for each area are given at the head of individual sections. Each *Carte de Randonnées* has major paths marked in red; GR10 and the HRP are highlighted, as are mountain huts, *gîtes d'étape* and official campsites.

For greater detail **IGN** produce their TOP 25 series of maps at 1:25,000 scale. As with the *Carte de Randonnées* series, these have major trails, huts etc highlighted in red. Details of these maps are also given at the head of of relevant sections in the main body of this guide.

Editorial Alpina publish a series of maps for walkers and climbers active on the Spanish side of the frontier. Whilst they fall short of standards of accuracy assumed by the IGN survey, improvements are made with successive editions. Most sheets are at a scale of 1:25,000, but some are 1:40,000, and have contours at 20 metre intervals. Walkers are warned that not all routes shown as paths on the maps are evident on the ground, and may be little more than wishful thinking on behalf of the cartographer. Each map in the Pyrenean series is published with an accompanying booklet (in Spanish) which gives useful information about walking and climbing routes, accommodation etc.

Both IGN and Editorial Alpina maps are generally available from major stockists in Britain – see Appendix A for addresses.

As for Continental guidebooks, **Rando Éditions** of Tarbes (address in Appendix A) publish a large number of excellent walking guides, in French, covering just about every valley in the Pyrenees, as well as a very useful handbook listing all refuges, *gîtes,* etc on both sides of the frontier; *Gîtes d'étape Refuges – France et Frontières.*

BIBLIOGRAPHY

The number of English-language books covering the Pyrenees has grown rapidly in recent years. The following list is necessarily selective, but may be considered useful to readers of the present guide. Some titles listed are out of print, but may be available through public libraries, specialist book suppliers or the internet.

1: General Guides

The Rough Guide to the Pyrenees by Marc Dubin (The Rough Guides, 1998); excellent coverage in typical no-nonsense Rough Guide style, of use to all visitors to the range.

Atlantic Coast and *Languedoc, Roussillon, Tarn Gorges* (Michelin, 1998); two general tourist guides of particular interest to motorised visitors.

Mountains of the Pyrenees by Kev Reynolds (Cicerone Press, 1982); a first attempt in English to record the history of climbing and exploration throughout the region covered by the present guidebook.

The Pyrenees by Bob Gibbons & Paul Davies (Batsford, 1990); one in a series of guides to the world's mountains, it gives brief information on various aspects of the range, including walking, climbing and skiing.

The Pyrenees – IGN Touring & Leisure Guide (IGN/Robertson McCarta, 1991); basic information, mainly for motorised visitors to the French side.

The French Pyrenees by John Sturrock (Faber & Faber, 1988); coast to coast guide giving good background information, history etc without actually getting into the mountains.

Languedoc & Roussillon and *South-West France* by Andrew Sanger (Christopher Helm, 1989/1990); history, background and touring information gathered in a readable form, lots of fine illustrations, but again, no mountain activity.

Landscapes of the Pyrenees by Paul Jenner & Christine Smith (Sunflower Books, 1990); a slim touring guide (with a handful of short walks) by the authors of the original Pyrenean Rough Guide.

Wild Spain by Frederic V. Grunfeld (Ebury Press, 1988); includes chapters on the Pyrenees of special interest to wildlife enthusiasts. Details where to go, what to see, and how to get there.

2: Walking and Climbing

Pyrenees West, *Pyrenees Central* and *Pyrenees East* by Arthur Battagel (Gastons/West Col); coverage in three volumes describing walks and modest ascents on both sides of the border.

Classic Walks in the Pyrenees by Kev Reynolds (Oxford Illustrated Press, 1989); a selection of the best walks throughout the range, illustrated with colour and black & white photographs.

Long Distance Walks in the Pyrenees by Chris Townsend (Crowood Press, 1991); similar to the above, ten multi-day routes are described in the High Pyrenees; well illustrated, and with useful planning information.

Rock Climbs in the Pyrenees by Derek L. Walker (Cicerone Press, 1990); the first English-language climber's guide (with topos) to the range, with routes on Pic du Midi, Ordesa cliffs, Riglos, Vignemale, in Valle de Tena and Sierra de Guara.

The Pyrenean Trail GR10 by Alan Castle (Cicerone Press, 1990); the classic long-distance walk from Hendaye to Banyuls described in 47 day stages, plus *variantes*.

Through the Spanish Pyrenees GR11 by Paul Lucia (Cicerone Press, 2000); a detailed guide to this long distance route which traverses the Spanish Pyrenees in 44 stages.

Walking the Pyrenees (Robertson McCarta, 1989); the GR10 in an English translation of the French topo guides, includes relevant sections of the IGN maps.

Pyrenees High Level Route by Georges Véron (Gastons/West Col, latest edition 1991); English edition guide to the magnificent coast to coast High Route described by its originator.

100 Walks in the French Pyrenees by Terry Marsh (Hodder & Stoughton, 1992); a handy guide to walks of varying grades in and neighbouring the PNP.

Trekking in Spain by Marc Dubin (Lonely Planet, 1990); multi-day walks in the wild regions of Spain, with sections devoted to parts of the Pyrenees.

Walking in Spain by Miles Roddis & others (Lonely Planet, 1999); much of mainland and island Spain covered, with a section on the Spanish Pyrenees and Andorra.

Trekking in the Pyrenees by Douglas Streatfeild-James (Trailblazer Publications, 1998), deals mostly with sections of GR10 and GR11.

The Enchanted Mountains by Robin Fedden (The Ernest Press, 2000); originally published in 1962, this lyrical account of three climbing trips to the Pyrenees in the mid-1950s is a minor classic of mountaineering literature that captures the romantic nature of the range as it was before tourist development. Deserves to be on the bookshelves of all who love these mountains.

ROUTE INDEX

Posets

Maladeta

Aigüestortes West – Besiberri Massif

CICERONE GUIDES TO FRANCE AND SPAIN

FRANCE

WALKING IN THE ARDENNES	Alan Castle
SELECTED ROCK CLIMBS IN BELGIUM AND LUXEMBOURG	Chris Craggs
THE BRITTANY COASTAL PATH	Alan Castle
CHAMONIX – MONT BLANC – A Walking Guide	Martin Collins
GR20: THE CORSICAN HIGH LEVEL ROUTE	Paddy Dillon
WALKING IN THE ECRINS NATIONAL PARK	Kev Reynolds
WALKING THE FRENCH ALPS: GR5	Martin Collins
WALKING THE FRENCH GORGES	Alan Castle
FRENCH ROCK	Bill Birkett
WALKING IN THE HAUTE SAVOIE	Janette Norton
WALKING IN THE LANGUEDOC	John Cross
TOUR OF THE OISANS: GR54	Andrew Harper
WALKING IN PROVENCE	Janette Norton
THE PYRENEAN TRAIL: GR10	Alan Castle
THE TOUR OF THE QUEYRAS	Alan Castle
THE ROBERT LOUIS STEVENSON TRAIL	Alan Castle
TOUR OF MONT BLANC	Andrew Harper

FRANCE/SPAIN

WALKING IN THE TARENTAISE AND BEAUFORTAIN ALPS	J.W. Akitt
ROCK CLIMBS IN THE VERDON – An Introduction	Rick Newcombe
TOUR OF THE VANOISE	Kev Reynolds
WALKS IN VOLCANO COUNTRY	Alan Castle
ROCK CLIMBS IN THE PYRENEES	Derek Walker
THE WAY OF ST JAMES: Le Puy to Santiago – A Cyclist's Guide	John Higginson
THE WAY OF ST JAMES: Le Puy to Santiago – A Walker's Guide	Alison Raju

SPAIN

ANDALUSIAN ROCK CLIMBS	Chris Craggs
COSTA BLANCA ROCK	Chris Craggs
MOUNTAIN WALKS ON THE COSTA BLANCA	Bob Stansfield
ROCK CLIMBS IN MALLORCA, IBIZA AND TENERIFE	Chris Craggs
WALKING IN MALLORCA	June Parker
BIRDWATCHING IN MALLORCA	Ken Stoba
THE MOUNTAINS OF CENTRAL SPAIN	Jaqueline Oglesby
THROUGH THE SPANISH PYRENEES: GR11 2nd Edition	Paul Lucia
WALKING IN THE SIERRA NEVADA	Andy Walmsley
WALKS AND CLIMBS IN THE PICOS DE EUROPA	Robin Walker

EXPLORE THE WORLD
WITH A CICERONE GUIDE

Cicerone publishes over 280 guides for walking, trekking, climbing and exploring the UK, Europe and worldwide. Cicerone guides are available from outdoor shops, quality book stores and from the publisher.

**Cicerone can be contacted on
Tel. 01539 562069
Fax: 01539 563417
www.cicerone.co.uk**

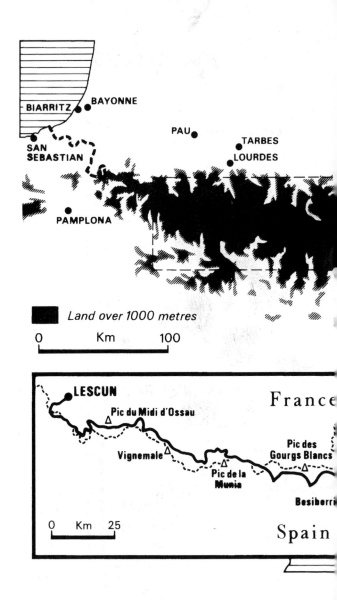

Land over 1000 metres

0   Km   100

LESCUN   France

Pic du Midi d'Ossau

Vignemale   Pic des
                                Gourgs Blancs

          Pic de la
          Munia

                                Besiberri

0   Km   25   Spain